Jonathan Boyes, BSc (Hons)

was born in England and studied in London and Heidelberg. A frequent visitor to Thailand during the 1980's, he set up an English language community school in Sawankhalok and spent a year in Chiang Saen. More recently he has lived for five years in a large Hmong hilltribe village to the east of Chiang Saen. He is an acknowledged authority on the collection of oral histories from among the tribal peoples of the region and, together with his Thai wife, is the author of *Hmong Voices, A Life Apart* and *Opium Fields*.

Tiger-Men and Tofu Dolls

Tribal Spirits in Northern Thailand

Jonathan Boyes

SILKWORM BOOKS
Chiang Mai

Text © Jonathan Boyes, 1997
Illustrations © Joanne Boyes, 1997
All rights reserved. No part of this publication may be reproduced, stored in a retrieval system, or transmitted, in any form or by any means, electronic, mechanical, photocopying, recording or otherwise, without the prior permission in writing of the publisher.

First published in 1997 by
Silkworm Books
54/1 Sridonchai Road, Chiang Mai 50100, Thailand
E-mail: Silkworm@pobox.com
http://www.muang.com/silkworm/

Silkworm Books is a registered trade mark of
 Trasvin Publications Limited Partnership.

ISBN 974-7100-35-5

Illustrations by Joanne Boyes
Set in 10 pt. Palatino by J. Boyes

Printed in Thailand

Contents

Illustrations		ix
Acknowledgements		x
Kiew Khan Update		xi

Introduction

1.	The Night of the Big Fire	1
2.	Living on the Mountain	4
3.	The Six Tribes of the North	10
4.	Dual Worlds: Spirits, Souls and the Afterlife	15
5.	On the Trail of the Spirits	20

Interviews

1) Nachai Sewa (*a Hmong shaman and mother of nine*)   29
    Spirit Heads
    In Need of a Luckier Name
    A Doll for the Tofu Spirit
    'Gong-goy' Spirits, and the Boy Who Farted
    First Signs of a Shamanic Calling

2) Laogee Sewang (*a Hmong shaman*)   47
    A Shaman's Lot

3) Aka My-yer (*an Akha village priest*)   55
    Apoe Miyeh: The Creator
    Our Village
    The Two Worlds of Humans and Spirits
    Two Spirit Practitioners

4)	Laojong (*a Hmong man*) Siting a New House	71
5)	Somboon Seejaow (*a former Yao headman*) Crossing to the Other Side	73
6)	Mano Leejar (*a Lisu headman*) The Power of Water Lisu Village Guardian Spirit Shrine The Black Magician	76
7)	Yiow-fun Selee (*a Yao shaman*) Fire-walker — A Shaman's Story	85
8)	Leur Prom-muang (*a former Karen headman*) House Spirits, and How Not to Offend Them The Karen Village Priest	90
9)	Mit Selee (*a young Hmong man*) Sexual Intercourse and the House Spirits	97
10)	Chan-jian Selee (*a young Yao man*) Ancient Writings	100
11)	Laojia - Sombat - Laopia (*three Hmong men*) Inviting the Spirit of the Three Ancestors: An Account of a Shamanic Curing Ritual	102
12)	Mai-gwa Selee (*a young Hmong woman*) Hmong Post-natal Precautions	108
13)	Gor-da Bierpa (*a former Lisu priest*) Great Balls of Fire Lisu Childbirth and Naming	112
14)	Ana Muangjai (*a young Lahu woman*) Giving Birth	116
15)	Laopia Selee (*a Hmong village elder*) A Curse on a Woman-hater Reading the Bones Hmong Soul-calling Bridges	118
16)	Anonymous (*a Hmong man*) The Good 'Tree Lord'	129
17)	Najeu Selee (*a Hmong woman*) Identification Marks for Wandering Souls A Hmong from Jin Haw Country	133

Contents

18)	Napur Muangjai (*a Lahu schoolgirl*) Chicken-bone Divination and Soul-calling Lahu Holy Days Solitary Chicks, Disappearing Pigs: Bad Death and Ghosts	138
19)	Narong Gangyang (*a young Karen man*) The Karen Afterworld	148
20)	Nayua Sewa (*a Hmong woman*) Hungry Ghosts Magic to Save Little Jeu A Messenger of Death	151
21)	Jonglao Selee (*a Hmong headman*) Poosu 'Have You Ever Seen a Spirit Walking down the Mountain?'	157
22)	Nasuo Selee (*a young Hmong woman*) Taken Away by the Spirit of the Rainbow	161
23)	Najia Selee (*a young Hmong woman*) 'Snake Splash', and the Rainbow-tooth Cure	164
24)	Laojia - Do - Yeh (*three young Hmong men*) A Shaman's Prophesy Ignored	169
25)	Boonchu (*a Hmong boy*) A Tale of Dark Deeds	179
26)	Malee Selee (*a Hmong girl*) Ghost Sighting	183
27)	Nachai Sewa (*a Hmong shaman*) Worldly Goods Bansia Married a Weretiger The Tiger-Man	185
28)	Abu Merlaygu (*an Akha youth*) Abu's Tale Chasing Out the Spirits	192
29)	Laoheu Selee (*a Christian Hmong man*) Tiger or Weretiger?	197
30)	Laoleuer Sewa (*a Hmong village elder*) A Strange Family from Laos	199

31)	Laosong Selee (*a young Hmong man*) Death Spell	204
32)	Nabai Sewa (*a Hmong girl*) A Curse on Nadoa's Babies	208
33)	Amer Merlaygu (*an Akha headman*) Rice Rituals Animal-name Day Omens	212
34)	Jantong Muangdee (*an elderly Karen man*) Rice Planting and Village Shrine	219
35)	Nai-wun (*a Yao schoolgirl*) Tourist Market	223
36)	Lortee (*an elderly Lahu woman*) Lahu New Year	229
37)	Laobor Seyang (*a young Hmong man*) Sending Away the Old Year's Misfortune	234
38)	Laodeng Sewa (*a Hmong hunter*) Paying One's Hunting Debts Christianity, or the Spirits?	237
39)	Janoo (*a former Lahu soldier*) Losing the Old Ways	242
40)	Laoseu Seyang (*an elderly Hmong man*) A Non-believer	246

Cultural Integrity Under Threat   249

Bibliography   255

Index   257

Illustrations

Maps

Hilltribe Migration Routes	xii
Northern Thai Provinces with Sizeable Hilltribe Populations	11
Northern Chiang Rai Province	23

Line drawings

Hmong spirit head	30
The egg-drop test	59
Village gate at Ban A-bey	61
Wooden figures placed by Akha gates	63
Hmong soul-calling bridge at Kiew Khan	127
Lahu soul-calling offering post	139
Lahu *Ku-ti* temple offering	142
Wooden swords used in the Akha 'chasing out' ritual	195
Akha rice spirit 'house'	216
Lahu 'Year tree'	231

Acknowledgements

I would like to acknowledge my gratitude to all the people who found time to talk to us in the course of writing this book. I would particularly like to thank Nachai Sewa, Laopia Selee, Jonglao Selee, Leur Prom-muang, Aka My-yer, Yiow-fun Selee and Mano Leejar.

As always, I owe a special debt of gratitude to my wife Suphawan, for it was she who conducted the majority of the interviews, and it was her position as honorary 'elder' in our Hmong village — a unique post for a Thai woman in a society known to be clannish and distrustful of outsiders — which has in many respects made our life in the hills possible.

A handful of people took the time and trouble to read and comment on part or all of the manuscript; Joanne Boyes, John Tallon, Peter Boyes, Martin Palmer and Francis Barry-Walsh were particularly helpful in their comments. Joanne Boyes was also kind enough to supply me with many fine illustrations, drawn, I might add, from very inferior photographs.

As to the type-setting, Steve Ottaway and Nigel Killick made useful design suggestions, and Dave Read and Brian James (and family) were kind enough to put printers and scanners at my disposal.

Finally, I would like to acknowledge the help received from the Society Of Authors, London. A generous grant from the K. Blundell Trust (which is administered by the Society) helped fund our researches at a particularly crucial stage. Thank you.

Kiew Khan Update

The road to Kiew Khan is now fully surfaced and brings ever-increasing numbers of tourists to the village. Illegal small-time logging in the area has been suppressed, and the hunting of wild game has been severely curtailed. Cash-cropping is becoming more common, and in some households oranges are replacing rice as the principal crop. Electricity has also reached the village, and money from the orange harvests is quickly disappearing into television sets and electric sewing machines. More and more families are also now able to afford motorbikes.

And finally, the village has recently been adopted by a Royal Project. The field co-ordinator's first step has been to tear down the existing school and rebuild it anew, complete with a formal garden, a new flagpole, and a large all-purpose playing field. To make room for these improvements the police post and five houses were ordered demolished. These included the homes of Laosong, Jonglao, Laoleuer and Nachai, and... Jon and Su.

JB, 1995

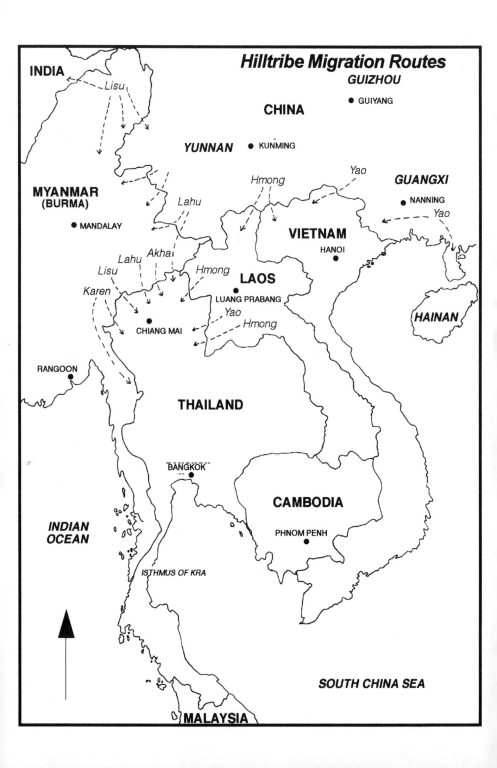

Introduction

1 - The Night of the Big Fire

The cool night air stirred momentarily, causing us all, even the mangy old dog lying in the corner, to raise our heads, listening for the tell-tale rustle of wind through leaves. Fortunately, much to everybody's relief there was only silence, and our friend Leuer Sewa continued with his bizarre story.

...what was really weird was that they were there with the dog. Normally when a dog sees a strange animal, like a lizard, it would bark a lot. But it didn't make a sound, it just lay there, quietly watching them.

We were in a tribal village high up in the hills of northern Thailand, sitting round a log fire in the kitchen of a government police post. It was three in the morning. Leuer was telling us of spirit possession and other eerie goings-on in a Hmong village over the nearby border in Laos (see Laoleuer Sewa, A Strange Family from Laos).

Only two hours before, we had been battling an out-of-control field fire whose flames had been directly threatening our bamboo and grass thatch homes — perfect kindling for a potentially horrendous mini fire-storm. At one stage, while we rested for a few minutes having spent more than two hours frantically rushing from incomplete firebreak to incomplete firebreak, desperately beating out the fast-moving flames with branches cut from nearby bushes, Leuer had surreptitiously pointed out a dark figure standing off to one side quietly watching the flames.

'That's the one, that's the son. It was his sister my friend Laoma went to see.' Whispering, he sketched out the story of how, late one night, while calling on his girlfriend, his friend Laoma had seen two one-metre long lizards lying by the fire, only inches from the family's dog. These he took to be the girl's disapproving parents who, by assuming a reptilian form, aspired to scare him off. 'No kidding, he saw them with his very own eyes. They were just lying there watching him and the girl. And him over there, that's her brother.'

Now we sat, exhausted and grimy from the long night's work, listening to Leuer's curious tale in full while we waited for the sunrise, and with it the end of our fire-watching obligations that March night: one person per family to remain awake during the night in case of a flare-up in the fields.

This incident with the lizards, insisted Leuer, strange though it was, was nonetheless just one in a whole catalogue of unusual and, to the neighbours, sinister goings-on associated with that particular family:

And sometimes at night people living close to them would hear a tiger's growl nearby, but strangely the dogs wouldn't start barking. And a few times they even saw tiger tracks right in front of their house. Everybody suspected the parents of being possessed.

And on some occasions when they returned home from the fields...

...they'd find fresh fish from the river left in a bowl in the house. Of course they'd think a friend must have left them there, but when they'd ask around, nobody would know anything about them.

Later, after the parents of the mysterious fire-fighter had died, the strange happenings ceased altogether, reported Leuer. Laoma eventually left the village and moved to Thailand. One day, however, he received a visitor from his old village. It was an elderly man, a shaman who had often performed rituals for the girl's parents. He spoke to the former boyfriend about the girl's family. In his opinion her parents had been possessed by the spirit of a dead Khamu tribesman, and it was therefore this spirit which was ultimately responsible for the strange events surrounding the household.

...no offerings are made to their spirits. So, of course, the spirits are hungry and wait for someone to come along.

As a consequence of the Khamu practice of burying their dead quickly and with very little ceremony, the Hmong believe the spirits of the Khamu dead do not ascend to the 'beyond', but instead, neglected and hungry, remain on the earth, harassing passers-by in a bid to coerce food offerings from them. Furthermore, if a person should die in his or her fields, it is here they are buried, following which the fields are immediately abandoned. Thus continued Leuer, in the shaman's opinion, the girl's parents had probably reclaimed some fields abandoned by the Khamu, and one-day had been 'followed home' by a spirit which had been lurking in the vicinity of an unmarked grave.

...the shaman said it was a spirit from the Khamu fields doing these things. And because they had eaten rice from the same bowl as the spirit – the spirit's leftovers – they too had become spirits, or rather, half-spirits, like being possessed. People shouldn't eat anything a spirit has left. After the spirit had done this it probably went away to be born again as a human.

An intriguing tale, but not the only one we heard that night. Later still, another man, having listened to the story of the strange family in Laos, related to us a second tale of the 'supernatural', a story of a local Lahu woman who is thought to have been possessed by a weretiger shortly before her death, and who, after her burial, herself became one of these fearful creatures (see Laoheu Selee, Tiger or Weretiger?). These two stories, told to us in Thai, were recorded on a Walkman, transcribed, and then translated into English.

In retrospect, this March night in our Hmong village of Kiew

Khan marked a beginning for my Thai wife Suphawan and me. For the tales we listened to during those quiet early morning hours after the hectic night of fire-fighting supplied the initial impetus which, in the following months, sent us into the nearby hills scouring village after tribal village, not only for similar fascinating accounts and recollections of mysterious goings-on, but also for personal descriptions of spirits, ghosts and other supernatural beings, as well as detailed explanations of spirit rituals and ceremonies, from soul-calling rituals to exorcisms, from simple naming ceremonies to the complex rituals which help despatch souls of the deceased to the land of the ancestors.

Through our efforts we hoped to capture, and then present, in as direct and simple a format as possible, some indication of the great scope and variety of the different religious and folk beliefs of the principal hilltribe peoples in the region: the Hmong, Yao, Lisu, Lahu, Akha and Karen.

2 - *Living on the Mountain*

We first came to Kiew Khan in 1987. I was still in England when Su (Suphawan), having spent two long months locked in delicate negotiations with Laogwa, the then headman of Kiew Khan, was finally given permission to build a three-roomed bamboo hut on the hill overlooking the village. We had already talked over the possibilities of building such a 'house' the winter before, but rather than wait for my arrival in Chiang Saen — Su's home town — that July, Su had gone on ahead, hoping to have our 'retreat' (from her small but busy guest house in Chiang Saen) completed before the summer.

Chiang Saen itself is a small pleasant Thai town nestling on the banks of the Mekong River. Once an ancient capital of the Lan Na kingdom of the Tai peoples, the town is studded with ruined temples and encircled on three sides by an impressive town wall and system of defensive moats.

On the surface a sleepy backwater, underneath it seethes with passion — and would-be secrets. Everybody, and I mean everybody, seems to have something to hide: from the senior policeman who

Introduction

moonlights as a major heroin trafficker (caught red-handed with thirty-seven kilogrammes; he's now in prison) and the jovial businessman big in illegal logging, to the sad, listless young girls in the brothels, many of whom are illegal immigrants from Burma...and not forgetting the small-time opium and marijuana sellers, the local government officer with the fake land certificates, the young lady with two (unknowing) Western husbands, the boy who burnt down his neighbour's house, the illegal gaming club, the guest house that's haunted, a second that secretly pays off the tricycle drivers and a third that's infested with cobras. The list is endless.

Despite the town's exotic charm, and it is charming in spite of everything, we nevertheless found ourselves in late 1987 and early 1988 passing more and more of our days with the Hmong in Kiew Khan.

By April 1988 we had decided to leave the relative comforts of Chiang Saen and move into Kiew Khan proper. Permission from the elders to move down the hill and into the village (closer to friends — and the water supply) was given without hesitation: they had got to know us by now and realised we were not intent on establishing an out-of-town brothel in their village. Strangely, or perhaps in hindsight not so strangely, this had been their major concern the year before.

As luck would have it, we managed to buy the empty house of a Thai forestry official living just seven kilometres from Kiew Khan. He was soon to move to the South in an attempt to rescue his marriage from imminent collapse. The timber, which he swore blind had been legally felled, was offered to us for a very reasonable £250.

Dismantled, carted up the hill by pick-up truck in four loads, and reassembled to our design with the help of four men from the Thai village, our house, complete with a veranda, a room for guests, and a grass thatch roof, was standing just four days later. We were now next-door neighbours to our good friend and sponsor in the village, Laoleuer — known affectionately by friends and others alike, and with good reason, as Lazy Leuer.

Though there is no electricity supply in the village — small home-made paraffin lamps are used for lighting — there is an adequate water supply which is piped from a small reservoir built by the villagers further up the mountain. Some people may see our house as a primitive shack on a mountainside. This may be so, but to us it is home, and unless it is raining, when the roof and walls leak, or it's extremely windy, when there is a chance the roof may blow off (it did in 1990 — twice), our home is relatively comfortable and, bearing in mind its singular location, entirely preferable to the brick suburban rabbit-hutch that may otherwise have been our home were we to live in England.

Looking from the veranda from where we eat our meals, out across a small maize field bounded on three sides by banana and papaya trees and over a narrow boulder-strewn dirt track which leads down the hill to the Thai village, there is a stunningly beautiful mountainside covered in thick, green, tropical primary jungle — home to wild boar, small Asian black bears, armadillos, civet cats, parrots, monitor lizards, cobras, pythons, vipers, kraits and, some say, tigers.

Despite the breathtaking beauty of the location and the sheer exuberance of tropical fauna and flora, our one overriding passion for the place is, however, based on something else entirely: on our being a part of a community. We feel at home in this society of nearly one thousand Hmong tribesmen and women. This does not mean we try and ape the Hmong lifestyle. We know we shall always be different, of course. We do not grow rice, for instance, an occupation in which almost every other man, woman and child in the village is employed for much of their time, and we do go on long hikes into the forested mountains, apparently just for the idle pleasure of it, an act which no one else in the village would ever contemplate doing. But this, I think, is largely irrelevant.

We are not the only non-Hmong living in Kiew Khan. There are almost one hundred Lahu villagers living in a small enclave at the highest level of the village. These are mainly of the Lahu Shi subgroup, although there are a few Lahu Nyi. And there are also two Kuomintang Chinese in the village, a father and son, refugees from the turmoil in China during the late forties and early fifties.

Some of the villagers are Christian converts, a few are Buddhists. A number of the men operate fare-paying pick-up services into town, and two have turned their small hut into an opium den — a sort of social centre for, in the most part, elderly Hmong addicts. The enterprising, though poverty-stricken duo also cater for occasional Thai devotees living in nearby villages.

There are practising shamans (both male and female), numerous blacksmiths, a handful of competent exponents of the Hmong musical pipes and, recently, the infamous *Kiew Khan Kickers* (my name), a company of ten teenage girls and two boys desperately trying to perfect a number of dance routines: Hmong traditional, Thai classical, disco and all three combined. They still have a long way to go.

There are also two families who run small shops from their houses, selling such items as Lux soap, White Horse and Cock torch batteries from China, buns bursting with sickly E-filled cream, plastic combs and other assorted essentials of twentieth century life. And finally, there is my wife and me, who quietly run the little village guest house and collect oral histories.

Having had the good fortune to be sponsored by a Hmong family we are expected to behave accordingly, and to accept all the responsibilities of a normal village household, such as in the contribution of labour for community work projects: repairs to the road, maintenance of the reservoir, and the upkeep of the village school, for example. Yet, being obviously non-Hmong, we still retain complete access to people of other clans and groupings.

As trusted outsiders villagers come to us asking for advice, such as the young boy who wanted to know where he could acquire a metal detector — illegal in Thailand — so he could locate and unearth his dead grandmother's lost hoard of silver that he'd been dreaming about for the past two weeks. Or the elderly man who had not experienced an erection since having a sexually transmitted disease ten years before, and who wanted to know whether the Western virility drug being offered to him by a Thai villager for four thousand baht (B40 = £1) was likely to be genuine or not.

Or, perhaps more seriously, the man who came to ask our advice on the behalf of a friend whose daughter was about to marry a Thai from a nearby village. The girl was sixteen and exquisitely beautiful. The Thai was in his early thirties, of smart appearance, and claimed to be a policeman. He had come to the village with two other men, seen the girl, and immediately asked her father for her hand in marriage. Why, our friend asked us, would a Thai with a good job want to marry a hilltribe girl? Surely there are plenty of Thai girls in his own village? And why the rush? Already suspicious of the groom's motives, the bride's father cancelled the wedding at the

Already suspicious of the groom's motives, the bride's father cancelled the wedding at the very last moment, and his daughter was saved from the almost certain horrors and privations of working in some dirty little brothel in the south.

Naturally enough, we also go to our neighbours when we need help, such as in thatching our roof, or for advice on where to get the best bamboo for making arrows for a crossbow. Or, more routinely, for information concerning their beliefs in spirits.

It is our acceptance into the community, yet still being obviously 'outsiders', that allows us such access to people's opinions, thoughts and experiences. In the two books *Hmong Voices* (1988, 1990) and *A Life Apart* (1989, 1992), our hope was to portray, through their words, glimpses of a traditional life-style that is so very different from our own in many ways, and yet show how their major concerns, love, marriage, children, work and status inevitably mirror our own.

In the past we interviewed people on any subject that cropped up: love and marriage, work in the fields, problems with Thais, school, the performance of shamanic curing rituals, land disputes, hunting, smoking opium, visiting the towns, and much, much more. However, during the winter of 1990–91 we felt circumstances compelled us to reassess our priorities regarding topics for interviews.

One sunny November afternoon Kiew Khan was visited for the first time by an organised tour group. Eight identical white Suzuki jeeps roared into the village carrying a Thai guide, sixteen middle-aged French tourists and eight two-man tents. They stayed one night, falsely led the headman to expect a large contribution to the school fund and left in their wake a rubbish-tip of seemingly urban-like proportions. The Thai guide was to return three further times that season, and has since indicated he will make this night in an 'authentic primitive hilltribe village' a standard feature of his 14-day tours. At present, it is the tourists who are in the zoo. They are the attraction for the gaping crowds. But it will change soon enough — it always does.

That same month a Thai development organisation of high repute began implementing a number of projects in Kiew Khan for 'the betterment of the people'. During a series of village meetings, to which one representative from every household was ordered to attend, the long-term development plan for Kiew Khan was outlined. Among the proposals: a rice bank, a credit scheme, waste paper baskets outside every house, terraced fields, the movement of all unsightly cow sheds away from the centre of the village, an increased effort in teaching Thai to children and adults, the enforcement of an opium smoking ban and the building of fences round every property. Laudabie aims, one and all (from the developers' perspective), but at what long-term cost to the indigenous culture?

Then in December, as if another portent of the future were needed, a group of seventeen Seventh Day Adventists (SDA) from the United States arrived in the village. High school students of mainly Japanese-American background, accompanied by a pastor from Los Angeles, and a Hmong co-ordinator from Bangkok, they came to Kiew Khan to build a church. For whom? For the SDA converts in the village (a mere handful). After ten days of hard toil the breeze-block basilica stood in all its glory, a worthy testament to the students' dedication, as well as to the unquenchable missionary zeal of the Adventists.

Changes had been expected for some time — the upgrading of the road running through the village has been in progress since before 1987. But the actual events of that winter finally brought home to us just how close Kiew Khan was to going the way of so many other formerly remote hilltribe villages in the North of Thailand: indeed, the way of so many thousands of similar communities the world over, from the great Amazon basin to the furthest reaches of the Indonesian Archipelago, from northern Siberia to southern Australasia. The long, all-powerful, ever-prevailing tentacles of the outside world were reaching out once again, as they have done, and are doing, all over this world of decreasing cultural diversity; stretching out to clasp and smoother the very uniqueness on which a minority culture bases so much of its identity.

Seeing this at first-hand, and well aware of the great wealth of tradition right on our doorstep, we decided in early 1991 to concentrate our interviewing efforts fully on the vast, rich area of belief and ritual. The story related to us in March by our close friend Lazy Leuer was therefore the catalyst which, already having been primed by the campers, developers and missionaries, finally sent us forth, hot on the trail of the spirits.

3 - The Six Tribes of the North

Before moving on to outlining our approach to collecting material in the field, I feel I should first say something on the individual tribal cultures themselves. The hilltribe peoples of northern Thailand are not native to Thailand: they originate further to the north, and north-west, in the mountains of South China, southwestern China and Tibet. They have been migrating slowly southwards for many centuries, and first moved into Thailand in the eighteenth century with the first Karen crossing over from Burma. However, it is the present century which has seen the largest influx of peoples into the kingdom, as highlanders have fled warfare and political instability in neighbouring lands.

There are now some half a million highlanders living in the North, with the six principal groups: the Hmong, Yao, Lisu, Lahu, Akha and Karen, representing ninety-five percent of the total. Each of these societies is uniquely individual, possessing its own distinct history, language, dress, values and beliefs.

Though unique, they do, however, share certain aspects of their lifestyle in common. They are all upland farmers living in small agricultural communities, with the family as the most important social unit and the belief in spirits and the spirit world of deep relevance to everyday life.

The Hmong

Adept embroiderers and master opium growers, the Hmong, whose marital prowess during the Vietnam war (particularly in Laos) led the Americans to lionise them as the 'Gurkhas of Southeast Asia', are perhaps the best known of all the tribal peoples of the region. With a total population of between four to six million, they are also one of the most numerous.

Originating in the mountains of South China (where the vast majority still reside) large numbers of Hmong are now found in northeastern Vietnam (200,000), Laos (200,000) and northern Thailand (80,000-100,000). They are known collectively as the Miao by the Chinese, and Meo by the Thai and Lao. However, the terms Miao and Meo are considered derogatory and they prefer others to call them by their own name: the Hmong.

Introduction

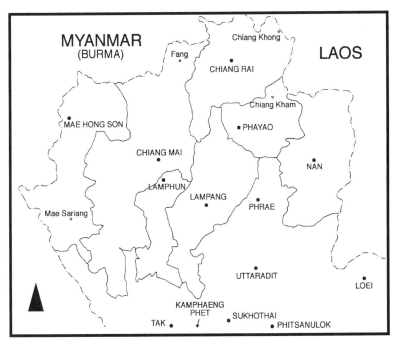

Northern Thai Provinces with Sizeable Hilltribe Populations

The Hmong in Thailand belong to two subgroups: the White Hmong and the Blue Hmong (also known as Green Hmong). It is possible to tell which subgroup a person is from by their traditional clothing, which most Hmong wear at all times. Each subgroup also speaks its own dialect of the Hmong language.

Provinces in Thailand with large concentrations of Hmong include Chiang Rai, Chiang Mai and Tak. Traditionally, settlements are found at high altitude: at least over one thousand metres. Villages consist of small clustered hamlets, generally without any central communal buildings, such as temple or meeting house.

The most recent wave of Hmong to arrive in Thailand have been refugees fleeing warfare and persecution at the hands of the post-1975 communist rulers of Laos. A Hmong anti-communist guerrilla army was financed and closely supported by the United States during the 1960's and early 1970's in Laos, and it was mostly these soldiers and their families that made to leave after the communist victory in 1975. Forty-four thousand fled in the months immediately following the change in government. Though the rate of arrivals slowed after the initial influx, by 1990 over one hundred and twenty thousand are thought to have packed up and moved to Thailand. The majority of these refugees ended up in refugee camps or detention centres. Many have since been resettled in third countries, principally the United States, where there are now thought to be over eighty thousand Hmong, almost fifty percent of whom live in California. Other third countries include Argentina, Australia, Canada, France, and French Guiana.

The Yao

The Yao, who are also known as the Mien, and who some regard as the most aristocratic of the Thai hilltribes, are an ethnic group of approximately two million people. Of these, some 1.5 million live in South China, 200,000 in Vietnam, perhaps 20,000 in Laos, and 38,000 in Thailand, the majority in the provinces of Chiang Rai, Phayao, Nan and Lampang. Like the Hmong, their villages have no central area or communal place, but consist of clusters of houses grouped around a senior lineage figure. Their religion is a colourful fusion of animism, ancestor worship and Taoism, with some elements of shamanism thrown in. The Taoism they follow is that of China in the thirteenth and fourteenth centuries, which differs somewhat from contemporary Chinese Taoism. A long-standing tradition of writing—using Chinese characters—makes the Yao unique among the hilltribes of Thailand.

The Lisu

The Lisu are a group of almost one million; nearly 600,000 are thought to live among the western borders of Yunnan in China, with over 250,000 in the far north of Burma, and several thousand in northwestern India, and about 25,000 in Thailand. Most of those in Thailand are thought to have come from China via Burma, and to have first crossed into Thailand during the opening decade of this century. Almost half of these now live in the mountains of Chiang Mai Province, with other concentrations being in western Chiang Rai Province—particularly along the Mae Kok River—and

Introduction

in the far north-west of the country in Mae Hong Son Province. Some Lisu groups live close to, or even with, Lahu Nyi or Lahu Shi communities, and many Lisu can also speak Lahu, as well as Yunnanese Chinese.

The Lahu

Skilled hunters and, some say, master practitioners of black magic, the Lahu are a multifarious group of over half a million people. Of these, over 350,000 live in southwestern Yunnan in China, roughly 200,000 in northeastern Burma, about sixty thousand in Thailand, and a few thousand in Laos. Nearly all those in Thailand have come from China (via Burma) within the last century, and are represented by five main subgroups: *Lahu Na* (Black Lahu), *Lahu Nyi* (Red Lahu), *Lahu Shi* (Yellow Lahu), *Lahu Sheh Leh* (Shehleh), and *Lahu Hpu* (White Lahu). Each of these subdivisions sports its own distinctive style of dress and, despite some discarding their traditional clothes – particularly those that have turned to Christianity – the full range and diversity of these groups can still easily be appreciated in Thailand.

The Akha

The Akha – perhaps the most distinctive of all the Thai hilltribes – are thought to originate from southwestern China, where there are now approximately 250,000 living today, mainly in Yunnan province. Many Akha in Thailand consider the Sipsongpanna region of southern Yunnan to be their original homeland. There are an estimated 200,000 Akha living in Kengtung state, Burma, 38,000 in northern Thailand, 15,000 or so in Laos, and a few thousand in northern Vietnam. In addition, there is a very closely related group in China known as Hani by the Chinese. The Hani number a million, of whom about 700,000 speak a dialect close to Akha.

The first Akha entered Thailand from Burma in the early years of this century and initially settled north of the Mae Kok river in Chiang Rai Province. The majority still live north of this river today. They can be divided into three main groups according to the style of dress worn – in particular the type of headdress worn. The 'U Lo-Akha', who have been domiciled in Thailand the longest, wear a pointed headdress, the 'Loimi-Akha', who are more recent migrants from the Loimi mountain region of Kengtung state, Burma, wear a flat headdress, and the 'Phami-Akha' wear a helmet-like headdress. The majority of these Akha in Thailand speak a common dialect of the Akha language.

The Karen

The Karen, called 'Kariang' or 'Yang' by the Thais, are thought to have originally come from either southwestern China or southeastern Tibet, and to have migrated southwards into eastern Burma, a land in which they have now been living for many centuries. They first began crossing the border into Thailand during the eighteenth century.

Most Karen still live in Burma, where there are estimated to be four million, of which the Pa-O, Kayan and the Kayah sub-groups are among the largest. Of the 280,000 living in Thailand over two-thirds, some 200,000 people, are Sgaw Karen living north of Mae Sariang in Mae Hong Son Province. Lesser concentrations are found to the north-east of Chiang Mai and west of Chiang Rai.

The other principal Karen group in Thailand are the Pwo Karen, who number around 80,000 and live south of Mae Sariang in a mountainous region stretching down the length of the border with Burma to the Kra of Isthmus in the south. A third and much smaller group are the Red Karen, or Kayah, who are found in a few villages in the extreme north-west of Mae Hong Son Province, and in isolated villages east of Chiang Rai.

The Karen remain culturally very different from either the other highland groups or the Thai lowlanders. Some live in villages at high altitudes, others live in lowland settlements close to ethnic Thai villages. There are even communities of Karen in some of the larger towns of the north, such as Chiang Mai, Mae Hong Son, Mae Sariang and Lamphun.

Though many Karens have adopted the Buddhist faith and speak Thai as a first language, and are in many ways almost indistinguishable from the Thais, there are still many, the majority even, who live their lives according to the ancient beliefs and strict codes of their ancestors.

Introduction

4 - Dual Worlds:
Spirits, Souls and the Afterlife

Although some Lahu groups have been more affected by Buddhism than others, and the Yao have a strong element of Chinese Taoism in their religion, the belief systems of all six of the above societies are intrinsically 'animist' in their make-up. Each also exhibits, to a greater or lesser degree, elements of ancestor worship and shamanism.

Animism is not a single creed or doctrine, but rather a view of the world consistent with a certain range of religious beliefs and practices. Essentially, animism is 'the belief in innumerable spiritual beings concerned with human affairs and capable of helping or harming men's interests.' (*Encyclopaedia Britannica* 16:576). Perhaps the most salient characteristics of all animistic religions is their particularism, as opposed to the universalism of the 'great religions', which conceive man as subject to higher powers and personal destiny. Particularistic religions identify a whole range of spirits, all acting independently of each other, from sojourning ghosts and mortal witches to perennial beings, whose natures and dispositions to man may be friendly, ambivalent or downright hostile, depending on the given circumstances.

Generally, spirits are conceived as being immaterial and, usually, as being diffused through space, although many are associated with specific places in the material world. Spirits recognised by Thai highlanders include:

1) Spirits associated with the elemental powers of nature: sun and moon, rain, thunder and lightning, the mountains and the forests.

2) 'Nature spirits', such as those found inhabiting certain trees, rocks, ponds, streams and pathways.

3) 'Owner' spirits, one of which owns all the wild pigs, and another, the locality spirit—a sort of spirit landlord—who owns a given area. Others are the rice owner and the maize spirit.

4) Protective spirits, for example the spirit associated with the Akha village gate, which keeps evil from entering a village, and the important and numerous house spirits: the spirit of the stove, the

spirit of the front door, the spirit of the central house post, and those associated with the marital bedroom, the loft, the fireplace and the household altar.

5) Malicious spirits, including the 'spirits of bad death'. These are the spirits of people who have suffered from deaths considered 'unnatural', for instance from downing, through childbirth, lightning, suicide and any bloody accident. Other evil spirits are the vampires, weretigers, the spirits of babies that have died before being named, and those associated with disease, in particular with smallpox and malaria.

6) Ghosts. Usually referred to as 'hungry ghosts', these are the spirits of the deceased who for one reason or another do not reside in the heavens, but remain on the earth to prey on the living.

The spirit categories listed above are all 'ordinary spirits', as opposed to the Gods, Lords and other supernatural spirits of the heavens. Ordinary spirits share the living world, or 'World of Light', with mankind, albeit a different sphere of this same world. These two co-existing spheres, the world of men, and the world of spirits, are held to be intricately linked. More than this, they are thought to mirror each other: the human's day is the spirit's night, and the spirit's wet season is the human's dry season. Just as men and women live out their human lives working in the fields and raising families in the world of men, so the spirits in their spirit world lead a spirit life, working in their fields and raising their own families.

In many ways the terms spirit and supernatural being are misleading, since the spirits, in a way, are all natural and physical. They are not exactly 'gods', nor are they functions or essences of things or people, but they have something of all these, and more. There is little suggestion that spirits have a demon-like or divine character, although hilltribe people will readily talk about a particular 'evil' or 'good' spirit, according to the function they are seen to fulfil, and some of the supernatural and powerful beings of the 'beyond' do come close to being regarded as 'gods'.

In most cases people do not consider there is anything sacred or profane about ordinary spirits. Neither do they live in fear of them, although they can, and do, live in fear of the actions of certain spirits. But even these less friendly spirits are still dealt with in a very human way, and may be bribed, negotiated with, or even frightened into a particular action.

This is typically the job of the shaman, an ecstatic figure believed to be able to communicate with the world beyond, and in so communicating, influence, and to some extent control and direct the spirits for the benefit of the community. For unlike in many of the advanced religions of the world, where the spirit, or God, is thought to be vastly greater and more powerful than men, and where the normal address to the spirit takes the form of humble entreaty, the relationship between men and spirits is far less one-sided in the 'simpler' religions. In fact, very often ghosts and spirits are thought of as being as much dependent on men, as men are on them. There are rights and obligations on both sides.

This is reflected in much of the ritual behaviour of hilltribe communities, in that an element of reciprocity or exchange is often clearly involved: people give food offerings to the spirits to evoke thanks, and hence, the spirits' blessings. Just as man needs the good-will and protection of the spirits if he is to prosper, so a spirit is thought to need the attentions of men if it is to be remembered, and thus honoured.

Standing separate from the everyday run-of-the-mill spirits, however, are the supreme beings, the deities and Lords of the non-living world, the so-called 'World of Dark', a metaphysical land of ancestors and other supernatural beings (what the West would regard as 'the beyond'). These 'higher spirits' include the two Lisu deities *Wu sa* (the 'Creator') and *Ida ma* (the 'Great One'), the Lahu supreme being *G'ui sha*, the Akha all powerful force *Apoe Miyeh*, and the Hmong 'Lord' *Ntxwj Nyug*. There are many other lesser deities. These are all spirits, but are spirits of a different nature to those ordinary spirits that co-exist alongside mankind. Most, if not all of these 'Lords' have their home in the heavens and are treated with respect by tribal people.

The Man Inside the Man

The Hmong, Yao, Lisu, Lahu, Akha and Karen all regard man as having one or more souls. A soul, which the eminent British anthropologist Frazer referred to as 'the man inside the man' (Frazer 1922:178), is the physical body's spiritual counterpart. It is generally conceived as being non-material and essentially immortal, and as existing before the body was formed.

Souls are considered very vulnerable to attack from outside, not only from malicious spirits such as vampires, weretigers and other 'bad death' spirits, but also from normally benign or indifferent spirits made angry for some imagined transgression on the part of the human. Such an attack and subsequent capture of the soul normally results in a deterioration in the health of the victim and, if urgent countermeasures are not undertaken, ultimately, in death.

Having first determined the circumstances behind a soul's loss, a shaman, or other knowledgeable practitioner will in most cases attempt to locate and recapture the missing soul. This is the purpose behind the majority of 'curing rituals'. If the soul cannot be retrieved, death will result. Death also occurs when a person's allotted time on earth has run out, following which one or more of a person's souls will depart for the 'land of the ancestors'.

Geography of the Afterlife

It is to 'the Otherworld' that a person's soul (or souls) travels after the death of the physical body. And it is from here that they (or some of them) return to the land of the living, when the time has come to be reincarnated. Some, however, remain in 'the beyond' to become ancestral spirits. These spirits are conceived as being able to influence events in the living world: subsequently, all of the tribal societies of northern Thailand regard it as only prudent to venerate and remember their deceased kinsfolk.

Each tribal group has its own, sometimes hazy view of the other side. The Karen travel to *phlyng*, where life for the disembodied soul mirrors that on Earth. The Taoist Yao, however, conceive of three distinct destinations: two earthly refuges, these being 'The Cave of the World' and 'The Inferior Cave of the World', and a heavenly abode called 'The Palace of Lao Chun the Ninth', or 'Ninth Heaven' for short. Which 'beyond' an individual ends up at depends largely on what qualifications one has picked up while in the world of men. Such 'qualifications' are gained by taking part in special merit-making and ordination ceremonies.

The Hmong 'Otherworld' is different again. We are told it is thought of as a harsh, mountainous landscape, similar to that inhabited by the Hmong in their mortal lives. As with Hades, it can often be entered through holes in the ground, or via underground caves. At a meeting point between the two worlds there is a large piece of water, crossed by a bridge. On this bridge the souls of men and spirits can communicate with each other. (Crossing water is a common feature in eschatological topography the world over.)

Passing into the Otherworld the souls of the dead come to twelve great mountains in order to receive judgement at the hands of the dreaded Lords of the Otherworld. The way is fraught with dangers, such as poisonous hairy caterpillars, over which the souls must pass, aided in this instance by a pair of slippers given to the soul during the funeral, before the start of the journey.

Reaching the highest mountain they come to the abode of the two fearful Lords, *Ntxwj Nyug* and *Nyuj Vaj Tuan Teem*. Here the souls are interviewed and an appropriate animal, vegetable, or human form of reincarnation is determined, following which licences for rebirth are issued. Not all souls are so lucky, however. The souls of people who have committed crimes such as stealing or murder while in the world of men will have their reincarnation delayed. They must first be punished, and are made to work as servants for the spirits of the sky world: a Hmong form of purgatory.

Those who have passed the judgement—and those who have served their time as servants—then proceed on to their ancestral villages where they will await reincarnation. Back in the mortal world, and usually within a year of the passing away, an important and joyous ceremony will be held in the soul's previous human village. This 'releases the soul' for rebirth. If all things are well, the family of the deceased can expect the disembodied soul to return to the world of men. With the proper observance of the rituals, the soul should enter the womb of a woman of the same lineage as the soul's previous incarnation.

The Hmong, in common with the Yao, Lisu, Lahu, Akha and Karen, therefore believe in a perpetual circle of life and death. They do not strive to find a way out of life and suffering, as do the Buddhists, nor do they hope to end their life by joining their Maker in heaven, as Christians do. Instead, they strive to keep the descent line strong. For by marrying and raising a large family they are providing bodies into which their ancestors may be reborn, ancestors who will in turn provide bodies into which they themselves will one day be reincarnated. It is this perpetual cycle of life and death which governs so much of everyday hilltribe life.

5 - On the Trail of the Spirits

As a result of the particular nature of the migration of tribal peoples into Thailand, there has developed over much of the northern mountains a hodgepodge of villages belonging to different ethnic groups: Karen, Hmong, Yao, Akha, Lahu, Lisu, Khamu, Lua, H'tin, and others. Although there are areas with concentrations of certain tribes, there are in Thailand no distinct tribal enclaves: there are no Lisu homelands, Yao enclaves, or Akha territories. Instead, a single mountainside may be home to three or four different peoples, and even a single village may consist of two distinct tribal groups, living their lives according to their own customs and traditions. It is this great cultural mishmash which makes northern Thailand so unique in Asia and which, coupled with the region's increasing accessibility, makes it so interesting to anthropologist and tourist alike. And it is this same cultural patchwork which we now hoped would facilitate our own collection of material.

From our home in Kiew Khan we have over the years travelled by motorbike to numerous other tribal villages in the region. Many of these villages we know well, having since 1986 made a concerted effort to establish contacts in as many communities as possible. Many of these 'contacts' have subsequently become close friends.

In Kiew Khan, and in other nearby Hmong and Lahu villages, our relationships are primarily based on our being neighbours. As outside-insiders we hear all the village gossip, ranging from who is having a 'secret' love affair with someone else's husband or wife, to who is engaged in certain illegal activities of which the Golden Triangle region is justifiably infamous.

Once we leave the immediate area, however, unless we are in a Hmong village, where acquaintances shared in common inevitably lead to invitations to stay, or are in a village that we have known for a number of years (and there are many), we necessarily revert to being strangers; strangers with an unusual appetite for anecdotes and explanations 'of the obvious'. For initially, until we have explained the reasons for our interest in tribal cultures, and especially so when our interest was directed rather more to people's 'ordinary' lives, most highlanders are, to say the least, rather perplexed at our enquires.

'Do they work for the district office?' 'Is there anything sinister in these apparently innocent questions?' 'Why do they want to talk with someone like me?' are the thoughts that likely go through many minds — as well as those of the 'Shit a post! Look at the size of that White Indian's nose' variety. However, despite their initial wariness, in our experience humour and an unassuming attitude usually opens the way to fruitful relationships remarkably quickly, and can often lead to meaningful friendships — and it must be said, to some of the best booze-ups ever! (at Yao weddings in particular).

Concentrating our efforts first on the place we knew best, we initially spent more than a month collecting accounts from our own Hmong neighbours in Kiew Khan. We spoke with men and women, the old and the young, often in their own houses, sometimes in the fields or when out hunting. One man spoke to us about the special rituals he performs as a hunter, and perhaps more interestingly, about the factors which led him to return to the ways of the spirits, having almost converted to Christianity. And Leuer's eldest daughter told us of the time she nearly came face to face with a 'hungry ghost'.

We heard of identification marks made on a baby's forehead which aid the return of its 'wandering soul', of mystical bones in far-off lands, of *gong-goy* spirits, weretigers, and a monkey-like spirit with 'vertical eyes', as well as a gripping account involving a 'wandering soul', a shaman, a powerful tree spirit, and a Thai Buddhist monk intent on felling a tall distinctive tree. And many, many others.

Excited by our early successes in Kiew Khan, and hurrying to beat the start of the monsoon rains which in June would turn the dirt roads into almost impassable quagmires, we hastily made plans for a trip into the hills to the west of Mae Chan. We chose the Mae Chan area for a number of reasons. Firstly, there were many tribal villages belonging to the different tribal groups in the area, many of which are easily accessible by motorbike. Secondly, it is an area we know particularly well, having conducted a series of interviews with tribal people in the area in 1989-90. And thirdly, we wanted an excuse to call in on some old friends, Thai and tribal, who we had not seen for more than eight months.

Allowing ourselves ten days and hoping to visit at least six villages: Pang Sa (Lisu), Lao Shi Guai (Yao), Bon Pa Kaem (Yao), Ja-pu'er (Lahu Shi-Lisu), Huai Pu (Lahu Nyi) and Ban Ar Lae (U Lo Akha), we stocked up on blank cassette tapes and camera film, packed up two large boxes, one containing basic medicines, the other school exercise books, pencils and coloured crayons — supplied to us for just such a purpose — and without further ado set off on the heavily rutted, dust-covered dirt track which, in a series of five drops, would lead us to the Chiang Saen road in the valley below.

This first trip proved surprisingly rewarding. In the large Lisu village of Pang Sa, the headman, a man named Mano Leejar, related to us a tale of black magic:

My father knew he had been attacked by do *— that's what we call black magic in Lisu, and he knew very well who had done it.*

And of the mountain spirit, *Ida ma*:

I think Ida ma is the same age as me. I am the headman of the village. I am the boss. If anyone has a problem, or if anyone needs some help, it is to me they come. They come to me to discuss the problem. And Ida ma, in my opinion, is like the headman of the spirits.

In the beautiful Akha village of Ban A-bey we met the village priest, Aka My-yer. He spoke of the two worlds of men and spirits:

The spirits stole many things, such as rice and vegetables from the fields. Finally the village elders and the senior spirits held a meeting to decide what to do. The elders ordered the spirits to leave the village and go and live in the jungle.

And of vampires:

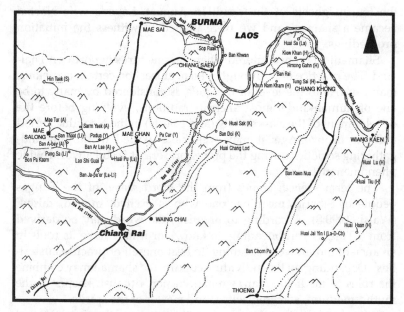

Northern Chiang Rai Province

Yes, yes, in the old days there were many of them. Now we don't get them so often, although there are still some around.

And in the Yao village of Lao Shi Guai, Yiow-fun, a Yao shaman, spoke of fire-walking and his summons to shamanism:

I could never ignore the drums...I'd hear them and come over all strange. My heart would start thumping and I wouldn't be able to relax. I'd have to go nearer and nearer, and then when I got really close my whole body would go cold and I'd start trembling and shaking.

Throughout the long wet summer months we busied ourselves once again with interviewing our friends and neighbours in and around Kiew Khan, hearing tales of weretigers, house spirits and the fearful ghosts of the dead. In August, Leuer's wife Nachai became a shaman, and we were invited to witness the initiation proceedings.

Shamanism is encountered wherever one turns in northern Thailand. The practice of it, through which, at least on certain occasions, man can rise to the level of the gods, is considered by many to be one of humankind's most ancient traditions, evolving before the development of the class society (and priests) in the Neolithic Period and the Bronze Age; it may well have existed in hunting-and-gathering societies during the prehistoric era. It is still a world-wide phenomenon today.

The term *shaman* comes from the word *saman* of the Tungas people of Siberia, meaning 'one who is excited, moved, raised' (Walsh 1990:8). According to linguists, the word may be derived from a Tungas verb meaning 'to know', or it may have its roots in an ancient Indian word meaning 'to heat oneself or practise austerities'. Depending on the individual culture, the shaman may combine the roles of medicine man/woman, healer, ritualist, keeper of the myths, medium, sorcerer/witch, and master of the spirits.

After her initiation, Nachai described some of the signs she had experienced as a child which were interpreted by those about her as being indications that she had been chosen by the spirits to be a shaman. She also told us of the practising shaman who, all those years ago, had managed to confine in a celestial prison the spirit which had been calling her, thus postponing her summons until she was older. That summer the old shaman passed away. The spirit returned to Nachai and she finally accepted her calling — much to our good fortune.

I told my father about the problem. He said the shaman who had put the spirit in jail all those years ago had died, and that the spirit wanted me again. He said I'd have to become a shaman.

The end of the wet season heralded the coming of winter: cold mornings and clear bright skies, every day like the best of English autumn days. Once again we set forth on the trail of the spirits, spending weeks in villages south of Chiang Khong, to the east and west of Mae Chan, and to the north of Mae Salong.

In October the maize harvests got under way, followed closely in November by the rice harvests. We visited Karen, Lahu, Yao and Hmong villages on our side of Mae Chan, and returned once more to the area around Mae Salong, visiting and staying in a number of Akha and Lisu villages. During these beautiful, crisp, clear days we heard descriptions and explanations of Lahu holy days, of divination, Karen taboos and house spirits, and the Lisu practice of blowing fire balls as part of an exorcism ritual.

Back in Kiew Khan we spoke with Mit Selee on the subject of courtship and the Hmong house spirits, and with his pretty wife Mai-gwa, on the topic of childbirth and post-natal precautions (against attack from malicious spirits). We also talked with a man named Laoseu Seyang. He related to us a fascinating tale of a non-believer:

There was once a man who didn't believe in the spirits. He didn't even try to understand why people carry out the rituals and live their lives aware of the spirits. Every time people began talking about the spirits he'd get angry and say they were talking rubbish.

In December, Hmong New Year came round again: a week-long celebration in which ancestor offerings, feasting, the wearing of newly-made clothes and, for the young at least, the playing of a ritual courtship game feature prominently. For a whole week each chilly dawn is greeted by the sounds of pigs being stuck — a most joyous sound to all Hmong.

During these relatively cold winter months we attended two funerals and three weddings, and were asked to perform a soul-calling ritual for a neighbour. Then, in quick succession came Yao, Lisu and Lahu New Year festivals, as winter gave way all too quickly to the dry, dusty hot season: the season of field clearings and burn-offs. And a whole year had passed, our fourth in Kiew Khan.

The following collection of interviews and accounts are the fruits of these inquiries into our neighbours' spiritual life. We have not tried to analyse every word spoken to us, for we are not social scientists trying to fit our data into a working modal of behaviour. And we have not judged the relative truth of stories. For what is truth? Surely, truth and belief are many different things to many different people. We have, however, tried to transcribe and translate their words faithfully, a task which has taken some time.

We only hope we have succeeded, no matter in how small a way, to convey some sense of the richness and diversity of beliefs held by the hilltribe peoples; for all whom we spoke with were eager and happy to share with us their thoughts and beliefs, believing that in so doing they would help others to know and understand them. For these 'ordinary' people living in the northern hills of Thailand are proud of their ways and, above all, proud to be true descendants of their forefathers, be they Hmong, Yao, Lisu, Lahu, Akha or Karen.

INTERVIEWS

1 – Nachai Sewa—Hmong

Nachai Sewa is in her mid-to-late forties and is the mother of nine children, of which three – Do, Nayua and Nabai – we will encounter in subsequent pages. She lives in the Hmong village of Kiew Khan, a large White Hmong community of over one hundred households situated on a site sheltered by two thickly forested hills nineteen kilometres north-west of Chiang Khong in Chiang Rai Province.

Nachai and her husband Leuer are particular friends of ours. Leuer is our official sponsor in the village, meaning it was he, supported by Laogwa, the former headman, and Jonglao, the present headman, who pressed our case with the elders when we first asked permission to settle in the village. And it is on his land, next to his own home, that we built our small house when we moved into the village five years ago.

Nachai is a born story teller, with a seemingly inexhaustible collection of tales from which to draw. Over the years she has been a valuable source of information for us concerning traditional Hmong myths, as well as having related to us many contemporary stories of unusual goings-on. In August 1991 she became a practising shaman. Since her initiation we have spoken with her at length on many subjects related to shamanism.

Spirit Heads

In the past there used to be many 'spirit heads' in Kiew Khan. Standing either side of the main doorways outside Hmong houses, they were still there when we first arrived in 1987. Carved at one end of a single wooden log about four feet long, the heads, though simply fashioned, seemed to bear an uncanny resemblance to the occupants of each house. And like the tribal people who carved them, they too had received knocks and scars over the years, a chip here, a deep machete cut there. Though most were still firmly embedded in the ground, some were leaning precariously to one side, while others lay abandoned in the dirt beside a pig pen or cow shed. I had asked whether I could take one. No, definitely not, I was informed, they were not to be removed by anyone, but left alone to rot on their own accord. Much later I heard the story behind them, but by then they had all gone. Rotted away into the soil.

Hmong spirit head

In the following account Nachai outlines the reasoning behind the creation of the 'spirit heads', and tells of the dreaded 'peanut spots', a disease which used to be inflicted upon villagers by an evil spirit in days gone by.

Oh, those heads. That's the *gunban* spirit, the spirit which stops evil spirits from entering our homes. We make those heads when the spots come, the ones we call 'peanut spots'. During an outbreak of spots every family in the village must make those heads to put outside their houses in front of the doors, one on either side. And at the same time we have to build spirit gates on all the paths leading into the village. These gates are to stop people from coming into the village, and also to stop us leaving. When the spots are in the area all the villages do it.

The gates the Hmong build at times of epidemics are simple affairs. They are built over the main tracks leading to the village, and consist of a rope made of grass attached to two wooden posts. Carved wooden knives are inserted between the strands of the rope. These are to frighten off evil spirits, particularly the one bringing the plague, and are placed there by the shaman. Sometimes a severed dog's head will be left on a gate across a main track, with the paws and lower legs hanging from gates across lesser paths. By sacrificing the dog, its soul is sent to the 'other side', there to protect the village from the evil spirit, just as in life the dog's job was to protect the household from strangers. This grisly display also serves to frighten off the evil disease-bringing spirit. A further protective measure is the tying of grass ropes around every house in the community, having first dipped them in the blood of the sacrificed dog.

The spots are serious. During a bad outbreak there could well be four or five people dying in the village every day. Their bodies go bad, pus oozes out from all over them. If they survive, they are left with scars all over their faces and bodies.

During an outbreak every house must carve the heads, and they also have to share in the costs of making offerings to the spirit of the gates, and for the services of the shaman.

The shaman has to fight off the bad spirit. He makes a big basket which he hands over to two men to carry for him. Then he gets hold of a black dog. Followed by the two men he takes the dog and a flaming torch to every house in the village. Inside each house he leads the dog round the house on the end of a piece of rope while all the time throwing rice powder over the torch causing the flames to shoot out and singe the dog. He goes into all the bedrooms, and to both the doors. Then when he has finished the householders give him some rice and cooked vegetables, some white and red pepper, and one live chicken which they place into the big basket carried by the two helpers.

The 'flaming torch dog-on-a-string' ritual is performed in Hmong villages during exorcisms of evil spirits. The fireballs are meant to frighten off the spirit. The one occasion when we witnessed such an event was when a shaman performed an exorcism of a spirit which had possessed Nachai's eldest daughter, Nayua. In this instance the poor dog's eventual fate was to have its throat cut and its four paws hacked off, these to be hung over the two house doors in an effort to bar the re-entry of the malicious spirit.

It all has to be done in a single day. When we did it we had one shaman for our side of the village, and another for the other side. The bad spirit inside each house leaves with the chickens we give to the shaman. The shaman takes it away from our homes. Once he has been to every house he takes the black dog to the spirit gate which has been built over the main path. Here he cuts its throat and severs the paws. The paws are then hung from the gate. This stops the spirit which brings the spots from coming to our village.

Oh, the gate is very strong, it frightens away the spirit. It also stops people coming to us. If anybody should ignore the gate they have to give a pig to be offered to the spirit of the gate. When the spots are in the area we build these gates on every single track coming into the village.

Many people in Thailand who come into contact with highland groups are often shocked by an apparent disregard for the suffering of animals shown by tribal peoples during ritual sacrifices. They consider the tribal peoples to be barbarous and brutish, and far too preoccupied with the killing of sacrificial animals. I, myself, remember regaling people with tales of how my neighbour's children would particularly enjoy watching an animal have its throat cut, how the youngest boy would sometimes prod his finger into the wound, just as another boy in another part of the world may dip his fingers into a pool of spilt paint; or how the fifteen year old girl next door would be happily teasing and playing with a puppy only minutes before picking up the furry little bundle and delivering it to a man with a cold, sharp knife.

But all this misses the cardinal point: sacrifice, in which an object is offered to a divinity in order to establish, maintain, or restore a right relationship of man to the sacred order, is a celebration of life, not death. Along with prayer, it is the fundamental act of worship. In a sense, what is always offered is, in one form or another, life itself. Through sacrifice, life is returned to its divine source, regenerating the power of that source; life is fed by life. By liberating the life-force of a sacrificial animal, man is thus guaranteeing the reciprocal flow of the divine life-force between its source and its manifestations.

Thus, the killing of a chicken, pig, cow or dog, or whatever, is a positive act which, in the eyes of the participants, brings benefits to all involved, including the victim. The actual killing may be bloody and distressing to some — myself included, but it is certainly not gratuitous or wanton.

We return to Nachai to ask who carves the heads that are placed outside the houses.

Anybody in the family can do it. We make them after the shaman has been. But now we don't have them, nobody gets the peanut spots now. I think it all finished many years ago. But it was different in the past, in the old days it used to be very bad. My mother has told me about it.

When she was a little girl everybody in her village in Laos was infected with the peanut spots. My mother and all her brothers and sisters got it. She lost a younger brother and one younger sister. She and my uncle have many scars, even to this day. They'll have'em forever.

She nearly died, too. In those days there were no Western medicines. All they had were herbs from the jungle. This was in Laos. There were medicines over the border in Thailand, though. So, whenever they got ill they'd go to the border and ask the Thais for help. An injection cost one haeng of silver [approximately 2500 baht]. Those without enough silver for the Thais would die. Those with enough paid and got the treatment. Then they wouldn't get the spots and could help bury all the corpses of those that died. My mother says the stink of the dead was terrible. The bodies were covered all over with worms and insects. The whole jungle stank of dead people.

Then Nachai told us of the time the plague struck when she was living on Doi Luang – the range of hills on whose northernmost slopes Kiew Khan is situated. The former village site overlooks Kiew Khan.

There was an outbreak in our village when I was a girl living on Doi Luang mountain. Every day I saw people die. Nobody would bury the corpses, everybody was too frightened of getting the disease. My mother knew how serious it was, she was really frightened that we'd all get it. The village carried out the rituals quickly. We killed some black cats, cooked them, and divided the meat around the village. But only among those families who hadn't yet caught the disease. We ate the meat to protect us. Then my family shut up the house and we went to live in our field house for a while. It was safer in the fields, many were dying in the village.

Here in Kiew Khan there has only been the one outbreak, that was when we made the spirit heads. That was the first and last time. A few years after that some government doctors came to vaccinate us. And since then nobody has ever got it. You see, when the smallpox spirit came to the village it saw the spirit heads outside our houses, and the heads said to the bad spirit, 'Ha! You're too late, they've already been vaccinated'.

Unfortunately, the day may be coming when it will be the 'AIDS spirit' threatening a community. I wonder will the spirit heads then be saying, 'Ha! You're too late, they've already got condoms'? I hope so.

In Need of a Luckier Name

In the following account Nachai explains why the name of her youngest son – a shy two year old – was changed from Namor (meaning 'to eat') to Bor-yeh (meaning 'big rock').

Namor is often ill. There is something wrong with his name. He doesn't want it any more. I went to the shaman to ask him to look at Namor's future. I took Namor along with me and asked the shaman to come to our house and examine my Namor. But he said he needn't visit us as Namor was already there, and he offered to examine him straight away. He took a look at him and told me there was no need to sacrifice a pig or chicken for the spirits, as there was nothing much the matter with Namor. He said Namor just wanted a new name, a luckier name.

He instructed me on what I should do. I had to get some white string and take it along with Namor over to the big boulder on the hillside by the big tree over there [pointing], just behind the village. I had to place the string on the stone and then gently rub it across the boulder while at the same time asking the rock if I could have its name for my son. I had to say, 'Oh, my son is often ill, he wants to have the same name as you, bor-yeh. Please can I give your name to my son?' Then I tied the string around one of Namor's wrists and told him his new name is Bor-yeh — Big Rock. Afterwards I told everyone to call him 'yeh', for short.

Bor-yeh took to his new name with little fuss, and now responds to both names.

A Doll for the Tofu Spirit

One morning on entering Nachai's house we saw a small, lumpy, doll-like object standing on the clay wall of the main hearth. Two red chillis were sticking out from its 'head'. On closer examination a face could be discerned. We asked Nachai, who was at the time making tofu, the meaning of this figure-like object made from dough.

Oh that, well, when we are making tofu we have to make that, too. Why are you laughing? It's not a doll, although I suppose it does look like one. We make it from soy bean. It's to ask the tofu spirit to help us when we are making tofu. No, I'm not joking. If we didn't make that first, the tofu spirit would cause the tofu to go bad, and it wouldn't set properly. Really, without that thing the spirit wouldn't help us to make tofu and in the end we'd have to throw away all the ingredients.

It'd never set, you see. Even if we were to boil it for a very long time, even for the whole day, and burn a big pile of firewood, in the end we still wouldn't have any tofu. We'd just have the runny soy bean stuff. No-one ever tries to make tofu without first making the doll. After all, it's no trouble to make the doll first.

We asked Nachai whether there were any other 'precautions' she must take when cooking.

Sometimes I have to do other things to make sure something I'm making turns out alright. For instance, I have to do something special when I get 'the big vegetable' from newly burnt fields. Before I cook this strange vegetable I first have to chop it up into very small pieces and mix it with water. Not just ordinary water, I have to use special water which has been filtered through ash from the fire. This makes it really clean. Then I boil the vegetable in the water.

But before I do all this I first have to tell the children to leave the house. Then I shut the door. This is because it's very important that nobody should ask what I'm doing. Nobody should say anything like 'Oh, are you cooking some vegetables?' This is why I have to order the children out.

If they were to stay inside, then for sure they'd ask what I'm doing. Or perhaps on seeing the strange vegetable before it's diced up, they'd say something like 'Oh, look, what a funny vegetable, it looks like a tiger. It might try and eat us'. Children always ask questions when they see something unusual.

If when I'm cooking it somebody asks me about it, then it won't go hard, and no matter how much it's boiled it would never thicken. It'll just become water. It'll even be ruined if someone outside calls through the door to ask what I'm doing. I'd have to stop cooking it and throw it away. Normally a family with many children can never cook this vegetable. It takes ages to cook, for sure one of the children would say something about it. It only takes just a few words and it'll have to be thrown away.

Why? It's because this vegetable is associated with the tiger spirit. We take it from the fields, we don't plant it. They are very big, and take a few years to grow. We call it 'tiger's paw', because of it's unusual shape.

'Gong-goy' Spirits, and the Boy Who Farted

Nachai tells of a boy's lucky escape from a gong-goy *spirit.*

You don't really believe in spirits do you? I tell you, they really exist. Buddhists go to temples, but they still believe in spirits, don't they. They sometimes see spirits. Well, I tell you, so do we. We sometimes see a *gong-goy* spirit. Sometimes it takes the form of a young woman, or a mother carrying a baby. Different people see the spirit in different forms. Men often see a woman *gong-goy* spirit.

My soul-force is strong, and I know some of the spells and chants to frighten off spirits, so I'm never troubled by ghosts. I know some of the special things only a shaman knows.

The Hmong, in common with other hilltribe groups, believe a person with a 'strong soul-force', that is, someone whose souls are not prone to wander, or easily be frightened off, and who consequently could be considered a healthy person, is less likely to be troubled by spirits. Thus Nachai, whose soul-force is strong, has never seen a spirit. Incidentally, this interview was conducted before Nachai became a shaman.

I've never seen a spirit. It's because I'm strong, a spirit can't attack my soul. But my daughter is different, her soul is weaker. Two years ago she saw a spirit—it was a young girl. It took away her soul and made her ill. We had to hold a special ceremony in which we killed and offered to the spirits a black puppy, a black goat and a chicken. We did this in order to get the soul back. You were there, I remember. Spirits are real, I tell you.

And then she tells us of two little boys and their encounter with a gong-goy *spirit.*

In Hmong Gahn village where my parents live, there is one

family with many cows. It's a small family. They haven't many hands to work in the fields. So when the parents and the older children go out to work the two youngest sons have to take care of the cows. Usually they take them out to graze in the fields near the waterfall.

One very hot day when the cows were happily grazing the two boys went to sleep under a big tree. When the younger of the two boys woke up he wasn't under the tree, but in a small hut in the middle of a field. He was alone and started to cry.

When the older boy woke he was still by the tree, but he wasn't in exactly the same place as before. And there was a stranger standing there looking at him. This man offered to carry the boy on his back and go looking for the missing brother. While this boy, who was six, was being carried on the stranger's back he let out a big fart that really stank.

Straight away the stranger dropped him to the ground saying, 'Blimey, what a stink, I don't want you, you'd be farting all the time and making such a terrible stink'. Then he walked off and disappeared into the jungle. The boy then carried on looking for his missing younger brother on his own, shouting out his brother's name as he went.

The younger boy was still crying, and really frightened having woken up in a different place from where he had lain down. The older boy heard the crying and followed the sound until at last he saw his little brother in the field hut. Reaching his brother he asked him why he had gone off on his own. But the crying boy just said he was frightened and didn't know what was happening.

After the older boy had told his brother about the stranger and the fart they decided to go back to get the cows and then return home quickly. Later they told their parents about the strange events, and the shaman was asked to check their souls. The shaman was also asked to find out who the stranger had been and what he had been up to. The shaman used his divining sticks made from goat horn to find out the answers.

Divination sticks, or horns, are often employed by the Hmong and other tribal groups in an attempt to shed light on a question under review. They may be made of bamboo, but are more likely to be made of horn. Horn is more robust and, according to tribesmen, has a much better feel to it. Their length varies from about ten to fourteen centimetres. Those made from buffalo horn curve to a point, having been cut from the end of one horn. They are used in pairs and have a flat and a rounded side – the original horn tip having been split into two.

The Hmong regard their horns as representing male and female, or yin and yang, and 'Lady and Lord Kuan' or 'Mother and Father Kuan'. These names highlight a Chinese Taoist origin. In throwing the horns, the holder first clicks them together in his right hand several times, and then, bending down, throws them to the ground. They are 'read' according to how they lie. The flat side is said to be the yang position, and the rounded side the yin position. A large range of position combinations are possible, suggesting different situations in the world of yin and the world of yang. They may be thrown several times during each session in order to get a clear reading.

And what did the shaman discover?

He discovered the man had been a spirit who had wanted to take the children into the jungle in order to make them become lost. But he must have changed his mind when one of them farted, and decided to leave them alone. You see, spirits don't like it when people fart.

If this had been a traditional story from the past one could interpret it as a homily to children warning them of strangers, while at the same time being a lesson on social etiquette – all peoples in the region regard the audible breaking of wind in public as socially undesirable. But the events in the account were both contemporary, and local, and were told to us as constituting fact. Was a bad dream responsible for the origin of the story? Or is it a case of a fertile imagination, or sleepwalking, or even a hoax on the part of the boys? Or, the physical presence of a spirit? In the context of this book, however, that a scientifically verifiable truth lies behind the events of the story is of rather less importance to us than knowing the account is perceived as true by the teller. And our experience suggests Nachai is sincere in her claims.

First Signs of a Shamanic Calling

As already stated Nachai has been a practising shaman since August 1991. In an interview conducted just two days after the initiation ritual Nachai describes some of the very first signs that indicated she had been chosen by the spirits to be a shaman.

You know there is a ritual we perform every year during the New Year festival. Every household does it. Each member of the family carries a lighted incense stick to the house of a neighbouring family of the same lineage. By doing this we take the good spirits from our house over to their house so that the spirits can eat New Year food there. Everyone does it. You do it for one family, and they do it for you. The children always enjoy it. When you arrive at the other house you have to run back and forwards between the door and the spirit altar three times. The children think it's great fun.

But when I was young I couldn't do this thing. I wasn't the same as everyone else. Whenever I smelt incense I'd start shaking uncontrollably. I could never go near them without shaking, so I had to keep away when the family performed this ritual. It was the same every year. And when I got older, when my father was a shaman, because of the burning incense I'd always have to leave the house when he was sacrificing an animal.

Whenever he held a ritual I'd get a weird feeling. I'd get fidgety, and feel I didn't want to be there. If I couldn't get away I'd start shaking and then feel a great strength coming into my limbs. I'd want to run and jump everywhere.

On one occasion during a ritual my body started jerking just like my father's did when the spirit came to him. I started to run and jump inside the house. I felt a strange power surge into my limbs, and even though they tried, they couldn't hold me down. I ran and jumped all over the place. Afterwards I was so embarrassed because everyone had been watching me.

At that time I had no idea why I should suddenly be filled with such strength and start shaking so much. I wasn't pretending, really, my heart would beat wildly, and my whole chest would shake. I didn't know where the power came from. I didn't realise then the spirits wanted me.

The Hmong are most adamant that it is not possible to learn shamanism from another person. It is the spirits themselves who choose a particular person to become the vehicle for their healing powers. Once the neeb, *which are friendly spirits that assist the shaman, have identified a potential shaman they generally inform the candidate through supernatural signs or dreams of their wish to be allowed to operate through them. If the man or woman chosen should remain unaware of the spirits' intentions, or perhaps be unwilling to become a shaman, the* neeb *will likely cause that person to suffer a minor, though lingering illness, or illnesses, such as mild fevers, headaches, general weakness and tiredness. Normal remedies will have no effect, and sooner or later the patient will consult a shaman. Eventually the true cause of the illness will be revealed. It will then be necessary for the shaman-to-be to seek help from a Master shaman.*

Nachai told us of the events which led up to the realisation that she had been called to be a shaman.

When I was a little girl I used to work in the family's fields with my mother. Often we'd sleep in the field hut at night. One day I was sitting alone under a tree when I saw a big black bird fly down and settle on a low branch just in front of me. It was big, about the size of a chicken. It just sat there looking at me. I waved my arms to frighten it off, but it didn't even flinch. It just sat there as if it didn't know where to go. As it wasn't frightened, it was easy for me to catch it. I cooked it and ate it.

Soon after I had this terrible fever, and someone said the bird I had told them about must have been a spirit bird. My mother went to see a shaman about it. He confirmed what my parents were thinking: it was a spirit bird.

Oh, I was really ill. I had a fever for days and days. Every week my mother consulted a shaman. She went to many different ones. I was really thin and could hardly walk. My life was hanging by a thread the whole time. You know, in the past we didn't use paraffin in our lamps, we used cooking fat. Because I was ill with fever my mother had to leave a light burning the whole night for three months. After those months our big earthenware jar of fat was all used up.

Then one day my mother went to Tung Sai village to see a shaman there. Later he came to our house to conduct a ritual. He went into a trance and journeyed 'up there'. Afterwards he told us not to worry. He said I had been chosen to be a shaman. I'd be alright, my illness would go.

But my mother was upset. She said, 'Oh, she's still so young, she doesn't know how to do it, she can't be a shaman.' At that time I was only about nine or ten. She asked the shaman to take the spirit away, and to keep it away from me, and not to let it come to disturb me again. So the shaman conducted a very special ritual to catch the spirit and put it in jail in the heavens for the sky spirit to keep watch over. My mother had to promise that if the spirit still wanted me when I was older I would become a shaman.

You see, in those days I was too young, my mother couldn't let me become one. Once the spirit had been sent to jail I started to get better. And since then I have been healthy, that is until last year.

Knowing that her father and uncle are shamans, we asked Nachai whether there had been many shamans in her family.

Oh, there have been quite a few. Both my grandfathers were shamans, and so was my mother's sister, my father's brother — he was the one that came to help my father for my initiation — and my father. And there's also my father's nephew. Oh, my father. It was terrible when my father first became a shaman. Once a terrible thing happened. I remember it so clearly. My father had come back from the fields. He was a little bit grumpy, complaining about a backache. He wanted to go for his hot shower, but the water was still on the fire. It was winter and very cold. He told my mother to take the water off the fire, and then right before my eyes he lay down with his back on the fire.

There were still some flames on the fire, and a lot of glowing embers. Really, I'm serious. He lay down on the fire, then stood up and walked on the embers, spreading them and the fire all over the place. My brothers and sisters, my mother and myself had to get away from the fire quickly. Oh, it was terrible, really frightening.

His back didn't burn, even though he hadn't a shirt on. He stayed there until the fire had died down. It was really something to see. He did it when the spirits came to him, came to his head. If he'd been a normal person he'd have been burnt all over and probably would've died.

This is what it was like when my father first became a shaman. He couldn't control himself. He can now though, he's alright now. He's been a shaman for a long time.

When he was a new shaman he was so strong. Whenever he summoned the spirits my mother would first have to tidy up the house, to make more space in the room for my father's spirits. My father would jump around a lot, if there had been anything in the way the spirit would have got angry.

We then asked to hear of the events of last year which finally led to her sitting the initiation ritual.

Last year the shaman who had put the spirit in the cage in the heavens died. Three months later my health started to deteriorate. I seemed to have a fever every day and had pains all over my body. I was often in a bad mood. I felt I was going crazy, often wanting to strike out at people that were making me angry. Particularly at night I felt bad. I couldn't sleep, even when it was past midnight. I'd lie awake, despite feeling really tired and yawning all the time.

I would often dream that a spirit was coming to get me. I would be walking to my fields when I'd fall head-over-heels down a steep slope. I'd feel as if I was falling down from the top of a very high mountain, right on down to the bottom and into some water. I'd struggle to get out, but it wouldn't be any good. I'd weaken quickly. But then at the very last moment someone would reach down to me and pull me out.

At this point the dream always ended. She'd wake up, frightened, believing her dream was a forewarning of her coming death. As a consequence of this dream – and it was the same dream many times – she would suffer a high temperature the following day and be beset by worries of her looming death. We remember noticing changes in her during this period. She became moody and argumentative, and at night was often beset with bouts of extremely loud yawning – much to our annoyance at the time. Later we realised loud prolonged yawning is a common manifestation that the spirits are with a person. Nachai is now clear about the dream's meaning: the spirits had chosen her, and if she had refused the call she would have died.

I told my father about the problem. He said the shaman who had put the spirit in jail all those years ago had died, and that the spirit wanted me again. He said I'd have to become a shaman. You see, that's why I was feeling strange. The spirit was back. My father is a shaman, he said he could help me.

My father helped me to become a shaman. He called up the good spirits to come to my head. He pleaded with them to come, to come for such a good reason. He told them only good ones could come, bad ones weren't wanted. They came to guide me.

Nachai's father thus performed the role of Master shaman for his daughter. A Master shaman is not considered a teacher of shamanism since the Hmong believe it is the neeb *alone that reveal the ways of the shaman. The Master is rather a guide, a counsellor and mentor to the newcomer. The Hmong support this contention by pointing out that if shamanism could be learnt, one would naturally expect older, more experienced practitioners to be much better than newer ones. Yet the opposite seems to be the case. New shamans tend to be much stronger in their words and movements. The Hmong suggest this is because newer shamans are that much closer to their original encounter with the* neeb *spirits and are thus still burning with unadulterated and undirected raw spiritual energy.*

The novice shaman learns from the Master, and from experience gained over time, how to control his or her movements, and how to allow himself (or herself) to be the medium through which the spirits may do their work.

With the Master's help the novice will invoke the neeb *spirits. These spirits, also known as 'familiar spirits', have among their numbers a whole host of natural and supernatural forces and figures including sparrowhawks, swallows, dragons, tigers, soldiers and cavalry, and a spider to stretch a bridge of copper and iron allowing the troops of the shaman to cross safely into the Otherworld. Their purpose is to assist and protect the shaman on his journeys into the potentially dangerous spirit world. The Master will also help the future shaman to construct a special spirit altar inside the shaman's house, and the familiar spirits invoked by them will them be divided between the altars and houses of the two shamans.*

When people first become shamans they usually don't know much about spiritual things. They learn about them slowly. It takes a few years to become a good shaman. Shamanism runs in the family. Some families always have shamans. Like my family. My grandfather helped my father, and now my father helps me. When I get too old I'll let one of my children become one.

Every Hmong village must have at least one practitioner, although a single village may have many. Kiew Khan village, with its one hundred households has five; three men and two women. There may be many others in the village qualified to do the job.

Often there are people who'd like to become a shaman, but they can't, the spirits don't want them. Not just anybody can learn to be a shaman. Oh no, many can't. The spirits only choose people with light bones. This is so the shamans won't be too heavy for the horses when they have to go somewhere [while in trance].

She then reinforces this view with the story of a woman in the village who had once been determined to have one of her children become a shaman. A hope, Nachai says, which naturally met with disappointment.

In Sombat's family they haven't got a shaman. His mother has four adult children who are old enough. So, one day she invited her stepfather, who's a shaman, to call down the spirits from the 'beyond' to come to one of her children. He summoned the spirits, offered spirit money, burnt bee's wax and banged the shaman's gong. But the spirits didn't want any of them.

The aroma of burning beeswax is thought to please the spirits, and act as an inducement to attend a ritual.

He tried first with Sombat's brothers and sister. Then it was Sombat's turn. He was the last of the four. When Sombat sat on the bench in front of the altar he started to laugh. He thought it was so funny, he just couldn't hold it back. But the shaman told him to carry on. The shaman thought the spirits were coming to Sombat in an unusual way — through laughter. He really believed the spirits were coming, just in a different way from normal.

He started telling Sombat to let the laughter come. He instructed Sombat not just to laugh, but to laugh in a 'spiritual' way. He wanted Sombat to enter the trance properly, by moving his arms and legs about. And Sombat [laughing], really this is true, and Sombat, who was still laughing said, 'But how can I do it? How? How? Nothing is shaking. I don't know how to do it. I really can't do it.'

Just before he said this everybody had been smiling and happy. They thought Sombat was going to be a shaman. But when he told them he couldn't do it, and said he was laughing because he thought it was funny that his mother so much wanted one of them to be a shaman, everybody stopped smiling. The shaman threw his gong to the ground and gave up. He brought the entire proceedings to an end. You see, it didn't matter what they did, the spirits didn't want them.

Sombat later confirmed the story.

As some of the original owner's familiar spirits will accompany the instruments, the shaman-to-be will receive the ritual paraphernalia of shamanism from a member of his (or her) own descent group. Thus to some extent Hmong shamanism is hereditary, since the supplier of the paraphernalia must also have been a shaman. The Master shaman does not necessarily have to be of the same lineage as the newcomer, but in practice this is usually the case. It is therefore often the Master who will help in the outfitting.

Once the new shaman, assisted by the Master shaman, has been on a first journey to the Otherworld, and has learnt some chants and spells he will then be left largely to his own devices. Much of the ritual procedure will already have been learnt from observations from everyday life, particularly during social discussions and the observation of ceremonies.

A shaman does not need to accept a heavy work load. When desired, it is still possible to live in a sort of semi-retirement from the shamanistic calling, helping only particularly close lineage members, and performing only certain important rituals.

Most people seem to become a shaman without regret. They accept the spirits have chosen them, and that a refusal to comply with their wishes would likely result in a long, protracted illness. They are also aware of the benefits in status and social position that a shaman normally acquires; as well as appreciating that the payments in meat and money they receive for services rendered normally constitute a significant addition to a family's well-being.

2 – Laogee Sewang—Hmong

Laogee Sewang is a twenty-six year old Hmong shaman from Kiew Khan. He is married and has three children. For a long time a Christian, he 'returned to the spirits' after a shaman summoned by his non-Christian mother diagnosed the cause of a particularly long bout of illness as the work of spirits informing him of their wish to be allowed to operate through him. Laogee consented and, with the help of a Master shaman, himself became a practising shaman.

A Shaman's Lot

The following interview, in which Laogee outlines some of the day to day practicalities of being a shaman was conducted in front of a large crowd of villagers, including many fellow students at Laogee's Thai language evening class – a class organised and financed by the 'Population and Community Development Association'.

INTERVIEWER: How did you become a shaman?
LAOGEE: I was ill, and even went to the hospital, which helped a bit. I wasn't seriously ill. It was just that I was constantly tired and weak, and ran a fever. Sometimes I had a really bad fever, but when the nurses took my temperature nothing showed on the thermometer. They gave me some pain relievers and said there was nothing else they could do. I returned to the village. But I still had a fever and for over one month I couldn't go to the fields.

At that time I was a Christian. But my mother wasn't, and so she called in the shaman. He discovered that a good spirit was causing my problems because it wanted me to become a shaman. He said the only thing I could do was stop being a Christian, to return to the spirits, and become a shaman. I agreed, and so me, my wife and my children went back to the spirits.

My father invited another shaman to help. He was related to us. He gave me the instruments of the shaman. I took over from him, from my teacher. Sometimes even now I consult him on certain points. He gives me advice.

The instruments, or accessories, of a Hmong shaman are essential for the performance of any shamanistic ritual. There is a gong which the shaman's assistant will beat to summon the neeb spirits as the shaman goes into a trance, and then again at the end of the seance; a ceremonial sword which he plants in the ground at the foot of the altar; a pair of divination horns, the same as those used by any household head; two bell-rings which he places on his index fingers; and a rattle made of an iron hoop with half a dozen or so small metal discs attached. This last instrument the shaman shakes regularly as he goes into the trance and then throughout the proceedings. It represents the harness bells of the shaman's winged horse that carries the shaman into the Otherworld – the horse itself being represented by a bench specially provided for the shaman by the household requiring his services. There is also a black cloth hood – sometimes dark blue or red – which the shaman wears over his face to cover his eyes so as to be able to 'see' the spirits.

The special altar of the shaman is located inside his house. It may be hanging against the wall, or standing on the floor, opposite the main door, and consists of either two or three tiers. To some extent its size will reflect the status of the shaman. It is thought to represent Siv Yis' grotto near the top of a supernatural mountain (Siv Yis is a mythical figure accredited with being the very first shaman). Below the grotto lies a pool, near to which grows the flower of immortality. This pool is represented by a bowl of water kept on the altar's shelf. Several cotton strings run from the altar to the central rafter of the house and down to the door frame. It is along these lines the neeb spirits travel when they visit the altar of the shaman.

Other symbolic objects typically found on the altar include a pork-fat candle to light the way into the beyond; a bowl of husked rice in the centre of which an egg is placed which represents the parakeet – the special spirit of the shaman, three sticks of incense, three small china cups which should contain respectively water, tea and rice liquor for the spirits, and a small pile of unhusked rice or maize which is offered on the altar as fodder for the shaman's horse. There is usually also a container of puffed maize which the shaman uses at the beginning and at the end of his trance, when he throws grains over his shoulder while shouting out commands to his spirit allies.

INTERVIEWER: For how long have you been a shaman?
LAOGEE: Four years. I didn't have to learn to be a shaman.

Laogee Sewang

Nobody can learn it. It is the spirits that call you. You become a shaman because they want you.

INTERVIEWER: Are there any things forbidden you?

LAOGEE: I don't understand. Do you mean food or something else?

INTERVIEWER: Anything?

LAOGEE: I can eat the same things as everybody else. And drink the same as well.

INTERVIEWER: As a new shaman how long was it before people began consulting you?

LAOGEE: Once I became a shaman my wife invited me to hold a ritual. This was two days later. We did it to practise. Now people come any time. I usually perform a ritual three days after the first consultation.

INTERVIEWER: How are you paid for your services?

LAOGEE: The family that consults me pays. I get the head and half the body of the pig. And I eat there with them as well. That's if they are related to me. For other people I usually get paid two or three hundred baht. It depends on how long it takes. Sometimes, if there is work in my fields that needs doing, the family that consults me offers to work for me for two days. You see, normally my wife works in the fields, as I do too. But when I'm helping somebody she has to be my assistant. She bangs the gong. So afterwards we need help in the fields. I never ask for much money. Usually I take whatever they offer. I make it cheap, that way they'll ask me again sometime. It's not good to charge too much.

When a family member falls ill and it is felt a shaman should be consulted, most Hmong would choose a shaman from their own clan, and, if possible, one from the same lineage. This does not necessarily mean the shaman will live in the same village as the patient. An especially highly respected practitioner may be called in from far afield when the occasion is thought to warrant it.

A simple divination ritual conducted by the household head helps in the decision as to which particular shaman to consult. One of the most common methods is to balance an egg on the back of the hand while repeating the name of the shaman one has in mind. If the egg stays in place, the chosen shaman is the one to contact. Another routine method is to balance the egg on a bottle. Other procedures include balancing either an egg or two chopsticks on top of an egg which has been placed standing upright in a bowl of rice. The Hmong stress that despite the apparent difficulty in balancing these objects, if the spirits accept the choice of shaman, the household head will manage these tasks with ease.

When it is decided which shaman to consult, the household head will visit him in his house and 'kowtow' with head and knuckles to the ground three times. The name of the sick person is given and the shaman's services are formally requested. The shaman will then cast divination sticks to determine the nature of the illness, and to check whether his familiar spirits are able to deal with the situation. As practically all sickness in a Hmong village is attributed to soul-loss, much of a shaman's workload is in trying to identify a missing soul's whereabouts, and the circumstances of its loss. This is then followed by the enticing back or recapture of the lost or kidnapped soul, thereby effecting a cure.

After identifying the problem the shaman will normally wait three days and nights to see whether the patient shows any sign of improvement in his condition. The shaman will be looking for an improved appetite or increased facial colour. If such an improvement is noted it is seen as a clear indication that the shaman's familiar spirits are sufficiently powerful to deal with the situation.

If the patient's condition should worsen during the three-day period, it is clear the shaman is unable to help in this instance and another practitioner will be approached. When this occurs there is no loss of face for the shaman, for it is fully recognised that it is the spirits working through the shaman, and not the shaman himself, who intervene (or not, as the case may be) in the workings of the spirit world.

INTERVIEWER: Is it true that a shaman cannot sleep with his wife the night before a ritual?

LAOGEE: Well, that one's easy to ask isn't it. Easy to ask but difficult to answer. You'd have to make it worth my while before I answer that one. Ask something different.

INTERVIEWER: No, this is the one you've got to answer. I can't change the question now.

LAOGEE: I don't think anybody would want to answer that in front of so many people. They'll only make fun of me tomorrow in class. You know, I go to the evening school now.

INTERVIEWER: No, come on, I'm interested to know. I want to know what secrets you and your wife have.

LAOGEE: [laughing] Alright, alright, I'll tell you, but I'm going to whisper. Usually I get three days notice of a session. I choose the day. The night before I cannot make love to my wife because if I did I'd lose my power, I wouldn't be any good. And when the spirits are taking me to the land of the spirits I think I'd make many mistakes and wouldn't be able to discover what was what. I'd be useless. Then afterwards, when the family questioned me about the cause of the illness I'd get it all wrong. And anyway, I'd feel unclean if I slept with my wife just before a session. I think the spirits would realise as well. I'd feel dirty and wouldn't be able to relax.

The shamanic session is normally divided into two parts. The first is to identify the cause of the illness, and the second, to attempt a cure. Often a few days, or even weeks will separate the two. If a clear picture of the cause of the illness cannot be obtained through the use of the divination horns, the shaman will proceed directly to the first part of the shamanic session for his diagnosis. This requires no sacrifice and can be performed at any time. The shaman will go to the patient's house accompanied by an assistant (usually a spouse) who will normally carry the shaman's tools. Inside the house a small altar for the shaman will have been set up against the wall facing the main door. In front of this will be the wooden bench, or 'horse', on which the shaman will 'ride' while in trance.

Having first thrown his divination horns a number of times, lit the incense sticks and burnt some paper spirit money, he will sit on the bench and, with his face covered by the black veil-like hood, almost immediately begin to jerk and tremble as he enters his trance. The movements will be the most pronounced in his legs and arms which will begin to take on a rhythm of their own and which, combined with his bumping motion up and down on the bench, closely resemble the movements of a rider on a cantering horse.

The sounds of the gong struck by the shaman's assistant standing just behind him, and those of the shaman's finger-bells, and the rattle which he holds in his right hand, together with the rhythmic motion of the body, the smell of the burning incense and the darkness caused by the veil, all combine to help the shaman enter his trance. Once there, the shaman can become the vehicle of the neeb *spirits. These spirits then descend and accompany him on his journey into the Otherworld in search of the afflicted soul.*

Throughout the trance – and it may last two hours or longer – the shaman cries invoking his spiritual helpers to aid and assist him in various ways. Many of the words used are unintelligible to the average Hmong. A good many may be unintelligible even to the shaman himself, for they are seen to have a spiritual origin.

On his return to the world of men the shaman will be exhausted and will be given time to rest and regain his strength. On recovering, he will be anxiously questioned by the patient's family for the results of his investigations.

It may be, for instance, that the family have failed, or delayed, in the performance of certain rituals, such as the post-mortuary rites held to assist an ancestor on his journey through the Otherworld towards rebirth, in which case the family must hold the rite and the shaman's services are no longer needed. Or it may be that the patient's soul has simply wandered off and got lost, which means a soul-calling bridge ceremony may be necessary (see Laopia Selee, Hmong Soul-calling Bridges). But the most usual cause of illness identified is the 'falling' of the wandering soul, either from a fall into a hole, or from having been caught by a malicious spirit. In this case the shaman must proceed to the second shamanic session to attempt to effect a cure.

After a delay of a few days or weeks, during which time the shaman can determine the progress of the patient and the family can obtain the requisite sacrificial animals, the healing ritual proper can get under way. The intricacies of any particular healing ritual depend on the circumstances of each case, yet whatever these may be, the session itself will normally be divided into five distinct parts.

The first part sees the shaman entering into the trance aided by his neeb. The second is formed by the procession of the shaman and all his troops and helpers to the home of the patient to search there for the afflicted soul. The third comprises of the hunt for the afflicted soul. This is followed by the return of the shaman and his allies bearing the soul back to his home. The fifth and final part sees the return of the neeb spirits to their altar, and the shaman to the world of mortals.

At some stage during the proceedings the shaman will call out for the animal sacrifice to be made in order to exchange the animal's soul for that of the patient. Usually a pig or chicken will be used. The decision as to which animal is required lies with the shaman and his familiar spirits.

Specially prepared 'spirit money' (votive paper) cut from sheets of plain white paper is burnt during the sacrifice, usually at the throat of the *animal while the shaman addresses a few words to its soul as to its expected conduct in the Otherworld. The burning of the spirit money is also used as a means of sending financial assistance to aid the stricken soul, who may need to offer bribes in the Otherworld. The patient, who would normally be sitting on a low stool behind the shaman during the ritual, will be daubed with the blood of the sacrifice as a means of identification for the spirits.*

In the course of the session a number of other actions may be performed by the shaman. He may, for instance, leap backwards from his bench to be caught by his assistant before he falls and, depending on the circumstances, may actually fall to the ground and appear to struggle with the evil spirit. At other times he blows sprays of water from the corner of his mouth in four directions, to 'wash away' any evil influences.

Afterwards there will be a great feast in the house, with meat from the sacrifice in plentiful supply. The shaman, who will be the guest of honour, will later return to his house with the head and a foreleg of the sacrificial animal as a payment for his services. For certain rituals he or she will receive money or silver.

INTERVIEWER: When you come out of a trance do you have any recollection of the language you have been using in the other world?

LAOGEE: No, no, I have no idea what I say. It's the spirits that come through my head that say the words. It's not really me talking. Sometimes I ask my wife, but she says she doesn't understand the words. Nobody understands them. She says I sometimes speak Chinese. She can recognise Chinese, but she can't speak it.

INTERVIEWER: Can you normally speak Chinese?

LAOGEE: Only a few words like 'to eat', 'to drink' and 'water'.

INTERVIEWER: How do you feel after the spirit has left you?

LAOGEE: Oh, I feel fine, not tired. I feel just like normal.

INTERVIEWER: Even though you have been bouncing and chanting for such a long time? Sometimes for four or five hours?

LAOGEE: No, really, after the spirit has left my head I feel fine. I think when the spirit comes my 'self' leaves my body and goes to rest somewhere. I never feel tired at all.

There are a great many occasions when a shaman's services are deemed necessary. He or she may, for instance, be engaged to change an unfortunate year into a fortunate one, to protect an entire village against an epidemic, to aid a childless couple to conceive, or to exorcise the malicious spirits of 'bad death', such as those associated with bloody accidents. The very frequency of their use in a community underlines the perceived value of the shaman's intervention.

The practice of shamanism confers many benefits on a community in addition to those perceived benefits of a purely spiritual nature. The conducting of shamanistic rituals is psycho-therapeutic. People believe action is needed, and Hmong shamanism is, at the very least, a psychodrama of great subtlety and power. An impressive performance increases the credibility of the cure, it relieves tensions and worries which in turn helps to promote better health and fortune.

Rituals are thought to offer a classic example of the workings of the so-called 'placebo effect', a powerful but little understood healing process in which, in the words of Hurley (1985) 'psychological factors such as belief and expectation trigger a healing response that can be as powerful as any conventional therapy – be it drugs, surgery or psychotherapy – for a wide range of medical and psychological problems.' Many shamanic rituals seem admirably designed to elicit this effect, as the workings of the effect are seen to be most noticeable when therapies are elaborate, detailed, expensive, time-consuming, fashionable or esoteric.

The practice of shamanism also increases social cohesion in that families and neighbours get together to share in the rituals and the feasting, and it can aid in disease prevention, such as when a shaman holds a ritual which bars people from an infected area entering a disease-free village, thus serving as a quarantine measure. Shamanic rituals also promote food redistribution. Families with a greater number of domestic animals are likely to consult the shaman more often, and thus conduct more sacrifices, which in turn leads to an increase in the amount of meat in the diet of all those that join in the feasting. Finally, the holding of a ritual involving a sacrifice and subsequent feast is of particular importance to the sick, as the input of vitamins and protein rich meat occurs just at the time they are in most need of it: an important factor in a community whose members are typically undernourished.

3 – Aka My-yer – Akha

Aka My-yer is forty-five years old and is the village priest and headman of Ban A-bey – a beautiful U Lo Akha village of about forty houses high up in the mountains to the south of Mae Salong in Chiang Rai Province. Aka has been both the village priest and headman of Ban A-bey for twelve years.

All tribal villages in Thailand have a headman (political headman), called phu yai ban *or* kae ban *in Thai, whose primary role is to be the representative of the village in all government matters. However, the existence of a distinct political headman in most groups is largely a matter of conforming to Thai law, and real power in village communities often lies elsewhere, such as with the village priest (ceremonial headman), who is often referred to as the 'father of the village', or with a group of village elders and household heads. A single man may combine the positions of village priest and* phu yai ban, *as does Aka My-yer, but more typically a different man will be chosen for each position.*

As village priest Aka is responsible for the health, welfare and ceremonial life of the village, as well as the upkeep of the sacred sites, these being the ceremonial swing, the spirit gates, the shrine to the 'Lord of Land and Water', the water source and the burial ground. For this service he receives no payment, although his position does offer certain material benefits, such as the right to a foreleg of every animal killed in the hunt.

Apoe Miyeh: The Creator

Though elected by the village elders, Aka is thought to receive his authority directly from the principal Akha deity, Apoe Miyeh, *the all powerful 'force', or 'prime cause' of the Akha. Apoe Miyeh – Apoe means 'male ancestor' in Akha – is regarded as having brought into the being the earth* (M Ma) *and the sky* (M G'ah). *From M G'ah came a succession of nine powerful spirits, the last of which was* Beh Sm, *from whom came* Sm-mi-o. *Sm-mi-o in turn parented the first human.*

Apoe Miyeh is the creator. He created us all. He is the great spirit. From him came the nine spirits. And after the ninth came Beh Sm.

From Beh Sm came Sm-mi-o, from whom all humans came. The first human was, *Ou-ter-leur*. From him came *Leur-be-do*, then *Do-mor-yeh*, *Mor-yeh-ja*, *Shehe-scher-lee*, *Lee-pwo-weh*, *Oo-weh-oo* and many, many more, altogether about fifty descendants.

All Akha traditions are contained in the Akhazan *or 'Akha Way'. This is the mass of oral traditions of the Akha which for centuries have been transmitted orally, generation to generation, along an unbroken line of masters and pupils known as* pee mas *(spirit priests). According to one tradition, Apoe Miyeh handed out 'books' to all peoples of the Earth. The Akha, however, lost their books. We asked Aka to account for the Akha's lack of a written language today.*

Yes, I know it. It is from long ago. The great spirit called representatives of all the peoples to his abode and gave out 'books' instructing them in his way. The Lahu were there, the Chinese, the Lisu, the Japanese, and many others. The 'book' given to the Akha representatives was written on the skin of a water buffalo.

On their way back the Akha saw several mysterious signs. They decided to roast the skin and eat it. And on that day we lost our book. The Akha have no books now. But we have the Creator's wisdom in our stomachs.

A second version of this myth tells how the Akha carried the writings whenever they had to move their villages, but eventually got tired of lugging around the weight and so decided to cook the skin and eat it, thinking they could preserve Apoe Miyeh's wisdom in their stomachs.

Many non-literate cultures who have lived near literate societies – in the case of the Akha, the Chinese – have similar myths to explain away their lack of writing. For instance, there is a legend among the Karen that at the dawn of time, when the Creator was dispensing books to the various peoples of the earth, the Karen overslept and missed out on the precious gift of literacy.

However, in the case of the Akha, there is some evidence, albeit slight, of a previous tradition of writing. According to eminent anthropologists (Grunfeld 1982:22), the oral verses of the Akhazan refer to a settled period in their history, when the Akha prospered in Yunnan, apparently for centuries. Here they farmed in the valley floors and at one time, according to the verses and confirmed by Chinese chroniclers, built an Akha walled city. During this settled period the Akha may have developed a writing system; old texts, written in a curious and as yet undeciphered script quite different from Chinese characters, have been discovered this century in Yunnan in the possession of groups related to the Akha.

The verses also describe a 'big burning' – a time of disasters when the Akha were forced to seek refuge in the forested mountains. Akha genealogical litanies, some of which go back to the names of the chiefs who ruled them before they were forced into the mountains, reveal that the flight took place some thirty generations – perhaps 700 years – ago. That would place it in the thirteenth century, the time of the Mongol invasion of China. It is thought the Mongol hordes of Kublai Khan, during their subjugation of China, may also have crushed the Akha mini-state in Yunnan, and it's entirely possible that the 'big burning' in the Akha verses may be a description of the troubles at that time. If they ever had books and a system of writing, it was probably at the time of the 'burning' that they disappeared.

We asked Aka whether the young people in the village believe in the old stories.

The young people now don't care too much about our ancestors. Some things they believe, but other things they don't believe. They tend to believe in new things that can be seen. Anything they can't see, can't hear, anything the can't see by themselves, like stories, they think isn't true.

Our Village

The village priest is chosen by the village elders, but in practice the position tends to be hereditary. This is because the detailed knowledge of the rituals and ceremonies necessary for the performance of the position can only realistically be obtained from many years of close examination of the ceremonies and the tutelage of the presiding village priest, who will normally want to pass on his expert knowledge to his son or other close relative.

For twelve years I've been the headman and the village priest. My grandfather was headman, and after him it was my father, and then my elder brother. And now it's me. My elder brother's name was A-bey. The village is named after him. My father's name was Ba-too-yur. This is the name of the village on the government maps—the border police maps.

Naming a village after a current or former village leader is common practice in the region. 'Ban A-bey' is thus 'the village of A-bey' — ban meaning 'village' in Thai. Similarly, the Yao village of Lao Shi Guai, or more correctly, Ban Lao Shi Guai, is 'the village of Lao Shi Guai'. Another practice is to name a village after some physical feature, such as 'Mountain Village' (Ban Doi), 'Climbing Gully Village (Ban Kiew Khan) and 'Sandy Plain Village' (Ban Tung Sai).

In the past we used to live in Hin Taek [Broken Rock] village. Since the opium war Hin Taek has been given a new name, now it's called Ban Therd Thai [Glorious Thai Village]. But we left a long time before the war. We've been here for twenty-nine years. It's not far from here to Mae Salong. Just along the track there is a Lisu village, and the town is a few kilometres beyond that.

There has been more than one 'opium war' in the region in recent times. The conflict alluded to by Aka is the attack on Ban Hin Taek by Thai government forces on 21 January 1982 in a bid to expel forces loyal to the infamous drug warlord Khun Sa, who were using the village as their principal heroin distribution centre on Thai soil. The engagement resulted in Khun Sa's troops withdrawing across the nearby Thai-Burmese border, and the reinstatement of government control in the area.

I can still remember when my brother and brother-in-law went off to look for a new village site. I was a child then. They took a load of provisions with them on their search. I helped them get everything ready. They eventually came to this place, and here they decided to build the village.

Yes, they had to ask the spirits for permission to settle. This is the Akha way. Once a good location has been found, namely one with a good supply of water and plenty of land, a perfect place in

The egg-drop test

which to build a new village, then you need to make a test to discover whether the 'Lord of Land and Water' allows you to settle there. We use an egg and some rice grains to conduct the test. The raw egg is dropped onto the ground. If it breaks you can build your village at that place. But if it doesn't break, you can't build because the 'Lord of Land and Water' withholds his permission. Only if it breaks can you build, because this means the Lord is happy to let you live there. Then you can start clearing the land.

On hearing the egg is dropped from ear-height onto a cleared spot on the bare ground, we asked Aka if it has ever happened that an egg has failed to break.

Yes, yes, it happens sometimes. Really, sometimes it doesn't break and then the searchers have to move on to another mountain to look for a good site.

All tribal groups in the region employ such a test as a means of ascertaining whether the spirits of the area, particularly the spiritual owner of a site, give their permission to settle there. But why an egg? And why drop it? The answer may lie in the symbolism of an egg with fertility. An egg breaks to give new life. One that resists breaking, especially having been dropped from ear-height, may suggest to tribesmen, infertility, ill-fortune, the withholding of prosperity by the spirit powers. However, one Akha man in Ban A-bey suggested an egg is used because of its perfect form. He pointed out how, with eggs it is easy to identify a perfect, blemish-free example, one that is worthy of being used in a spirit ritual.

Another widely employed method to divine an auspicious site for a village is the so-called 'rice grain test'. This involves the placing of three or four grains of uncooked rice in a shallow depression in the ground on the proposed site. The grains, which are so positioned so as to radiate out from a common centre, are then covered by an upturned bowl and left for a certain predetermined length of time – usually a matter of three or four days. If on later inspection the grains are found to lie undisturbed it is assumed the site meets with the approval of the ancestors and other spirits. Once again, an idea of fertility is represented, this time in the guise of uncooked grains of rice.

The clearing of the land starts almost immediately after conducing a successful test. The first house to be built will be that of the priest. Once his house has been completed the village has been established. The rest of the houses will be grouped around his house in an egalitarian fashion.

The Two Worlds of Humans and Spirits

According to Akha myth, in the past humans and spirits lived together in an idyllic relationship, with the humans tilling their fields during the day, and the spirits theirs during the night. Not only this, but all animals, wild and domesticated, lived together in perfect harmony. Hawks and chickens passed the night in the same basket, and tigers and domesticated livestock slept in shared pens. All was cosy and very amicable until the humans and spirits began stealing from each other. The humans stole cucumbers from the spirits' fields during the day, and the spirits stole eggs from the humans at night. The Akha do not make clear whom was to blame for this breakdown in relations. Some accounts suggest it was the

Aka My-yer 61

Village gate at Ban A-bey

humans who started the pilfering, but in others the blame is laid squarely at the feet of the spirits. The conflict grew, until finally it was decided the two sides should separate. Aka My-yer, who clearly lays the blame on the spirits, continues the story:

The spirits stole many things, such as rice and vegetables from the fields. Finally the village elders and the senior spirits held a meeting to decide what to do. The elders ordered the spirits to leave the village and go and live in the jungle. Then they gave some land to the spirits for them to farm. But this land was covered in huge boulders and was therefore unsuitable for farming. There were far too many rocks. You see, the humans were very clever. They took the land which could be cultivated, and gave the spirits only bad land.

Having separated, the Akha elders realised that a clear demarcation between the human and spirit realms was needed. So, it was decided that gates should be erected at the upper and lower ends of an Akha village.

We have two spirit gates in the village. One is at the head of the village, the other at the tail. Every year we give a sacrifice to the spirit of the gate. We call the gate *law kaw* in Akha. The spirit gate is there to protect the village. The *law kaw* is a good spirit. It makes sure bad spirits outside the gate cannot enter the village.

Perhaps it should be emphasised that the law kaw *– the spirit gate – which Aka states 'is a good spirit' is not the actual spirit, but rather the seat, or home, of a spirit. Such a distinction, which to many tribespeople is only all too obvious is in our experience seldom made during explanations or discussions of spirit-related topics.*

There are many of these bad spirits outside. They are called *pee-hah*. There is one that eats ducks, chickens, cows and lots of other animals. Sometimes many of our animals die. This is because *pee-hah* have come to the village to eat them. This spirit is really bad. The spirit gates have to struggle with the *pee-hah* to keep them out. It also stops vampires and *pong* spirits coming in. The gate is our security.

Every Akha village in which the traditional beliefs are followed – and this is by far the majority in Thailand – will have at least two sets of these village gates, one at either end of the village. Consisting of two uprights and a crossbar, they are built over the main pathways leading into the village and are unconnected to any fence or wall. They are sacred and on no account may be touched.
The crossbar is usually festooned with a large number of taboo devices – flimsy bamboo constructions – designed to ward off evil and prevent spirits from entering the village. Carved wooden replicas of objects which feature in Akha daily life are also attached alongside the taboo devices. On occasion replicas of M-16 assault rifles and carved model helicopters are added as a further signal to the spirits that beyond the gate lies the realm of mankind.
Positioned next to the gate there is normally at least one pair of carved wooden figures, representing a male and a female. They are naked, about

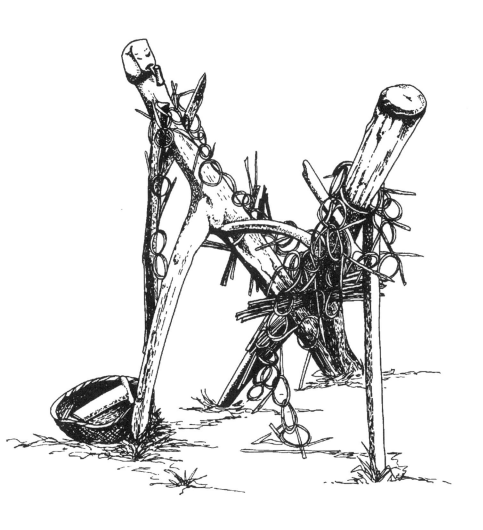
Wooden figures placed by Akha gates

half life-size, and stand facing each other, with the male figure always on the upper side of the path, as the Akha believe 'men should not live under women'. Despite possibly having some association with human reproduction – the male figures often have very prominent genitals – it is thought the primary function of these figures is to indicate that beyond the gate lies the world of the humans.

Unfortunately, these figures command a high price in souvenir and antique shops in Bangkok and Chiang Mai, and it has been known for non-Akhas – usually Thai lowlanders – to steal into Akha villages under the cover of darkness and remove them.

The gates – and associated carvings – are renewed each year by young men under the direction of the village priest, as Akha outlines:

The village priest makes incantations during the building of the village gates. I am the village priest, so I do it. I take some rice, some water, some raw eggs and a few one baht coins to the site of the gate. Once the post holes are dug I place the water and rice into the bottom of the holes. Then I take the coins and scrape shavings off over the holes. After that I put the eggs in, too. Actually, I don't really put the eggs in, I just pretend to, later I take them back home to cook. After that the posts are put in and we erect the gate. When the work is finished I recite special incantations and sacrifice a pig to the spirits of the gate.

The eggs symbolise good health and fertility for all in the community, the rice invites plentiful harvests, the water represents rainfall, and the shavings from the coins seek prosperity for the entire village. The eggs are saved for a ritual meal later in the day.

Once completed the gate should not be touched. If anyone breaks this rule a fine is payable and a further sacrifice to the spirit of the gate is held. The following year the gate is not dismantled, but left to slowly rot and disintegrate naturally. The replacement gate is built on the same site, thus producing over time a tunnel of rotting timbers leading into the village. If the villagers follow the ritual requirements fully, each time they enter the village they must pass through one of the gates. This is to decontaminate themselves from the dark forces of the jungle. Outsiders, such as tourists, should not walk through the gates unless they intend going into the village properly and entering at least one house.

We asked Aka to tell us about some of the 'bad spirits' that roam 'outside', beyond the protective gates. First we asked him to elaborate on the vampires which threaten the Akha.

They look just like us, but they like to bite people, especially children. They also attack adults, particularly when someone is ill. If you are weak they are able to kill you very easily. But usually they prefer to attack children, especially if the children are sleeping alone. When a vampire comes to drink blood from someone's neck there's no puncture mark to be seen. There's just two black marks. A child who is attacked loses weight and becomes weak from the loss of blood. And then dies.

The vampire is very much feared by most tribal people in the region, who consider the vampire to be a particularly dangerous spirit which originates from the bloody deaths of humans. Vampires are thought to go to people, particularly the weak and defenceless, such as sleeping children and the sick, enter them, and then bite their souls, with or without the person's knowledge. Once bitten and possessed, that person too becomes a vampire. As the affliction is considered to be communicable, this person then becomes a threat, both to the household and to the community at large.

In common with the other tribes, the Akha believe a person possessed by a vampire may take the form of a cat, or dog, or some other animal, which goes out at night, biting and sucking the blood of people and animals. They regard the cat form as one of the more common manifestations of the vampire, and suggest it may be recognised by the cat's human-looking mouth. This may explain why cats are so rarely seen in tribal villages.

It was a staving, rain-sodden stray cat rescued from the jungle by a well-meaning Suphawan which, having been killed one night by a neighbour who feared it was a vampire, and who then witnessed Su burying the corpse and, shock of all shocks, muttering something to the dead body, almost led her to being accused of practising witchcraft. This all happened during our very first month in Kiew Khan, when a number of people considered the presence of outsiders in the village as constituting a threat to the well-being of the community. Fortunately for us, the old man who witnessed Su's corrupt behaviour was, and still is, considered something of an eccentric in the village – largely because of his resourcefulness, hard work and subsequent relative wealth – and the incident was quickly forgotten. We have had three cats since, none of which have come to any harm. Significantly, all three came from the town and not from the spirit-infested jungle.

Asked whether he thought vampires may have been more rampant in the past, Aka replies:

Yes, yes, in the old days there were many of them. Now we don't get them so often, although there are still some around. These days there are Thai policemen in the villages, border policemen. They often fire their guns up into the air for fun. This frightens any bad spirits which may be lurking in the village, and they leave to go and live in the jungle a long way away. This includes the vampires.

And if a person is unlucky enough to be confronted by a vampire...

You get uncooked rice, say a spell, and throw it at the vampire. That should make it scream and run away.

And once possessed, can the vampire be made to leave a man?

Yes, we can exorcise it. A village elder can do it. He uses a fang from a wild animal. He punches the body of the victim with the fang at the place where it hurts, and this in turn hurts the spirit, the vampire. Then the vampire leaves. Whenever a spirit has entered someone there is usually a hard lump somewhere on their body. We can also use a 'sky stone' to do the job, instead of a fang.

'Sky stones' are stone age implements, such as axe heads, found in the fields and which the Akha believe have been cast down from the sky by the sky spirit for their use. They are thought to contain magical properties.

And the pong *spirits?*

Pong are bad spirits that like to eat at night. They often lurk in the paddy fields looking for frogs and fish to eat. At night their faces are all lit up with a bright light that's as powerful as a torch. I don't know exactly where on the face the light comes from, whether from the eyes, nose or mouth, but I know it is very bright. If a man is not too scared he can fire off his gun to frighten them away. You don't need to try and shoot them, you just fire off into the air to frighten them. When a gun is fired, the *pong's* light goes out and the spirit disappears.

Pong are the same as people: they are people. At night, when someone is sleeping, they can come to your body and possess you. The possessed doesn't know they're possessed. He or she still sleeps, but the body goes out into the night to hunt for food. If anybody were to shoot a *pong* spirit, the person whose body it is using would surely die. Then the spirit would leave, because the body isn't its body. They like to eat fresh food, especially frogs and fish. But they don't eat people. They are different from vampires. Vampires like to attack children at night.

We asked whether pong *spirits can possess both men and women, and whether one has ever been caught in Ban A-bey.*

It can be a man or woman. If the husband is a *pong* spirit, then the wife too can be one. I don't know why. And yes, it is possible to catch one if you're not too frightened. If one is caught it'd say something like, 'You don't know me, and I'm not going to tell you my name because I've forgotten it. But I'll tell you where my house is'. Sometimes a person who has been possessed by a *pong* spirit has come to my house. I'm still friendly when this happens. I still offer that person some water and something to eat. I'm friendly because I know *pong* don't harm people.

If you try and kill the spirit, the person whose body has been possessed will die. So you can't try and kill them. Most people who are *pong* don't realise they are, so it's no good trying to tell them. And they wouldn't be able to do anything about it anyway, because they can't control their own will. A spell can be said which should make the spirit leave. This is the only way. People who have been bad in a previous life often become *pong*. The village spirit gate helps give us protection against *pong* spirits, it tries to keep them out of the village.

A particularly vicious spirit much feared by the Akha is the spirit called neh mui neh ceh. *This spirit originates from the death of newly-born* babies who leave the 'world of the living' before being named. They live in the jungle, each tending to have its own place. Akha staying out in the jungle report they sometimes hear them. What they hear is the sound of the evil little monsters throwing boulders, sticks and rocks about, as though in a tantrum. Despite the fearsome noise, nobody ever gets struck by anything. However, this does not mean they are not considered dangerous, for this they certainly are, as it is thought neh mui neh ceh actually hunt man. If they manage to catch a human, say the Akha, they hold him or her down and eat out the living heart, after which the victim dies. The heart is not physically eaten, rather its essence in the spiritual plane is destroyed. An Akha thus suffering a heart attack in the jungle would be said to have been attacked by the fiendish 'unnamed baby spirits'.

Two Spirit Practitioners

In the following interview, in which Aka differentiates between the two spirit practitioners, the shaman (nyi pa) *and the spirit priest* (pee ma), *the subject of soul-loss and soul-calling is raised. It is the Akha spirit priest, referred to as the reciter by some anthropologists, who is summoned to repeat spirit incantations and call back the wandering soul of a person suspected of 'spirit affliction' or 'soul-loss'. He is a chanter of incantations and performer of offerings, and is paid for his work in food and money. In contrast, the Akha shaman, or* nyi pa, *who may be male or female, is a mediator between the spirit and human worlds. He is the great communicator, a negotiator and general fixer of spirit-related problems. It is his task to travel in trance into the Otherworld where the spirits and ancestors live, there to seek out the missing soul of a patient and try and discover what is happening to it. And it is through him that the patient's family try and make amends with the spirits, such as by the offering of a sacrifice.*

In this village we have a blacksmith [*ba ji*], a village priest, a spirit priest, and a shaman. The blacksmith makes the ceremonial knife for the spirit priest, and also the tools to harvest the rice. The village priest, that's me, is in charge of the spirit gates and the swing, and sets the dates of the ceremonies.

The spirit priest and the shaman are spirit specialists who help the people when they are ill. They have different roles to perform. If a person goes into the fields and attracts bad luck or sickness to themselves, say from the mountain spirit or the water spirit, then it is the spirit priest who can help them. He would walk through the jungle to the fields at night, chanting as he went. He'd follow exactly in the footsteps of the sick person. While walking he'd make up incantations, and keep on repeating the patient's name in order to call back the missing soul.

He has to try and retrieve the lost or wandering soul. He'd take with him a chicken's egg and a bottle of rice whisky to offer to the spirit when he meets him. Then he'd bring the soul back to the patient, and then together the spirit priest and the patient would take the soul to the shaman for him to sort it out.

Once soul-loss is suspected to be the cause of a person's illness a soul-calling ritual will be performed. Depending on the individual case, and the particular ritual deemed necessary, this may be conducted either by a specialist, such as a shaman, or a layman with the required knowledge.

This is different from the shaman, who helps people when they have done something wrong and have angered the spirits, such as when someone has cut down a tree on the wrong day or has disturbed a termite hill, thus angering the termite spirit. It is the shaman who has to help people make amends with the spirits.

This is the most common cause of soul-loss, when a nature spirit — an ordinary spirit — is offended by the action of a man or woman. For instance, if a man curses after tripping while walking along a jungle trail, tribal people believe the trail spirit will feel slighted and may seek revenge. Or if an Akha disturbs a termite hill, the termite hill spirit will retaliate. Similarly, the jungle spirit, the mountain spirit, spirits of particular caves and streams, trees and rocks, and many others, if offended, will retaliate by capturing the souls of the offenders. This form of soul-loss necessitates the holding of special ceremonies in which food offerings are made to the disturbed spirits in order to procure the return of the missing souls.

The shaman is there to help people when they get into trouble with the spirits. Sometimes people go into the jungle looking for mushrooms or wild vegetables and get attacked by spirits. The spirits eat their souls, thus making them ill. The shaman helps such people. He tries to discover what the problem is.

Sometimes it is because the spirits want a dog from a person, that's why that particular person is attacked. The shaman discovers this and informs the patient's family to carry out the sacrifice to the spirits. It may be a dog, or pig, or chicken or some other animal. Whatever the spirits want, must be sacrificed to them.

Or it may be that the spirits have harmed a person because that person has trespassed. The spirits have a law that says humans have no right to walk on the spirits' land. So they attack the trespasser and then demand an offering. It is the shaman's job to help them.

The shaman is paid for his services in food and money. A single practitioner may serve more than one village, and a single village may have more than one shaman.

4 – Laojong – Hmong

Laojong is a thirty-four year old Blue Hmong man from the Blue-White Hmong village of Huai Lu, which lies five kilometres south of the small town of Wiang Kaen in eastern Chiang Rai Province. The village consists of almost equal numbers of Blue and White Hmong, each group wearing its own traditional style of dress. Though rice is cultivated in the surrounding fields, their principal crop is maize, and many small elevated storehouses for the latter line the track leading into the village.

Laojong is married and has six children, one of which, a boy, boards at a special school for tribal children in Nan Province.

Siting a New House

Just as an egg-drop or rice-grain test may be employed by highlanders to help locate a new village, so too may these tests be used when siting an individual house, as Laojong illustrates in the following short account.

Before we can build a new house we have to make sure the site we have chosen meets with the approval of the spirits. We have to see whether or not it's a lucky site, a healthy site. First we clear a small patch and make a shallow depression. We must make sure it's really neat and tidy. Then we place one grain of rice for every person in the family into the depression. We cover them with a bowl and leave them there for one night. We must place them on the ground very carefully. It's important that we remember the exact position of each grain. To make it easy for us we form the grains into a star shape.

Then the following morning we come to look. We pick up the bowl and examine the grains. If the rice is still in exactly the same place, it's alright to build on that site. If just a single grain has moved we cannot build our house there, it wouldn't be any good for us. This is how it is.

If a person ignores the results of this test, that is, if the grains moved, but they still went ahead and built their house on that site; well, for sure someone in their family would soon die. You see, they would lose someone in their family, just the same as they lost the rice grain.

We asked whether a sacrifice is made prior to the actual building of the house.

No, we don't have to kill anything before we start building. We do that later, when the house is finished and we are about to move in. We celebrate a new house by having a party. This is when we make an offering to the house spirits.

Hmong houses are always built on the ground and have earth-packed floors. After the first two posts of a new house have been erected the household head – the oldest male – announces in a loud voice 'I am living here! From now on let all evil spirits stay away'. A fireplace is then installed and a temporary altar made, after which construction is resumed. The house walls are made of wood planking or flattened bamboo, and the roofs of grass thatch or shingles – or, in some villages, tin.

When the house is complete two chickens are sacrificed at the altar and the ancestors and other household spirits are cordially invited to move in. Following this a hen and a rooster are sacrificed and offered at the main door, the seat of one of the more important of the household spirits. An appeal is made to the door spirit to protect the family's domestic animals and crops, and to bring good fortune to the family members. Afterwards a number of roughly made wooden knives are attached to a grass rope and hung outside, and to one side of the door to prevent the entry of evil spirits. They remain above the door until they either rot away or are replaced by a freshly made set installed as part of an exorcism ritual.

5 – Somboon Seejaow – Yao

Somboon Seejaow is 67 years old and is a former headman of the Yao village of Pa Car, a large settlement lying about eight kilometres to the east of Mae Chan. The village lies on a partly surfaced track leading to the main Chiang Rai - Mae Sai road. As a consequence of its easy access it is visited by tourists travelling on organised tours out of Chiang Mai and Chiang Rai. An average day during the tourist high season, between November and April, sees a steady stream of white Toyota mini-buses bringing in tourists (usually Westerners) to the makeshift village market, where local women sell handicraft products brought into the village by a Thai supplier from Mae Sai. Few visitors stray from the immediate market area, and the average length of stay is barely twenty minutes.

Though the income derived from the tourists is significant, most families remain wedded to the land, as it is from selling their cash crops that the greater proportion of their income is derived. The principal cash crops are maize, peanuts, soy beans and various fruits and vegetables. Paddy rice is cultivated for domestic consumption.

Crossing to the Other Side

Having heard of a Yao man who had once been interviewed by a journalist, only subsequently to find his words grossly distorted on the printed page, Somboon Seejaow chose to remain steadfastly silent. That is, until our recording Walkman had been withdrawn, whereupon he happily agreed to share his knowledge with us. One topic on which he spoke was that of the very beginnings of the Yao race. He related to us the myth of 'The Crossing of the Sea at the Mercy of the Waves', *also known as* 'Crossing to the Other Side.'

Before the Yao people came into existence they lived on the other side of the sea. This sea was immense, far too big to be able to see across. If the Yao spirits wanted to be born as humans they'd have to cross the sea in a boat. One group of spirits decided to try. They realised it would be risky to cross the sea, but even so, they decided to give it a go.

So they went onto the sea in boats. These boats were like Chinese boats, you could go inside them and keep away from the weather. The spirits sat deep inside the boats and couldn't see anything, not even the sky. They had to rely on the wind to take them somewhere. They were at the mercy of the wind and the waves.

They knew if they were on the boats for more than three days they would sink down into the sea's navel. This they knew because some Yao spirits had already tried to cross the sea once before, and this is what happened to them.

They began to get worried. They were frightened of sinking. Then some of them had the idea of asking the sea spirit for help to take the boats across to the other side. One of them called out, 'Oh sea spirit, if you take us to the other side, then when we arrive and are born as humans we will sacrifice and offer to you a pig or chicken. And thereafter, every time we have a ceremony we will make offerings to you. This we promise. We will make offerings to the sea spirit forever more. All our descendants will sacrifice to you. This we shall do for you if you help us now.'

So the sea spirit helped them and took the boats to the other side, to the human world. And so they were saved. They were the first Yao to be born as humans. All the Yao people ever since have come from these original ones — the ones who crossed the sea.

Somboon continued by relating how most Yao hold true to the promise made to the sea spirit, and added that when a Yao man or woman dies, a boat is made out of paper and banana leaves and offered to the deceased in order for the deceased's soul to be taken back across the sea to the other side. He mentioned, however, that many Yao today are largely unaware as to why the boat is made during a funeral.

They don't even know why. They just do it because it's what's done. Even people who should know better, people in their forties or fifties, even they don't really know why they do it.

It would appear this myth may have developed from an episode in Yao history recorded by the Chinese. It is thought the Yao fled a drought in the coastal mountains of Chekiang province in the fourteenth century by taking to the China Seas in rented boats. They became lost and were driven to the coasts of Guangdong province. From here it is thought they made their way first to the mountainous districts of Shaochow and Lo Chang, and from here spread out over much of South China; to Hunan in the north, and Kweichow, Kwangsi and Yunnan in the west.

6 – Mano Leejar – Lisu

Mano Leejar is the thirty-six year old headman of the Lisu village of Pang Sa. The village lies alongside a river in a narrow valley about twenty-three kilometres west of Mae Chan. It is a large and fairly prosperous settlement: the number of pick-up trucks and tin roofs in the village attest to this. There is a small shop in the centre of the village, which is run as a co-operative by a man named Bierpa, and a roadside stall serving a concoction of tofu, chilli and pickle, a Yunnanese speciality.

All houses are ground-built, like rural Yunnanese houses. Some have walls of sun baked mud; others of flattened bamboo or timber planks. Despite the large number of tin roofs, the majority still have roofs of grass thatch.

According to his neighbours, Mano is an exceptionally able headman, being described to us as a good father, a good communicator, and extremely hard-working. He is also fairly wealthy, certainly by Lisu village standards, and is the proud owner of a new blue Toyota pick-up. At first wary of us – and our questions – he soon relaxed and, even during our first meeting, sat for hours explaining various points of Lisu belief and culture, as well as relating to us a number of bizarre stories from his own past.

The Power of Water

The Lisu are particularly anxious about a mystical power residing in water. This concern is reflected in their choice of village site. The setting they like best is one where they can live on one side of a ridge, with a stream on the other. This makes it possible to bring fresh running water around the ridge and into the village by means of bamboo aqueducts, without exposing themselves unduly to this mystical power. Mano explains further:

The prosperity of the village depends on the soil, the location, the existence of a good water supply, and the security of the area. And the spirits! When choosing the place to build a village we look for a place where there is a mountain in front, and one behind. Then we build on the slope of one mountain, leaving the other one in front of us. Once we have finished building the village we have to sacrifice a cock and a hen to the spirit that owns the mountain, the mountain spirit.

It's very important that the water for the village doesn't come straight down the mountain, but instead comes around the side of the mountain. It would be very bad if we were to make the water come straight down. The water spirit, whom we call *In-jia-nee*, would take the harmony away from our village.

You see, if the water were to come straight down, the mountain would be split in two. Then the mountain spirit would be angry and would likewise divide the village into two, causing the villagers to argue. So we must bring the water around the mountain, and not down it.

Lisu houses are usually built on posts raised above the ground, using available local materials, such as hardwood planks and flattened bamboo slats, with roofs of either grass thatch or tin sheet. Some homes are built on the ground in the Chinese style, as in Pang Sa, which reflects the mixed origin of the Lisu in Thailand. Whether ground-built or elevated, the Lisu orientate their houses so the ridge-pole of the house follows the contours of the hillside, with the only door to the house always made in the middle of the lower side, opposite the ancestral altar. This then places the altar on the uphill side of the house, and thus keeps the altar 'above the people'. On completion of the house structure the first cooking fire must be started by an older person, preferably someone who has parented at least one child – this is in the hope that some of the fertility and good fortune will rub off onto the younger inhabitants. Once the altar has been installed the ancestral spirits are asked to take up residence. Two cocks and a hen are then killed, and the meat, some of which is cooked and some left raw, is placed on the altar.

The ancestral spirits, who are also referred to as the house spirits, protect the household, and also its guests, as Mano explains:

Every house has a house spirit to take care of the family. The shrine to this spirit is called the *ta-biea*. In my house we have the shrine upstairs. Every time we have guests in the house we light some candles and incense sticks on the altar and offer some water and freshly cut flowers to the spirit. In this way we let the house spirit know we have guests staying. This is so he can protect them when they are sleeping. This is important because they may have crossed a river, or passed through an area of jungle on their way to the village, and the spirits of the jungle and those of the rivers and streams may have followed them. And then, when the guests are sleeping, the spirits may try and taunt them, giving them bad dreams. The house spirit can help protect them.

Mano's house is unique in Pang Sa in that it is a two-storey concrete dwelling. All traditional hilltribe houses are single-storeyed, thus of course, having no upper floor. It appears he has chosen such a design, which is closer to an urban Chinese house than Thai, as a reflection – and enhancement – of his status in the village.

We then asked about lu khwa *leaves. The leaves of this aromatic herb are traditionally burnt by the Lisu during offerings to the ancestral spirits – the aroma is thought pleasing to the spirits. Mano, however, only knew of the following use for this plant:*

We use the *lu khwa* leaves for washing up. We don't use washing powder. The *lu khwa* leaves have a nice smell. In the old days our parents always preferred these leaves to washing powder.

Only after asking around a large part of the village did we come across one old lady who remembered using such leaves during ancestor offerings. But that, she said, 'was a long time ago'. Instead, the people of Pang Sa now use shop-bought incense sticks when conducting ancestor offerings.

Lisu Village Guardian Spirit Shrine

All Lisu villages have a village guardian spirit shrine which is always located in a fenced compound a little way above the village, usually under the spreading branches of a large leafy tree. It is roofed and contains a shelf on which are kept four small rice bowls containing water – one for each point of the compass – as well as a bowl of water for each of the clans represented in the village. The shrine is dedicated to the village guardian spirit, also known as 'Old Grandfather', who is responsible for the protection of the village from thieves, drought, disease and the attentions of evil spirits. He is considered powerful and potentially fierce, and therefore polite avoidance behaviour is observed towards him and his shrine at all times. Also located in the shrine are two other less elaborate altars. One is to the 'Lord of Land and Water', and the other to the ruler of the area, the important spirit-cum-god, Ida ma.

In the following extract Mano Leejar describes the guardian spirit shrine in his village.

It's on the slope over there at the back of the village. It's like a small hut, but it's not too small, there's still enough room for people to sit inside. There's a fence around it. In Lisu we call it *mao fun-nye*. Every family in the village makes offerings at the shrine to the village guardian spirit during the New Year festival. This is held at the same time as the Chinese New Year festival. We also make offerings a second time, about two months after New Year. And later once more again. Altogether there are three big ceremonies in a year.

The village priest, who is my brother, changes the water at the shrine during every special day, that's every holy day. We have one every fifteen days. The priest puts fresh water in the cups, lights the candles and incense sticks, and asks the village guardian spirit to look after the village, our village. There is also an altar to Ida ma in the shrine. My brother also takes care of this one.

Women are not allowed to go anyway near the shrine. But any man can go inside the compound and into the shrine proper. It is the men's job to keep the place tidy, to cut the grass and keep everything clean. Nobody should go to the toilet near the fence, or say rude things near the shrine. If someone were to say something bad nearby, the guardian spirit would cause them to fall ill. Then that person would have to offer two chickens to the spirit in order to be excused for his bad behaviour. Our shrine is very sacred.

We asked Mano about Ida ma.

Ida ma is the mountain spirit. He is the spirit who owns the mountain. If people are ill after they come back to the village from the fields or jungle, they kill a pig or a chicken for Ida ma in order to ask for forgiveness for the thing they must have done wrong. You see, if they are ill they must have done something against Ida ma, and that's why he made them ill. They'd have to offer the pig to him in order to right matters. They'd have to ask him to help them get better.

Ida ma is a powerful spirit, everyone is very frightened of him. He owns all the mountains. There is the spirit which owns the water, and the one which owns the trees, and the village guardian spirit which looks after the village, but it is Ida ma who owns the mountains where we live.

And his personal opinion of Ida ma:

I think Ida ma is the same age as me. I am the headman of the village. I am the boss. If anyone has a problem, or if anyone needs some help, it is to me they come. They come to me to discuss the problem. And Ida ma, in my opinion, is like the headman of the spirits.

We then enquired about **Wu sa**, *the principal Lisu deity, or 'High God'. Lisu tradition has it that Wu sa looks after the living and never brings trouble to them. It is he who determines everybody's lifespan, and who sends a 'letter' when a person's time has come to return to the land of the ancestors. The letter is, in effect, the person's actual death.*

This is expressed in a song which mourners sing to a person when he dies: '...Wu sa made this the time for you to die. He makes the sky take your strength, and he makes the earth take your bones. Wu sa wrote the date for you to die. Now your letter has arrived. Today Wu sa's letter has reached you...and now you must go up there...'

Wu sa is the spirit who is the parent of the Lisu people. It is he who sends us into the world to be born as humans. And it is he who decides how long we are going to live. He decides when we have to die. He is a good spirit, we call him 'mother and father of birth'. But these days most people don't talk much about Wu sa, they have almost forgotten him.

This is perhaps surprising, for one would have expected 'the Creator' to have played a significant role in Lisu ceremonial life. We asked Mano whether he knew of the Lisu creation myth which tells of a great drought from which only a boy and his younger sister survived.

According to this myth the boy and girl lived inside a water gourd and were facing starvation. In desperation they pleaded with Wu sa, the Creator, to send rain and save them. Eventually their request was granted and the world became fertile once more. However, they were the only two humans left. Realising they were the only hope for mankind, they nevertheless worried that an incestuous relationship would be wrong. They talked over their dilemma and decided to conduct a test to determine whether or not it would be permissible for them to sleep together. They rolled two huge boulders down opposite sides of a mountain. When these stones reached the bottom they continued rolling around the mountain until they came to rest beside each other. Other tests were made giving similar results. They deduced from this that it was right and proper for them to marry.

In time their union produced a water gourd. The brother was mystified and asked Wu sa the meaning of it. He was told there were 101 languages (ethnic groups) and 201 people inside the gourd. On hearing this they opened it up and released the 201 people. There were one hundred couples, one of which were the forebearers of the Lisu. But there was one man without a partner. This was the Akha man. Wu sa ordered him to go into the jungle and marry a monkey.

Yes, of course I know of the creation of the world. This is a very old story which tells of the distant past. Wu sa is the Creator, he is a powerful spirit, but it is Ida ma who is important in our everyday lives. It is to Ida ma that we must pay respect, to honour.

Interestingly, the Lisu myth suggests the Akha are the descendants of an Akha man and a monkey, and are therefore only partially human. A similar outcome is found in another version of this myth, this one based on a flood, with the boy and his younger sister saving themselves by riding out the waters in either a gourd or a pumpkin. Again their union produces a gourd containing all the forebearers of the various tribes. And once again the Akha man has to go off into the jungle to find himself a monkey to marry.

The Black Magician

The belief that a person's death may be caused by means of placing death spells on a victim is widespread in northern Thailand. The Lahu are thought by many to be particularly adept at sending death by such means, and have a fearful reputation among the other tribes. One especially fearful death-sending practice said to be employed by them involves the practitioner shooting arrows into a grass effigy representing the intended victim. Once enough arrows have pierced the 'victim' in this voodoo-like ritual, the 'life' string supporting the doll is cut. The string is then buried, and the effigy burned. The victim is expected to die soon after.

One of the most common forms of traditional black magic found in the hills, however, is the sending of pieces of animal hide, paper, nails, bamboo chips, pieces of rope and various other objects into the body of the person the practitioner wishes to harm. The Lisu believe a man who knows the right incantations may put certain objects into a cup and while holding his hand over the cup, repeat a secret spell, so that on removing his hand the object will fly out and almost simultaneously enter the intended victim, usually in the region of the victim's stomach. Once inside the body, the object is expected to cause severe stabbing pains in the area in which it is located, and if not quickly 'sucked out' by a skilled person would likely cause the death of the victim. Much sickness among the Lisu has traditionally been attributed to such attacks.

In the following account Mano Leejar recounts how his father was once attacked by someone using black magic. The 'someone' turned out to be his father's brother-in-law, Mano's uncle.

These days people don't use black magic. Anyone who does is killed straight away. But we had it in the past when I was a young boy. I've seen it with my very own eyes. It's true, I tell you. When a person is attacked by magic he or she falls ill for no apparent reason. But they don't die quickly. They are in pain for a long time. Often they'd have to sell their cows and water buffalo to buy medicines. But they'd never get better. In the end they get through all their money.

I'm not sure how to describe where it hurts. Sometimes it's in the heart, or sometimes it seems to hurt a little bit, but all over the body, not in any particular spot. And at other times it hurts in a different place every day. But the heart and the head are the common places.

The person who has this power to hurt people in this way sends a piece of cow hide, or a small knife or nail, or even a piece of rope into the person's body. Anything that would hurt can be sent. The victims never get better, even after going to hospital it's never any better.

It happened to my father once. My mother's brother sent it; he did the black magic on my father. He wanted my father's musket, but my father only had one and so wouldn't give it to him. My uncle really wanted it. In those days guns were really expensive. But my father wouldn't give it to him. So my uncle decided to hurt my father by sending an object into him. He sent it, and after two days my father had a very bad stomach-ache. He had severe pains, really bad ones. He knew immediately what it was all about, he knew what was causing the pains. He told my mother about it. She ordered her brother to remove whatever he had sent into her husband's stomach. She was very angry, after all it was a serious thing to do.

My uncle agreed to remove it. He got a big silver coin, a very old Thai one, and rubbed it over the painful place. At the same time he recited a special spell. I actually saw the bump on my father disappear. And with it, went my father's pains. And I also saw something in the palm of my uncle's hand: it was a small plastic bag of salt wrapped in silver paper, like the paper from a cigarette packet.

My father knew he had been attacked by *do* — that's what we call black magic in Lisu, and he knew very well who had done it. My uncle quickly explained that he hadn't wanted to kill his sister's husband, that he only wanted to hurt him to make him agree to hand over the musket. He said he was sorry for what he had done, and in the end my father did give him the gun.

Mano then told us of his uncle's other magical powers.

My father used to run the little village store. Among the things he sold was headache powder. You know, the sort you can mix with opium to help the opium burn. Well, my uncle used to smoke opium. Often he would steal some of this powder from my father. Whenever he got caught they'd be a terrible row and he'd be forced to pay for what he'd stolen.

Sometimes when he was broke he'd be particularly friendly with me. I was young then. Once he said to me, 'Hey, if you want to see something special I'll show you something, but first you've got to go and get some powder for me.' I also had to get a leaf from a nearby tree for him. Then he put the leaf into an empty bowl and covered the top. He shock the bowl and said a spell. All of a sudden I could hear the sound of a bee coming from inside the bowl. He told me to open it. I did. There was a bee flying around inside it. It didn't try and fly away, it just stayed there inside the bowl. This is what he showed me.

Every time he wanted me to steal some of the powder he'd show me something different. Sometimes he'd take hold of a leaf, say something to it, and it would become a piece of wood the size of my arm.

I really saw these things. He's dead now, somebody killed him. In the past the villagers didn't like it if someone practised magic to attack people. They'd kill such people. You know, it was the bad people that particularly didn't like it if someone could use magic, they knew that one day it might be used against them.

The practice of black magic, or witchcraft, is considered a serious offence in all tribal societies in the region. In the past the guilt or innocence of a suspect would often have been determined by trial by ordeal, a Lisu example of which involved the accused handling hot iron, or being made to retrieve a piece of silver from a pot of boiling water or oil. Should the accused accomplish the task unharmed he was judged innocent. An accused person failing the trail by ordeal would have been put to death, or at the very least be subject to expulsion from the village. When asked for details about the death of his uncle, Mano was not disposed to comment further. Whether his uncle suffered in this way, or whether he was simply shot one dark night we shall probably never know.

7 – Yiow-fun Selee — Yao

Yiow-fun is a forty-seven year old Yao shaman living in the small Yao village of Lao Shi Guai, situated sixteen kilometres to the west of Mae Chan. The village lies astride a narrow track which runs off from a dirt road (presently being upgraded) officially known as route 1089. There are fifteen households in the settlement. The headman, a man named Shi Guai, is also the founder.

Yiow-fun is a widower and father of six. He has been a practising shaman for the last fourteen years. We first met Yiow-fun in 1988 when we were invited to his daughter's wedding one cold winter's day. His home is a typical ground-built Yao house, though somewhat smaller than that of his neighbours. It stands in a rather dilapidated state, with holes in the thatched roof and daylight showing through the flattened-bamboo walls. As Yiow-fun himself says, 'shamanism doesn't pay, it's the Yao priests who make the money' – there are none in Lao Shi Guai. Apart from a certain status acquired through performing his work, Yiow-fun's only payment for his services is the food his neighbours wish to offer him.

Fire-walker — A Shaman's Story

This interview was conducted inside Yiow-fun's house. He was sitting with his four year old granddaughter asleep in his arms.

I didn't really learn to be a shaman, I could do it naturally. I became one by myself. In the past I would always watch the 'walking on fire' ceremony held at New Year. I liked to go to the house where it was being performed. Well, no, that's not exactly right. It's not that I particularly liked going, it's more that I couldn't stop myself going. I just had to watch, I had to see it.

I could never ignore the drums that were beaten to announce the ritual. I'd hear them and come over all strange. My heart would start thumping and I wouldn't be able to relax. I'd have to go nearer and nearer, and then when I got really close my whole body would go cold and I'd start trembling and shaking. Then I'd lose control of my head and body. I'd be taken over by a special power. What I think it was, is that when I got near to it the spirit would enter me. So, I became a shaman. I've been one for fourteen years now.

One year during the New Year celebrations in Lao Shi Guai we were invited to witness the 'walking on fire' ritual. All afternoon during the feasting and drinking the villagers had been talking about the spectacular fire-walking to be held that night in one of the houses. Everybody promised we would be terribly impressed by the special ritual.

At eight o'clock we made our way in darkness to the designated house and joined the excited crowd of men, women and children already gathered inside. Small flickering oil lamps helped to illuminate the scene. We watched as four men holding white hens made their way to the centre of the floor to gather around a low round table beneath the ancestral altar, on which four small bowls of cooked rice, four tiny cups of rice whisky, some paper spirit money and a number of burning incense sticks had been placed. While a fifth man – a priest – repeated incantations, and others off to the side beat a drum and gong, each man in turn picked up the ceremonial knife and, holding the bird over the bowls of rice, carefully slit the hen's throat, allowing the blood to drip slowly onto the rice.

Then, with the offering completed, the crowd became quiet, as Yiow-fun, the shaman, wearing his everyday dirty white shirt and black loose fitting Chinese trousers, apparently in a trance, walked over towards a large pile of hot embers spread over the ground beside the fireplace. Desperate little children pushed forward at the last moment for a clearer view; a comely Yao woman turned her face to watch for my reaction as, very quickly, he stepped onto the glowing embers, bent down, and with his bare hands scooped up handfuls of hot ash and embers throwing them wildly over himself, and anybody foolish enough to be standing too close – mainly those same eager little children who had been so intent to get to the front.

In fifteen seconds it was all over. The beating of the drum and gong ceased and the women and children began to drift off, but only after all those present, myself included, had refused to be cajoled into attempting to emulate the 'fire-walker'. A while later we too retired, and only the men remained, sitting around the fireplace excitedly discussing the evening's performance.

Yiow-fun continues his story:

You know, not just anyone can perform the 'walking on fire' ritual. Only shamans can do it. It's very dangerous to walk on burning fire, for sure if a person wasn't a shaman he'd burn himself. Shamans know the right spells, they know how to prepare themselves. Before I do it I first have to make an offering to the spirits.

See that shelf over there [pointing], that's the altar. I light incense sticks and recite a special incantation. Then I go and wash my whole body in specially prepared water. First I put some scent into a bucket, then I fill it with water. I use this water to wash with. Then I go to the house where I am to walk on fire.

As soon as I arrive I begin to feel strange. I am no longer in complete control of myself. When I look at the fire on the ground I don't see the fire, what I see is a river. I go to splash about in the 'river'. At the time I don't realise there are hot coals and ash everywhere. I imagine it's water. People tell me later what it really was. After 'swimming' I feel really refreshed and invigorated. I never get burnt. I feel really good.

If someone has this special power they can't stop themselves when they hear the drum. They can't hold back, they lose all control. Before I became a shaman I'd sometimes hear them a long way off. I wouldn't be able to stop myself going to them. This sort of thing happens to people with a weak soul.

On another occasion we asked Yiow-fun for the reason behind this ritual which he performs every year during the New Year celebrations. After some moments he replied that he does it to purify himself, and to renew his powers, as though sharpening a knife. And the connection between fire and water? His answer was simple: fire in the human world is water in the world of the spirits, and visa versa.

We return to Yiow-fun, who outlines his role in the village.

There aren't any priests in our village. All we have is me, the shaman. I know about spirits and can help with sickness. But for the big things, such as fighting off a particularly evil spirit we have to invite a high ranking priest to come and help us. We either get one from Bong Pa Kehm village or from Lao Sip [nearby Yao villages].

Dietary restrictions? No, there are none. I can eat anything, well most things. I can't eat dog because a dog is a low animal, I'd be demeaning myself if I ate such an animal. And I can't eat snake. If I were to eat either of these two by mistake I'd be sick later.

Most hilltribe people do not eat snake, believing some snakes to be particularly evil spirits. This attitude may have its origin simply in recognising that many snakes are indeed dangerous, both to hunt and to eat. Once a Hmong friend in Kiew Khan — who happened to be a Christian convert — shot a two metre-long king-cobra on a jungle track just outside the village. He left it there, but later mentioned it to us in passing. Jokingly, we rebuked him for the waste of edible meat, whereupon he immediately rushed back to reclaim the abandoned (and now profitable) reptile from the ants.

Having skinned the snake we hung the bloody corpse to dry over a log fire in the kitchen at the nearby village police post: a post manned in the main by local Hmong recruits. That evening a number of the men avoided the kitchen. They were frightened of the spirit which may have been living in the snake's body, much to the amusement of those Hmong who for some reason did not fear the bloody serpent. One man in particular was adamant he would go nowhere near it. Unfortunately, in our excitement (this was the first king-cobra I'd seen in the wild) we failed to make a mental note of the clans of those who feared, and those who did not, for possibly different clan beliefs may have played a part in this. The snake meat was delicious, but sadly, nobody would share it with us.

My job is to help people in the village. They often come to me to divine the future for them. Usually I use chicken bones. I often have to ask the spirits to help sort out problems for them. For instance, sometimes the spirits in the fields make people ill. The sick people come to me for help. I have to try and discover which spirit it was that attacked them, and find out what has to be done to right matters. I do this for my relatives and for most of the other people in the village. I don't always get paid. They only pay me if they have some money. If they have nothing, I get nothing. I do it to help them. Then they give me whatever they can.

Hoping we were not being too indelicate, we asked Yiow-fun whether or not he was able to practise black magic.

No, no, I can't do it, neither can Mr Shi Guai the headman. Nobody in the village can do it, though in the old days when we lived in our former village there was someone who could perform black magic. The elders sometimes talk of it. My father told me about him. He lives in a village near Chiang Khan now. He'd be very old by now, he probably stopped doing it a long time ago. And if he hadn't stopped on his own accord then someone would have killed him by now anyway.

Of course you can't do this sort of thing for long before people begin to realise. I don't think anybody would do it these days, it's too much trouble killing that way, using a gun is so much easier. And anyway, anybody who can do these magic things would be very frightened of the gun.

I remember when I was young there was one man from our village who was always stealing. He was bad. Sometimes he'd even steal cows and water buffaloes. One day he fell ill with severe pains in his chest and stomach. His family called in the shaman to see what was the matter. They wanted the shaman to try and determine the outcome of the illness. Straight away the shaman realised his patient had been attacked through black magic. There was no hope for the victim. He died shortly after.

Later my father told me a sorcerer had done it. He had sent something into the thief's stomach to kill him. Everybody in the village knew what had happened. Someone had written the thief's name on a piece of paper and then while repeating a spell had put the paper inside a chick's mouth. Then that person had chopped off the chick's head at the neck, to separate the head and the piece of paper from the rest of the body. This is the only way to kill someone by magic. It takes about two or three days, during which time the victim falls mysteriously ill and suffers great pain. Then he dies. Only someone who knows the spells can do this sort of thing.

8 – Leur Prom-muang – Karen

Leur Prom-muang is sixty-eight years old, and is a former headman of Ban Doi, a lowland Karen village situated in an area of fertile rice paddies to the south-east of Chiang Saen.

The village was founded in 1915 by an advance party of Karen from Lamphun Province further to the south, and now has over six hundred inhabitants. It was the first settlement in the valley, pre-dating all of the many Thai villages now in the area. Many of the houses in Ban Doi are very large, completely dwarfing the single-room houses typically seen in upland Karen villages.

Leur Prom-muang's house is particularly large – by anyone's standards. Half hidden in a garden of banana trees and frangipani bushes, it is forty paces long and fifteen wide. Its single floor is raised two metres off the ground on fifty-six tree-trunk size supporting posts. On first sight it has the appearance of a long-house more typical of the Rajang River of Sarawak, only more sturdily built. Inside there are three bedrooms, an open cooking place and a large open communal area. Apart from the supporting posts, which are mahogany, the entire house is built of teak. The construction of this magnificent house took Leur's father eight long years from start to finish.

There are few ornaments or pieces of furniture in the communal area. On one wall there is a small Buddhist altar flanked by portraits of the Thai King and Queen. To its right is a small collection of photographs. An old black and white one depicts a former Karen leader sitting atop an elephant somewhere in the jungles of Burma. Just below this there is a picture of a former Chiang Rai governor standing outside Leur's house. Half a dozen others are of Leur's children, one of which shows a son standing proudly in the uniform of the Black Tigers, an elite commando unit of the Thai army.

Only Leur and his wife now live in the house. Sons and daughters have all either moved out into their own houses in the village, or are away working in Bangkok. We have known Leur since 1989, and are frequent visitors.

House Spirits, and How Not to Offend

Leur Prom-muang

House Spirits, and How Not to Offend Them

Leur spoke with us on the subject of house spirits and the rules of prohibition associated with such spirits, taboos which cover so many aspects of Karen behaviour.

You want to know about siting a Karen house? Well, let me think for a while. There are many rules. There are right places and wrong places to build a house. A house can be built as close to another house as you like, as long as it's in the correct position. For example, a son or daughter cannot build a house directly in front or directly behind their parents' house [he uses his hands to illustrate the point]. If they were to do this it would displease the house spirit of their parents' house, because you see, behind the house is the head of the house and in front is the face. It wouldn't be right to build right in front or right behind. They'd have to build their house off to one side, either a little bit in front or a little bit behind.

It would also be wrong, for instance, if a son built his house behind the parents' house — but not directly behind — and then someone from a different lineage came along and built a house between the two. If this happens the house spirits would be in conflict. It would be the same if, say, two brothers built a house near each other and then someone from a different lineage built between them. This can't be done, it'd be contrary to the wishes of the house spirits. The spirits would bring illness to all those involved, even death perhaps.

Fearing we may have missed the point, he then supplied us with an analogy.

Think of it like this. When you roast a piece of chicken, you use two small sticks to hold the meat over the fire. If you get too close to the fire the two sticks will burn. They will burn first, but later so will the chicken. So, if someone of a different lineage was to build his house between two others who share the same lineage, he will then be giving them trouble with their house spirits. But later, he also will suffer from the same problem.

It's also taboo to build a house between two rice stores. If you were to do this you'd be in for really serious trouble. The spirit of the rice is very, very important. Another vital point is that no three houses may form an equidistant triangle. In all these matters we believe in, and follow, the ways of our ancestors.

The Karen afford great reverence and respect to their house spirits, and take great pains not to cause the spirits any offence. In addition to the complex set of rules governing where one may, and may not, build one's house, there are many other taboos that must be adhered to so as not to cause the house spirits' displeasure, as Leur Prom-muang recounts:

If a couple staying in a Karen house were to make love, the house spirit would be very, very upset. So, our traditions dictate that a couple cannot share the same room. Well, no, really our traditions don't actually say they can't share a room for the night. It's just that we can't trust people not to sleep together that we have to forbid the sharing of a single room. Of course, the husband and wife of the household can sleep together, that's no problem.

We therefore have to make guests sleep in different rooms, or on the veranda. Oh, you know, sometimes it's very difficult telling people this. Naturally, if they are Karen they understand the situation. But when the guests are Thais, then we have problems.

It's very embarrassing to have to explain the reasons for making them sleep separately. It's not easy at all. If they do share a room and don't make love, that's fine. But how do we trust them? How do we know they won't? I know what people are like [he laughs], if a couple are sharing a room, for sure they cannot wait. They would make love and our house spirit would be angry. Then the spirit will cause a family member to fall ill, and we'd have to sacrifice a pig to appease him.

It is not only inconsiderate guests that offend the house spirit however, but also, it seems, any sow belonging to the family which produces an all male or all female litter.

Yes, if a sow gives birth to piglets that are all of the same sex they must be killed. You see, it's not normal. We can't keep them, it would anger the house spirit. If we were to keep them, then

Leur Prom-muang

sometime later when we were in the forest a tiger or bear would come and kill us, and then eat us. If the house spirit is angry then for sure some misfortune will befall you. He will harm you in some way. For example, if you were to chop a tree down in the forest, or perhaps go out to cut bamboo, then if the spirit is angry he'd make you chop yourself by mistake.

It's the same with chickens, you know. If a hen with new chicks makes a noise like a cock, she has to be killed, along with the chicks. Again, it's because it's not normal. If we tried to keep the chicken we'd be eaten by a tiger the next time we went to the fields or entered the forest.

A similar belief concerning the crowing of a hen (whether with chicks or not) was held by many in the British Isles until the present century; in some country districts it may still flourish. An old Scottish proverb recounts how 'A crooning cow, a crowing hen, and a whistling maid boded never luck to a house' (Kelly 1721 - in Opie & Tatem). And in 1887, in her book 'Superstitions of Ireland', Lady Wilde (Oscar Wilde's mother) wrote: 'A hen that crows is very unlucky and should be killed; very often the hen is stoned, for it is believed that she is bewitched by the fairies.'

And sometimes a sow eats some of her own offspring, and doesn't give milk to the others, and is always gnashing her teeth. Whenever we witness this sort of behaviour we have to kill the sow and her remaining piglets. This type of pig has to be evil. Maybe one day it would eat its owner. Its behaviour is unnatural, it's evil, so it must be killed.

On enquiring how a pig could eat its owner, Leur clarified the point further.

No, not really eat its owner. The evil pig's spirit would make the person become ill. It's possible the owner would die. What happens is that the spirit eats the owner's soul, his life-force.

The Karen Village Priest

Referred to as 'sapwa hi akhu' by the Sgaw Karen, and 'shasha g'ae akhu' by the Pwo Karen, the Karen village priest is the most important person in a Karen village. He announces and directs all the village ceremonies, the most important of which is the twice yearly ceremony held for the 'Lord of Land and Water'. He also watches over the moral conduct of the village, particularly in sexual matters. This last duty is of the utmost importance to the Karen, as they believe a break in their moral code will result in repercussions from the offended spirits in the form of disease, crop failure and loss of livestock. The position is hereditary, with the duties being passed on to the oldest willing male relative in the village who is related on his father's side to the former priest, i.e. brothers, sons and cousins on the father's side.

Leur explains how a new priest is chosen.

The village priest is chosen by everyone in the village. Everyone has to be present when we elect a priest, and the choice has to be unanimous. Usually we choose someone from the same family that has always supplied the village with priests—for generations and generations. It's the same in my family. I was a soldier during the Second World War. I trained in Lampang and Chiang Mai, and then went to help the Japanese Army. And now my son is in the army, too. It's often like this, sons follow in their father's footsteps. It's the same with the village priests.

A thought then occurred to Leur. He asked me whether I had been in the army. I hadn't. 'Never mind', he said, a sympathetic expression (perhaps disappointment) briefly showing on his face before continuing with his account.

The village decides who they want to be the village priest, and then by means of divination we look to see if that person is suitable. We use a chicken's thigh bones. You see, normally there are small holes on the bones. If the holes on both bones are exactly the same, then the person we are asking about is the right man. Then everything is good, and he can become the next priest.

Leur Prom-muang

The practice of divination is a worldwide phenomenon, and so it has been since time immemorial. In the temple of Apollo Diradiotes at Argos, a lamb was sacrificed once a month; by tasting the lamb's blood a woman of proven chastity became inspired by the god and prophesied or divined. The ancient Germans, we are told (Frazer 1922:97), employed sacred women to look on eddying rivers and listen to the sounds of the flowing waters, and from the sight and sound foretold what would come to pass. And today, the screech of a barn owl in Thailand, as it flies in a westward direction over one's house signals that a death in the household will follow shortly, for the owl is the messenger of the spirit of Death, and the setting sun symbolises death. Whatever method employed, whether using the entrails of animals sacrificed (hieroscopy), currents in water (bletonism), passages in books (stichomancy) or through dreams (oneiromancy), the diviner is hoping to read some 'sign' or 'omen' which can help him in forming a prediction.

We shall run across many instances of divination throughout the pages of this book. By obtaining readings from rice grains, raw eggs (see Aka My-yer, Our Village), chicken bones (see below, and Laopia Selee and Napur Muangjai), feathers, divination horns (see Nachai Sewa, 'Gong-goy' Spirits), crying babies, and extracted pigs' livers (see Abu Merlaygu, Chasing Out the Spirits), to name just a few methods, the hilltribe diviner will be trying to ascertain the wishes of the unseen powers in a whole host of different situations, some of which are listed below:

1) Choosing a site, such as for a new village, a house, a burial or a shrine.
2) Enquiring into the cause of sickness.
3) Examining whether a shaman's familiar spirits can help in a matter.
4) Determining the result of a curing ritual.
5) Helping one decide on a certain course of action, such as which crops to plant, or whether or not to undertake a certain business venture.
6) Selecting an auspicious day for undertaking an action, such as building a house, burning a field, beginning a journey.
7) Testing the compatibility of a couple before marriage, or the suitability of a candidate for the post of village priest.
8) Naming a child.

> *In all these cases of divination, whether practised by village priests, shamans, spirit specialists, elders or household heads, definite, concrete answers are not provided, nor expected. The results are rather seen as an omen, an indication only, of the standing of the unseen powers in such matters. In a sense, the activities of the diviner have a practical social value by indicating a choice of action which has the sanction of the supernatural. Thus, the diviner relieves the client of the burden of decision; an important psychological service in a world filled with spirits, many of which are malevolent and easily wronged. In the words of the American anthropologist, George Park, the diviner is able 'to remove the agency and the responsibility for a decision from the actor himself, casting it upon the heavens where it lies beyond cavil and beyond reproach.' (in Middleton [ed.] 1967.)*
>
> *We return to Leur and the search for a village priest.*

How many chickens? What colour? Oh, the colour doesn't matter. Black or white, that's not too important. Sometimes we have to go through twenty birds before we find what we're looking for. You see, if you want a particular person to be the priest, sometimes one pair of bones isn't enough. You have to examine more until they are exactly right. It's not only the holes that have to match. The two bones have to be straight and regular.

Sometimes the bones are perfect, but the candidate doesn't want to be the priest. This sort of thing can happen when the man's wife and children are against it. When this happens, that is to say when the whole village wants a man, and the bones are perfect, but the man doesn't agree, and there is no one else in the village that's suitable, well, then we have to order that man and his family to leave the village. He has to go because he's going against the wishes of the community.

> *Thus, the villagers use the reading of chicken bones to satisfy themselves they have selected the right candidate for the post of village priest. Since, by examining enough bones, they must ultimately discover the 'right' signs which, conveniently, allows them to pass on the responsibility of their choice to the spirits.*

9 – Mit Selee – Hmong

Mit Selee is a friendly, energetic twenty-six year old Hmong man from Kiew Khan. He is married with four children and lives with his parents and married brothers and their families in a single, large ground-built house of traditional Hmong design. With its wooden plank walls and roof of thatch grass, the house is typical of most dwellings in the village.

Living in large extended families under a single roof is the norm for many Hmong, but Mit's family is considered large even by his neighbours, and much good-natured banter is directed to his father – a slightly-built man well into his sixties – for spawning such a vast crowd: from his two wives he has managed to father fourteen children, eleven of them sons. Now four of these sons, Mit included, have married and have children of their own, and Mit jokes that at meal times they are forced to work a shift system, with supper consisting of three sittings.

Sexual Intercourse and the House Spirits

With the exception of the Karen, who are altogether more reserved and stricter in their sexual codes, all tribal groups in the region afford their young a great degree of freedom in meeting and getting to know members of the opposite sex. However, there are certain restrictions on where sexual intercourse may take place. Mit explains some of the taboos pertaining to courtship in Hmong village society, with particular reference to the spirits of the house.

If a young man and a young woman want to see each other, the male has to go to the female's house. He can't take her to his house because that would anger his family's house spirits. If he did such a thing, oh, it'd be terrible, he'd be in a lot of trouble. All the family's good fortune, money, silver and good health would leave the house and never return. No matter what the family did, no matter how hard they worked they'd never be prosperous again. That's why we have this custom stopping men from taking women to their houses.

A man can visit a woman in her house, however. But only in

her bedroom. When I say 'visit', what I mean is go and chat her up and then sleep with her. They can sleep together in her room, but nowhere else. They can't do it in the main room, and especially not in the cooking area by the hearth. That would displease the spirits, and if the parents found out about it later both of them would be in serious trouble.

The interior of a Hmong house consists of a large main room, in which the fireplace and spirit altar are found, where the family eats its meals and entertains its guests. A bamboo sleeping platform for guests is located off to one side. Bedrooms for parents and some of the children are positioned along two of the walls, and are partitioned with boards or hanging mats. The eldest unmarried daughter in a White Hmong family usually has her own private room just inside the main door. This location allows easy access for suitors. Callers would normally only be invited in after the woman's family have already retired.

We asked Mit how serious an offence it would be for a couple to sleep together in the main room of a Hmong house.

How serious? Well, Jon, Najia [Najia is Su's Hmong name], the house spirits would make someone in the family fall ill. Then the parents would consult a shaman. He would hold a ritual to try and determine the cause of the illness, and he'd discover that two people had done something terrible. He'd find out they had made love together outside of the bedroom. The parents would then ask their daughter if it were true. She'd have to own up to it. You can't do these things and get away with it.

Once it had all come out the parents would then have to make amends to the house spirits. They'd have to apologise to the spirits. Oh, it'd be a lot of trouble. The shaman would have to do something as well. He'd make two little figures out of grass stalks.

How big? Oh, about this big [He indicates about twenty centimetres]. He'd make them so that they are joined together as though making love. The naughty couple would then be told to carry the figures out of the house and throw them away somewhere beyond the village. The sick person in the family would then get better.

But all this is very rare. Maybe in the last twenty or thirty years it has only happened once or twice in our village. Everyone is far too frightened to do such a thing. And anyway, if the woman hasn't got a bedroom they can always see each other outside. That's no problem.

Young Hmong men sometimes carry a blanket with them at night when calling on a woman they know does not have her own private room. They then invite the woman to spend the night with them under the stars in some quiet spot on the outskirts of the village, with only the thin blanket — and their passion — to keep them warm.

10 – Chan-jian Selee—Yao

Chan-jian Selee is twenty-two years old and lives in the Yao village of Lao Shi Guai. He has recently married and has one baby daughter.

Ancient Writings

The Yao have a tradition of writing using Chinese characters, and most Yao communities possess a number of 'old' hand-written books and pamphlets. The 'Book of Days' is of particular importance. It is referred to before a young couple is betrothed, for by comparing the day, month and year of their births, it can be determined whether the union will be harmonious or not. A second book, of equal importance, is the 'Ancestor Book', which contains the ceremonial names of the ancestors going back at least nine generations.

Another document, formerly found in Yao communities but rarely seen nowadays, is the so-called 'Yao Charter', or 'Mien Passport'. This unique document of great historical interest includes in it a copy of an Imperial Edict issued by the early Chinese Emperor Pien Hung to the Yao people living in China, permitting them to migrate and engage in cultivation anywhere in the mountainous areas of China. The Edict also stated that the Yao were to be accorded certain special rights as 'children of Emperor Hung'.

We asked Chan-jian whether there were any Yao books in the village.

Yao books? Yes, there are some. The headman has them in his house. He is the founder of the village, he can read and write Chinese. I can only read Thai, I can't read Chinese characters.

Asked what sort of books the headman possessed, he told us of an old book which is traditionally consulted when building a new house.

We use an old Yao book to help us decide where to build our houses. It's a very old book written in Chinese characters. I can't read it, but the headman can.

It's very important to choose exactly the right place for a house. I know it says in the book that we should never build on a piece of ground which is uneven, or if there's a water-filled hole nearby. Also we shouldn't build anywhere near a termite hill, that wouldn't be any good at all. I think there are many other factors to take into consideration.

There are many restrictions, but the only ones I can think of now are those that I've already mentioned. I'm sure there are very good reasons to be careful when siting a house, so it's essential to consult the old book.

If the book says don't build your house on land which has a hole nearby, I'm sure there must be a very good reason for this. Usually when we need to build a house we ask the elders to help us locate it. They know all about these things.

From what Chan-jian remembers from the above book it would appear it contains down-to-earth (no pun intended), common-sense advice. Not building your wooden house near a termite hill seems sensible, as does avoiding particularly uneven ground – Yao houses are ground-built, and usually when building such a house more than half the time needed for construction is spent simply levelling the ground. Naturally, the more level the ground to start with the better!

11 – Laojia - Sombat - Laopia — Hmong

In the following interview with three Hmong men from Kiew Khan we hear of a curing ritual held the week previously for the elder brother of one of the interviewees. Laojia is twenty-two, and is the younger brother of the patient. His friend Sombat is twenty-five (the same 'laughing Sombat' from Nachai's account of a failed shamanic initiation), and Laopia, forty-seven years old, is a family friend.

Inviting the Spirit of the Three Ancestors: An Account of a Shamanic Curing Ritual

LAOJIA: We're doing a special ritual tonight. It's for my brother. He's been seriously ill recently. He's better now, so tonight we are going to thank the spirit that came to help us. We asked the spirit of the three ancestors for help. He's a very important spirit, not many people make offerings to this spirit. It all happened last week. Now everything is alright.

INTERVIEWER: Can you tell us something of the ritual?

LAOJIA: It was very long and complicated. It's not a normal sort of ritual. Before we started my father asked six men to help. It had to be men, it couldn't be women. And the shaman came with two helpers as well. The helpers worked in pairs. Each pair had a different task. One pair killed the pig and took care of the cooking, another went to find some bamboo to make the special table, and the others constructed a temporary stove.

When everything was ready the shaman asked my father for a tray on which he put some corn and red and white peppers. Then he shook the tray to mix everything together, and started throwing the stuff around the house. While doing this he repeated a spell ordering the bad spirit who had made my brother ill to leave the house.

He finished by throwing some of the corn and peppers in front of the door. After this he put on a white hood and stood outside the front door. He shouted out to anybody who might have been nearby. He said 'If there's anyone walking around outside go home quickly. If anybody's children are out playing, take them inside now. Girls and boys, wherever you are, go inside now. There is a very powerful spirit coming. He'll be riding a very old horse. Be careful everyone, the horse may kick you. If he kicks you in the mouth your mouth will become deformed. If he kicks you in the eyes your eyes will be misshapened. And if he gets you in the ears, your ears will be all twisted.'

Then he called out for the spirit to come. I can't tell you what he said, it's strictly forbidden, but after calling him he informed the spirit that the women and children of the village were all in bed sleeping.

It is possible the spirit summoned by the shaman may be the same spirit which is thought by the Hmong to have guided their 'ancestors of long ago' in their flight from China. A ritual to honour this special ancestral spirit is performed by some descent groups – ideally once every three years. It is held indoors and at night, and no women are allowed to witness the proceedings. Significantly, the spirit summoned to Laojia's house that night is thought to have travelled from a great distance.

LAOJIA: Then he asked the spirit to come into his body. A short while later the spirit spoke through the shaman saying 'Err, I am coming, riding on an old horse. Is this the right house? Is this the one that has invited me to come and eat pork?' Then the spirit, still speaking through the shaman, asked the people sitting in the house if entry to the house had been barred. We were sitting inside and replied that the house was open and he was welcome to enter.

INTERVIEWER: What were those words the shaman used to call the spirit?

LAOJIA: Oh, well, they're just words to call the spirit.

INTERVIEWER: Oh, come on, you must know. Why not just tell me a few of them? And also, why does the shaman tell everyone to go to bed? Is this ritual held late at night?

LAOJIA: Yes, at night. At midnight. We have to wait until the village is asleep because this spirit we summon is not a normal spirit. When he comes on his ancient horse and sees anyone out and about he will cause their faces to become twisted and deformed. And if anybody other than the shaman should use those special words to invite him, he will harm them too in the same way. Nobody can say these words other than the shaman. Please believe me. This spirit is very powerful, we have to be careful not to offend him.

INTERVIEWER: Um, maybe it is something you want to keep for yourselves. Go on, tell me some of it. I'm sure the spirit wouldn't mind.

At this point Laopia and Sombat join in.

LAOPIA: Really, these words cannot be repeated. If anybody says them the spirit causes their mouths to become all deformed. Nobody can repeat these words. If someone says them the spirit will think he is being summoned. If he comes and there is no offering for him he'll get angry and then make the caller's mouth twist out of shape. In order to rectify this the shaman would have to be called. He'd have to offer a pig to the spirit and then rub his divining sticks three times over the victim's mouth in order to bring it back to normal. This really happens, it's all true.

SOMBAT: It happened to my father once. It was about ten years ago. He had been out hunting deep in the jungle and had come across what looked like a bag hanging from a tree. He didn't realise it was something used in the ritual held for the spirit of the three ancestors.

You see, after this ritual everything that is used in it has to be taken out of the house and left somewhere in a part of the jungle where nobody usually goes. Somewhere a long way from any paths or tracks. This is what my father came across accidentally. He walked too close to it. By the time he got back home his mouth was already all out of shape.

LAOPIA: The table made for this ritual, as well as all the ash from the firewood used for cooking and the pig's bones have to be cleared up and thrown away in the forest, somewhere remote in the forest. If anybody should accidentally come across them they must make a big detour around the area and not simply walk right past them. If they make the detour everything is alright.

Laojia continues the account.

LAOJIA: This is why we had to wait until the women and children had all gone to bed. Otherwise the children may have heard the secret words and repeated them sometime. And then the spirit would come to them and harm them.

While the shaman was calling out to the spirit that night the rest of us were inside preparing the food. A piece of each part of the pig was put into nine separate bowls. Altogether there were twelve parts. That's some of the leg, ear, heart, snout, lung, liver, tail, intestine, kidney, tongue, some good meat and some blood. Just a little piece of each was placed into each bowl.

The bowls weren't normal ones. They had to be specially made for the ceremony from half sections of bamboo. As the shaman placed the meat and other things into them he repeated some incantations and invited the spirit to come to eat. Afterwards the meat in the bowls was eaten by all the people who came to help. Each helper also got a small pile of meat which he could take back home with him. When the pig is a big one there is usually also some left over for the family who held the ritual.

As the spirit left the house the shaman and the family members called out to the spirit saying 'Err, you are going, do not come back. Go for ever, go a long way and don't return. Not until the rocks become flowers and the Mekong river flows backwards. Not until the cocks start to lay eggs and the hens begin to crow. Only then can you come back. You took the pork, don't come back, err.'

We have to say this because we invited the spirit to come and eat in our house. We asked him to come and help fight off the evil spirit that was harming my brother. But after eating, the spirit must go. If we didn't say these words the spirit would probably come back again for more pork.

INTERVIEWER: Do you really think the spirit comes to help? And that he enters the shaman and fights off a bad spirit?

LAOJIA: Yes, it must be true because we can't see the spirit. We've been asking for help from spirits for many, many generations.

INTERVIEWER: But how do you know the spirit comes if you can't see it?

LAOJIA: Because we can see its effects. We know it comes.

INTERVIEWER: Are you frightened of it?

Laopia answers.

LAOPIA: Even though we can't see the spirit we are still frightened of it. Once someone who was not a shaman tried to summon this spirit. He spoke the secret words and the spirit made his mouth become distorted. This really happened, it's true. It's not a good idea to try it out.

There was an occasion when a family was holding this special ritual and one of their children was only pretending to be asleep. Really he was awake and waiting to hear the special words to summon the spirit. The following morning he tried them out for a joke. At this time the spirit was still on his way back to the land of the spirits. He was a long, long way away when he heard the boy call him back. So he came back expecting another pig to be offered to him. But there was nothing, the boy was just playing games. The spirit then caused the boy's mouth to deform. The parents went to the shaman and were told they had to sacrifice another pig to the spirit. And then a little while later the mouth went back to normal. After this nobody else wanted to play around like that again.

INTERVIEWER: What happens if the spirit comes across people when he's leaving? Does he harm them?

LAOPIA: Oh no, not when he leaves. Once the offering has been made and the spirit has eaten, he is happy to go. He wishes the family good luck and informs them he's leaving. He tells them to remain inside. Then he goes.

We turned to Laojia.

INTERVIEWER: Laojia, where were your little brothers and sisters on the night your family summoned the spirit of the three ancestors to your house?

LAOJIA: They went to bed early and we locked them in their rooms so they couldn't come to look.

INTERVIEWER: Doesn't the beating of the shaman's gong wake them? Surely they can hear what's going on?

LAOJIA: Oh, the shaman doesn't use his gong for this ritual. My brothers and sisters are always asleep by midnight. And with my mother is doesn't matter whether she hears or not. She's too scared of her mouth being deformed to come and look.

You know, if the spirit was to come across someone outside, or was called by someone other than a shaman, and he didn't cause their mouth to deform, it would mean he had lost his power. And then the evil spirit who had caused the patient's sickness in the first place would return to make that person ill again.

My family held this ritual because my elder brother was seriously ill. He had been in hospital for many days and wasn't getting better. So my father asked the spirit to help. He promised a big pig to the spirit if he would help my brother get better. It had to be a big sow that had had three litters. You see, an old spirit should receive an old pig.

The ritual finished at about 3.30 a.m. The shaman's two helpers took everything away into the jungle. It had to be taken off immediately the ritual was over. Even the ash from the fire and the leftover firewood had to go. It was especially important that all the bones were taken off. We had to make sure there were no bones mixed up with the leftover meat. It's important because it's the bones that make up the pig. If any bones are left in the house the spirit may think there's another pig for him and come back for it. Everything used in the ritual had to be disposed of.

This ritual was held on 15 June 1991. Ten days later we were told the presiding shaman himself had fallen ill. According to Laojia the shaman was demanding one hundred baht (£2.50) from Laojia's father so he could buy a chicken to offer to the spirits on his own behalf. Such a development is considered extremely inauspicious for the future health of Laojia's elder brother.

12 – Mai-gwa Selee — Hmong

Mai-gwa is a twenty year old Hmong woman from Kiew Khan. She is the mother of four children and the wife of Mit, with whom we spoke earlier on the subject of courtship and the house spirits.

Hmong Post-natal Precautions

Mai-gwa, who is a recent mother for the fourth time, describes the birthing practice of the Hmong and outlines some of the precautions a mother must take to ensure the good health of her baby. Not all tribal groups follow the exact procedure of the Hmong in these matters, although in practice the general outlines are similar.

Some tribeswomen today are having their babies in lowland hospitals. This occurs relatively infrequently, and is usually due to some irregularity in the mother's condition. Many Hmong women, for instance, would rather undergo a difficult birth at home, and in private, than have strangers (doctors and nurses) see them at such an intimate time. For at home, even the midwife – or husband – does not witness the actual delivery. We asked whether a woman has help during the delivery.

Yes, we have help. If it's your first, a midwife will help, or maybe your grandmother. They have to cut the umbilical cord. Once you've had four or five your husband can manage on his own, or the mother could do it by herself. It's only at first that you need help.

The birth takes place in the couple's bedroom, and no one but the midwife, the woman's mother-in-law, or her husband can be present to assist in the delivery. She gives birth sitting perched between two low stools set on top of the sleeping platform. This allows the baby to drop the few inches onto the springy bamboo. The delivery is done in complete silence. There are three reasons for this. Firstly, the Hmong consider any noise made by the mother would shame the household. Secondly, they fear any noise made may alert wild spirits outside the house which may then come to attack the child. And thirdly, they worry moans or screams made by the mother may cause the unborn baby to think the world into which it is about to come is an unhappy place, and therefore decide not to come out of the womb.

Immediately after birth two plaited hemp cords are tied around the baby's neck. One is white, the other is red. The white is thought to tie in the two souls the baby is born with; the red, to protect the infant from evil spirits and harm during the three days before the child fully joins the human world. The midwife or mother-in-law then ties a white thread around the umbilical cord in two places, and cuts the flesh, either with a sharp sliver of freshly cut bamboo, or with a pair of sewing scissors cleaned in ash. The baby is wrapped in a piece of cloth and laid on the bed.

As soon as we give birth we go to lie down on a bed of rice stalks next to the fire. We lie with our stomachs facing the fire. We stay there for four or five days, until we are able to walk about again. After five days we can cook for ourselves whenever the husband is not there.

Usually we stay at home for thirty days—that's one month. Every day we eat chicken. If your family is wealthy the mother can keep eating chicken even after the thirty days. We eat very hot rice with it. You can't eat any leftover rice, it has to be very hot every time. And we drink a lot of hot water. We have to eat hot food because when we give birth we lose a lot of blood, so we need the hot food to keep us warm.

Immediately after the birth the husband collects the sarong worn by the mother during the birth and washes it, being careful to collect up all the effluent from the birthing process which he then quickly buries in a hole outside the house. It is important the spirits don't see any of this blood, as they may be tempted to try and get more. While the husband carries out this task, the mother boils an egg on the fire, which she eats, giving a small portion to the newly born baby as a meal of welcome.

During her time confined to the house the mother only eats freshly cooked rice and chicken. These warm foods are thought to promote good blood circulation. She lies on a camp bed beside the household fire. This helps to ensure that all the stale blood flows from her body, so that her uterus, which the Hmong refer to as 'the house of the child' (Symmonds 1991), will be cleansed and ready for the next child.

And what of the placenta?

The placenta? We bury it in the bedroom, in the corner by the door. We never take it outside the house. You know, if we were to bury it outside the baby would grow up to be very bad, a really bad child, one that stays away from the parents. The sort of child who goes away and never misses home. We bury it inside the house so as to keep the child's soul. Then when he's older he'll still love the family, and he'll still want to be with his parents. You never see Hmong people staying away from their families for long periods of time. They always want to be with their families, no matter how poor they are.

If the baby is male the placenta is buried at the base of the main house post, where the lineage spirits are thought to reside. If the child is female the placenta will be buried under the couple's bed. Great care is taken in this operation. It is usually wrapped in leaves and placed flat into the hole, and then quickly covered up. It is essential no insects eat any of the afterbirth, as it is thought this would cause the baby's health to suffer. Upon death, each person is admonished to go back to the place of birth to retrieve the 'birth shirt', or placenta, in order to wear it back to the land of the ancestors. Without a birth shirt, say the Hmong, one cannot be reborn as a human being (Symmonds).

After thirty or forty days we go back to work in the fields. Oh yes, during those thirty days, if you feel strong enough you can walk around outside the house, but you mustn't go far. You can't go to the town, or do anything strenuous. Whenever you go outside, even just to go to the toilet, you must carry a piece of smouldering cotton rope behind your back. This is to keep the spirits away. The smoke does it. Then when you go back inside the house to see how your baby is, the evil spirits can't follow you and disturb the sleeping infant.

One thing you can't do is to enter another house. And if people from another household come to see you during the first thirty days they mustn't take away any burning wood from the fire [to light their own fires], nor must they take a lighter or box of matches or any cooking pots out of the house. If they did take away any of these things, it'd be the same as if they were taking away the baby's milk. The milk would dry up and there'd be nothing for the baby.

Not only are women thought particularly vulnerable to attack from spirits during times of childbirth, and pregnancy and menstruation, but they themselves are seen as constituting something of a threat, in that they are thought of as being somewhat out of balance and likely to attract evil influences. Thus, there may be more to stopping a neighbour from removing burning brands from a fire than simply not allowing people to deplete a much needed fire. It may also be a measure to protect people from attracting bad influences or misfortune from the new mother to their own homes.

At birth a child's body is not yet in full possession of its souls. Of the two souls that every human is born with, one is attained by the infant as its bones grow while still in the mother's uterus, and the other is acquired from the 'wind' when the child takes its first breath on emerging from its 'house'. However, the third soul; is still part of the pool of souls – the ancestral mass – which belongs to the descent group in the land of the ancestors. These are souls in need of a body in which to be reborn. Only after the baby has survived the first three days of life is this third soul summoned.

This soul-calling ritual marks the child's formal adoption into the world of human beings. The ceremony is conducted by the oldest male of the lineage who knows the ritual chant. He offers thanks to the 'Baby Goddess' – a deity believed to reside in the Otherworld who is thought to send babies into the world – and invites the soul to take up permanent residence within the child's body. The child is now given its formal name and introduced to the household and lineage spirits who are expected from that moment on to give it their protection. If a child should die before the three days are up it is thought the child's time for life has not arrived for some reason, and the body, still belonging to the spirit world, is buried quickly and unceremoniously.

13 – Gor-da Bierpa – Lisu

Gor-da Bierpa is a grey-haired, bespectacled sixty-two year old living in the Lisu village of Pang Sa. He runs the local store which operates along the lines of a village co-operative. He tells us the shop had originally been owned one hundred percent by the villagers, however, they had found it difficult finding people to take on the responsibility of running it, and eventually it was decided to allow Gor-da to take over control in return for a thirty percent share of the profits. This agreement seems to suit both the village and Gor-da perfectly.

Gor-da is a former Lisu priest. Realising this when we first met him, we immediately set about interrogating him, hoping (rather optimistically) to learn something of weretigers and black magic: two subjects which other people in the village seemed reluctant to talk about.

On enquiring about the possibility of there being weretigers in the vicinity, Gor-da replied:

You mean that people become tigers? No, we don't have that now. There may have been some in the old days, when I was a baby, but I've not heard of any around here nowadays. These days any tigers here would be frightened of us humans. Look around you! There's no thick jungle around here anymore. No undergrowth for them to live in. For sure there are no tigers here. We've got guns now. Any weretigers would have moved deeper into the forest by now, the same as with the vampires.

And black magic?

Black magic? Oh yes, I know what you mean, I've heard about it. In the past, before we had guns or good knives, like bowie knives, the only way to hurt people was by sending something to kill them through black magic. But I tell you, we don't do it now. Sending nails or bits of paper into your victim's stomach is a slow way to kill him. It's much easier to use a gun.

People don't bother with black magic anymore. Evan an expert at black magic would be frightened of someone with a gun. These are technology days we are living in now.

But on other, perhaps less controversial, subjects such as curing rituals and childbirth, Gor-da has since proved a mine of information.

Great Balls of Fire

When a person is ill, and it is believed the presence of an evil spirit is the cause of the sickness, the Lisu may conduct a 'spraying' of the sickness. The ritual, in which a shaman blows fire balls over the patient in an effort to frighten off the spirit, exhibits certain similarities with the 'flaming torch dog-on-a-string' component of the Hmong exorcism ritual mentioned earlier by Nachai. Gor-da Bierpa describes a 'spraying':

It's not dangerous, but only a shaman can do it. He sprays oil onto a fire to fight off the bad spirits. He blows fireballs. This is done when someone is ill, in order to fight off the spirits. It's also done during the New Year festival, but on this occasion he does it to renew his powers, and not to fight off spirits. This is when he blows fireballs out of the houses through the open doors. He goes to every house to perform this.

When he blows fireballs to cure people he spits the fire onto the patient's body. He does it by collecting together a handful of sticks which he then lights to make a burning torch. He sucks up some burning cooking oil into his mouth and spits the oil over the flaming branches. And this makes the fireballs.

As a safety measure, the patient usually sits with his or her head covered by a shawl or sarong.

Only shamans who know the right spells can do this. Not every shaman does it. Me? No, I can't do it, only shamans can do it. If I tried to do it I'd burn myself. Normal people can't blow fireballs without burning themselves.

I wonder what Gor-da would make of some of the fire-blowing stunts commonly seen in London's Covent Garden or outside Paris' Pompidou Centre?

Lisu Childbirth and Naming

A Lisu women may deliver her baby in her bedroom or in the main room of the house close to a specially prepared fire, referred to by the Lisu as the 'mother roasting' fire. After delivery she lies by the fire for a month in order to keep warm. The placenta may be buried under the spot where the fire was built, or it may be placed high up in a tree in the jungle. The day after the birth the village priest makes offerings of pork and other items (supplied by the family) to the village guardian spirit. The priest asks the spirit to give its blessings to the child, to help keep the child from harm, to allow the baby to 'become big like a huge cucumber' (Lewis 1984:269), and to give it a long life and much power. It is taboo for visitors to enter the house for the first seven days after the birth. During this time the baby is not considered a human being, but as still belonging to the spirit world.

Gor-da furnishes us with some further details:

A Lisu husband helps his wife when she gives birth to their child. He gets the sharpened bamboo sliver to cut the umbilical cord. If the baby is a boy he is given a name after three days. If it's a girl she's named after only two days. The village priest gives the name to the baby. If the parents don't want to ask the priest they can ask their own parents or a village elder to find a name for the child instead. After giving birth the mother cannot go to work for one month. She has to stay home near the fire. Her husband does all the cooking and all the jobs around the house.

At first the mother can only eat chicken—boiled chicken. This is for the first two weeks. After this she can eat pork if she wants, but only the meat from a very black pig, one that hasn't any white colouring at all.

Seven days after the birth an old lady in the village who knows about herbs and things like that, collects some herbs and boils them close to the new mother. The old woman makes the steam smother the mother. This is repeated every seven days for a month. It helps the blood circulation. If this is done the mother will remain healthy and not suffer from backaches when she's old.

After one month the 'mother-roasting' fire is extinguished and the ancestors are informed there is a new member to the clan. The mother then returns to a normal life, and taboos on certain everyday actions, such as cooking for the family, carrying water and using agricultural tools are lifted.

The naming ceremony for a Lisu child is held the day after the birth. A priest divines a name using one of a number of methods. One such means is by first dropping a silver rupee into a bowl of water, and then dropping into the water two cowrie shells, having first called out the name desired. If one shell should land with its closed side up, and the other with the open side up, the name just called becomes the official name. This process is repeated with alternative names being called until the right shell configuration appears. Usually the first names tried are those of famous ancestors, these being names the Lisu consider auspicious. Names once given may be changed at a later date if found to be unlucky for the child concerned.

An alternative method to divine a name is given by Gor-da:

We can use two Thai one baht coins to find a name. We drop them to the ground while at the same time saying the name we have chosen. For every name called, we drop them three times. If both coins should land the same side up all three times, then that is the name we adopt. For instance, if the King's head shows every time on both coins, then the name just called is the name we take. It is very easy to do, anyone can do it. I often used to divine names for children in the village. Sometimes I'd use small pieces of wood instead of coins.

14 – Ana Muangjai – Lahu

Ana Muangjai is nineteen years old and lives in the large, prosperous Lahu-Lisu village of Ja-pu'er. The village, which is just two kilometres south of the Yao village Lao Shi Guai, was founded by a man named Ja-pu'er, who subsequently became its first headman. He originally came from the Doi Chang area close to Fang. According to Ja-pu'er's reckoning – he still lives in the village – he was one of the very first Lisu to be born in Thailand. He is now ninety years old and still in reasonably good health. Many of the village's inhabitants, including Ana, are descended from this remarkable man. Although of a Lisu father and Shan mother, Ja-pu'er considers himself Lahu. His wife is a Lahu woman, as are many of the women in the community, and it is largely Lahu traditions (Lahu Shi and Lahu Nyi) that are followed in the village. There are some purely Lahu families in the settlement, as there are Lisu, but the vast majority are of mixed Lahu-Lisu descent. Ana is Lahu. She is married and has two young children.

Giving Birth

Very little ritual accompanies a Lahu birth, unless difficulties arise, in which case prayers are normally offered to G'ui sha for assistance. G'ui sha is the Lahu supreme being who is credited with creating the heavens, and whose wife Ai Ma created the earth. Most Lahu pray to one or both of these beings – more usually to G'ui sha – for blessings and good health. The birth normally takes place in the home, with the mother-to-be kneeling on a mat and supporting herself by hanging onto ropes or clothes suspended from a rafter of the house. Usually she would be supported from behind by an old woman, or sometimes by her husband, who gently massages her abdomen to aid the birth of the child. As with the Hmong, the father buries the placenta. The Lahu practice is to bury it beneath the porch steps, paying particular attention that no insects should eat any of it. Ana explains further:

These days those people with money go to the hospital to give birth. Other people have'em at home with the help of their mothers.

Those at the hospital take Western medicine and drink a lot of hot water. Those at home sit by the fire and drink hot water. I had my children at home.

Lahu women lie down on the floor next to the fire after giving birth. They don't lie flat, like if they were sleeping, but half recline. The husband heats up a big, flat stone which he lays on his wife's stomach to help dry up her insides. For three days he keeps rewarming the stone and putting it back on her stomach—they aren't too heavy. The mother sits by the fire for two weeks, drinking hot water with herbs added, and eating chicken and plain rice until her blood has dried up completely. She also eats salt. Later she can go back to her bedroom. During this time she cannot eat any chilli or spice of any kind.

The stones are used to help stop the blood coagulating - the Karen do the same. After giving birth a woman is considered to be 'raw', thus chilli and any other spicy foods are avoided for fear of damaging the woman's sensitive 'insides'.

During those first few days they have to think about a name for the baby. The father usually invites the village priest to come and name it. He selects a name by throwing divination horns while calling out different names. When they find the right name they kill a chicken and cook it, and tie white stings around the baby's wrists.

The white string is used to tie the baby's soul more firmly to its body, thus preventing the soul from wandering off. The string is tied onto the wrists: the wrists are not tied together!

Sometimes after they have chosen a name the baby falls ill, this is because it doesn't like the name. When this happens the parents call in the shaman to try and determine the cause of the illness. When the shaman discovers it's because of the name he will find out who in the village is able to help the baby by sharing his name with it. It's the baby's soul which lets it be known he wants a new name. When the baby is renamed the illness goes. The person who gave the new name becomes the child's godparent.

15 – Laopia Selee – Hmong

Laopia Selee, whom we spoke with in the 'Three Ancestor' interview, is forty-seven years old and is an important village elder in Kiew Khan. He is married with seven children, the oldest being twenty-six, the youngest just two years old.

Laopia is a local recruit to the police post in the village. Under the command of three Thai NCO's, the fifteen or so Hmong 'policemen' at the post constitute the village defence force. As such, their principal role is to act as a deterrent to any would-be Thai robbers who may consider the silver-bedecked Hmong – or 'dung beetles' as some Thais like to call the highlanders – as legitimate targets for opportunistic attacks. Generally, relations with Thais living nearby are good, however, and disturbances are few and far between.

Officially, as part-time members of the paramilitary Border Patrol Police (BPP), Laopia and the others are also obliged to intercept heroin and opium shipments being smuggled across the hills, detain illegal immigrants from nearby Laos, and put a stop to illegal logging in the immediate area. In reality, and perhaps prudently, they rarely do anything at all but sit about their post keeping an eye on their children while the women are out working in the fields.

A Curse on a Woman-hater

Laopia believes a curse is blighting his life, for all his female babies except one – and this one he gave to his younger sister to raise immediately after birth – have died soon after birth, or in infancy. His sons, all seven of them, have survived, and are, and have always been, in the best of health. The curse was laid more than twenty-five years ago by an old woman living in the village who wished to punish him for his hatred of women. The old woman is now dead, but according to Laopia her curse continues. This state of affairs greatly upsets Laopia, for he desperately wishes to have a daughter. The situation is exacerbated by the fact that his first and second sons, who have been married six and three years respectively, are yet to have children. This, Laopia fears, may in some way be connected with the curse on himself.

One cold winter's day while we were sitting at the village police post talking with the men gathered there, Laopia told us his story.

It's my fault. Every female baby I have dies soon after birth. I only have sons, seven altogether. And my two oldest, despite being married for six and three years have yet to have children. There is something wrong with us. It's because of something I did when I was young. I've been cursed.

When I was a boy I hated all women except my mother. I even hated my sisters. But of all the women in the village there was one in particular that I hated with my whole being. She was an old woman who was always dressed in dirty rags. She lived near my parent's house.

Oh, she was so dirty. She lived on her own. People in the village thought she was rich. We thought she had a lot of money hidden away somewhere. And we thought she was evil. You know, at night she'd sneak off to the fields and steal other people's chickens. She'd eat them alive! She'd also steal vegetables; she was too lazy to grow her own. Everybody knew what she was up to, but her relatives in the village asked for everyone to turn a blind eye because she was so old and wouldn't last long anyway. So disputes were kept to a minimum.

I would see her almost every day at the water tap—we shared the same water source. I was always rude to her because I hated her so much. Sometimes I'd even throw pieces of wood and lengths of bamboo up onto her roof, hoping to make a hole in the thatch. I know, I know, I was bad in those days, but you see, I hated her so much.

Once when she was really angry with something I had done she said to me 'Before I die I will curse you. I know you hate all women. But one day you'll have to marry one. Do you realise that? But I tell you, you will never have a daughter that lives, they will all die.' See, she cursed me.

Eventually she died, and I met the woman who later became my wife. My first three children were all boys. All three were healthy. But the fourth and fifth were girls and both of them died soon after birth. The sixth was another healthy boy, and the seventh, a girl. This girl, my daughter, I decided to give to my younger sister for her to look after. You see, if I had kept her she would have died, too. I couldn't keep her. I did it to save her life. She is eight years old now and very healthy.

The daughter sent to live with Laopia's sister is a happy, healthy eight year old. Laopia firmly believes that by sending this girl away from his curse-plagued household he has thus managed to negate the death spell on her life.

And now we have another baby, another son. He, too, is healthy and strong like all the other boys. It was the old witch that has caused all my daughters to die. This is all her doing, and it's my fault. It's really because of me, because of the way I behaved when I was younger that all this has happened. I'm very sorry now. I really wanted to have a daughter in the family, I think about this all the time. I'm especially sorry for my sons who have been married a long time but still haven't had any children. I am to blame.

Reading the Bones

The reading of chicken bones is one of the most common methods of divination practised by the highlanders in the northern hills. There is no right or wrong way to read the bones. Not only does each tribe have its own idea as to which features of the bones are 'readable' (see Leur Prom-muang, The Karen Village Priest), and the subsequent interpretation of such signs, but in many cases each clan, and even each lineage, has its personal understanding of the significance of particular markings, colouring and shape of the bones.
  Yiow-fun Selee, the Yao shaman from Lao Shi Guai:

Yes, we boil the chicken and then afterwards examine the thigh bones, the claws and the skull. We do this to help people decide on a course of action, such as choosing a marriage partner, or buying something important, or before going on a long journey. We don't usually bother if we are just going somewhere for fun. It's business trips that are important.

And Gor-da Bierpa, the former Lisu priest from Pang Sa:

Only the elders can do it [reading the bones]. They look at the thigh bones. We don't examine the skull, only the Chinese can do that. Another way is to use divination horns, although these days this is seldom done. Most people use the bones.

The standard Hmong practice is to kill a healthy bird and boil it whole in a large pot of water. The body is later dissected and the bones examined. Traditionally, it is the thigh bones, the tongue bone, the skull and the claws that are inspected.

In the following account, Laopia describes in detail the White Hmong 'reading' of chicken bones for the purpose of divination.

We use the chicken's thigh bones, its tongue, toes and skull to help us see into the future. Not everyone knows how to read the bones. I can do it. People often ask me to check the bones for them before they undertake some action, such as planting a new crop, or buying a pick-up truck. The bird we use has to be a perfect specimen. We throw it into the cooking pot whole: legs, wings, head, everything. And it has to be very well cooked.

When we examine the tongue we look to see if it's red. It's a good omen if the middle bone of the tongue is straight and doesn't turn either to the left or right. It's a very good omen if it's straight, doesn't turn, and also has no little marks on it.

With the skull we take note of its colour. A bad sign concerning money is when it's white and clear of any blemishes. Good luck in money matters is shown by a red colouring. Red is the colour of a one hundred baht bank note. But it's a bad sign if there's any black on the red.

The Blue Hmong interpret an entirely white chicken's skull as indicating very good fortune, with medium fortune being shown by a white skull exhibiting patches of grey/black. A reddish coloured skull is considered a very bad omen indeed. These can be seen to be in sharp contrast to the remarks made by Laopia.

With the thigh bones we look at the small holes. Only people who know about these things can tell whether the bones show good fortune or bad. It's not that easy to read them, you have to learn it.

We use the right thigh bone to represent the man, and the left for the woman. The right and the left bones aren't always the same, they can be different. So, if a man wants to buy a truck, I'd use the right bone, but if it's a woman who wants to buy it, I'd use the left one. Of course, women don't buy trucks [laughing], but whatever they are thinking of buying or doing, I'd always use the left thigh bone for them.

The number of holes in the thigh bone is important. Four holes is a good sign. Three or five holes is not good. Three holes means there is a husband or wife left over. Do you see? There is an odd number, one is left over. You see, they must match to be in harmony. So, if there are three holes, the third hole will hinder your undertaking.

With four holes, two represent your legs, one is your mouth, and the other one your heart. The two for the legs means you are able to walk, and therefore work. The mouth one indicates people will listen to you and take your advice. This one therefore will help you in communicating with people. And the one for the heart means you will be able to use your head to be clever. With four holes, no matter what your aim, it should turn out alright.

And three holes?

Three holes indicates bad luck. This means if you were to buy a truck you'd have problems with it later on. No matter what the trouble, nobody would be able to help you with it. Five holes is also no good. It's bad to have an odd number of holes, one hole would always be left over. It's especially bad if the fifth hole—the odd one—is in the middle of the others.

You see, with five holes there's one for the mouth, one for the heart, and two for the legs. This is fine. But you'd still have the fifth one. This one would stop any good fortune indicated by the others. For example, if you wanted to buy a pick-up truck and the bones showed five holes, this would indicate you'd probably have an accident and lose all your money if you went ahead and bought it.

Two, four or six holes are good for business. Odd numbers are never any good. For example, seven holes, like this [he draws a rough sketch], shows that when you walk away from a house having completed some business, you will be attacked and have all your money stolen.

And six holes?

Six holes would be much better. Six holes stand for your two legs, your heart, mouth and brain, with the sixth representing people buying and selling from you. Six holes means you'll profit from the transaction.

A normal chicken's thigh bone will have many holes, maybe as many as ten or twelve. But I will only take note of the important ones. This is the difficult bit. I have to know which ones are significant, and which ones can be ignored.

If all the bones of a single chicken show bad fortune I might kill a second, or even a third bird. If all three were to indicate bad luck then the undertaking planned must be given up. The enquirer has to wait for the return of good luck. This may take many months, or even a year to come back. But it doesn't happen often because a chicken has many different bones. We can examine them all for the right sign. Not being able to find a good sign at all is really a very, very bad sign.

The number of chickens examined is restricted to an upper limit of three, in contrast to the Karen practice of repeating the entire procedure until the right signs are found (see Leur Prom-muang). Does this imply a greater respect of the omens by the Hmong? Not necessarily. With there being so many bones available for examination, the chances of finding the right sign using a maximum of three birds are high. The differences between the Hmong and the Karen in the number of chickens that can be examined, may therefore, in most instances, prove to be immaterial.

It's not only for business matters that we look at the bones. We also use them to divine the future for other reasons, such as before a wedding. Quite often a young Hmong couple will live together before actually getting married. When they decide to hold the ceremony they first have to consult the chicken bones. If the bones show bad fortune they have to postpone the wedding until the bones are alright again. Once the bones are okay, they can then proceed with the celebrations.

And other omens?

Even when the bones are auspicious and a couple decide to get married they still have to be wary of other omens. For instance, when the groom's family are travelling to the bride's house for the wedding, if they see a snake on the path they must stop and return home. And the marriage will have to be cancelled.

Seeing a snake is a sign that one of the bride's parents will die a short time after the wedding. Or it could even mean the bride will die. It's serious if you see a snake during a wedding.

To the majority of tribespeople, those omens that manifest themselves independent of man possess much more significance than those obtained via divination. This is particularly so as many of these 'naturally occurring' omens are taken as warnings of ill fortune to come. Great care is therefore taken to act upon these omens in the prescribed manner.

The Hmong often associate birds with bad omens. Certain birds if seen by a Hmong hunting party are a particularly inauspicious omen. A new spider's web, however, is considered a highly favourable hunting omen. A cat in the house is seen as a good sign, as a cat is thought unlikely to stay in a house haunted by many spirits. A stray dog wanting to enter one's house is likewise a favourable sign, as dogs are thought able to see spirits and therefore would be unlikely to want to enter a house inhabited by them.

The sight of a snake, or the sight or sound of a barking deer is considered a bad omen by all, necessitating a quick return to the safety of one's home, as does hearing the cry of a wildcat (Karen), and seeing someone pass by carrying a spade over their shoulder (Yao). Likewise, if a Karen starting out on a journey should sneeze, or be told of someone's death, he should at once delay his departure for another day or else risk his family meeting with some misfortune. Another bad omen for the Karen is for a green pigeon to fly past a house under construction. When this occurs the house must be abandoned.

Laopia Selee

Hmong Soul-calling Bridges

Much sickness in a Hmong community is attributed to soul-loss, and the Hmong are therefore particularly concerned with the protection of their wandering soul, which according to tradition is the one soul which every human possesses which is easily frightened, playful, and apt to wander off and get lost. Such souls are considered easy prey to malevolent spirits. They are also thought likely at some time during their wanderings to fall through a hole in the Earth into the Otherworld. In both cases the soul is said to have 'fallen'.

There are a number of techniques for bringing back a lost, or 'fallen' soul. One of these is through the holding of a soul-calling 'bridge' ceremony. This is a one-day affair which is normally held just beyond a village perimeter.

In the following account Laopia outlines the various bridge ceremonies held by the Hmong in order to effect the recovery of a missing soul.

We build bridges to help retrieve lost souls. When someone is ill we go to see the shaman. He tells us what we have to do. There are different types of bridges, he tells us which one to build. There's one type we build when we want to call back the souls of young children. We build this bridge at the junction of three tracks, a little way from the village.

The child's parents have to ask a neighbour to help. This helper must be someone blessed with many, strong, healthy children. It is his job to call back the missing soul. First the parents sacrifice two chickens at the bridge site. Then they tie white strings around their child's wrists.

The ritual of thread-tying in order to bind the souls more firmly to the body is common to all tribes. It is not only done as a remedy, but is sometimes performed simply as a precaution, such as before a long journey is undertaken. Usually it is done for an individual, but occasionally may be employed for a group, such as when it is thought the souls of a family may have wandered off in different directions causing discord within the family, in which case it may be felt necessary to temporarily bind an entire family with a single rope during a curing ritual. Occasionally a soul is not bound into the owner's body at all, but to an object, such as a house, or to a large distinctive tree whose possessive spirit is thought able to protect it from harm (see Anonymous, The Good 'Tree Lord').

After this they construct the bridge. It's just pieces of wood set into the ground. When it's ready the helper walks across the bridge while the father waits on the other side. Then he walks back over the bridge as the father calls out 'Did you see my child's soul?' The helper replies 'Yes, I'm bringing it with me now.' Then speaking loudly he says 'OK, your parents are here, you go back to live with them. Live a healthy life with them.' And that's it, that's all we have to do when we call back a wandering soul. We also do this type of bridge ceremony for girls.

There's another type of bridge we often build, this one usually has a roof over it. The bridge is raised like a seat, like a bench. There are two planks on the ground, and two raised on small posts. The shaman tells the parents where to build it. It's usually on a track leading into the village. The shaman takes the patient to the bridge. This is the place for the child to sit while waiting for his parents. First the child asks the shaman if he has seen his parents. The shaman then asks for the names of his parents. Then he crosses the bridge and calls out the two names, telling the parents their child is waiting for them and that they should come to see him. The parents then reply, saying 'Son, we are coming now. Here we are.' It's very important they sound enthusiastic when they say this. And that's it.

A bridge is used only once. After the ceremony it is abandoned and allowed to decay over time. There are numerous old bridges along the little paths and tracks around Kiew Khan. Sometimes there will be a succession of three or four in various states of collapse along a single thirty metre stretch of path. Bridges are not only built along pathways, however, but also over streams, as Laopia explains.

Sometimes we build a bridge over a stream. This type is usually done for an older boy. When somebody's boy is ill, they would go and ask the shaman for help. The shaman then goes into a trance and journeys to the other world to look for the boy's soul.

Sometimes he finds the soul and discovers it cannot cross a stream to get back home. He then tells the parents to build a bridge

Hmong soul-calling bridge at Kiew Khan

across a stream so their son may return. Still in the other world, the shaman informs the soul what the parents are going to do. He then usually tells the parents to kill a pig and two chickens to offer to the 'Lord of the Land'. They do this at the site where the bridge will be built.

Before returning back to the human world, the shaman goes to see the 'Lord of the Land' to ask for permission to build the bridge across the stream. After burning some incense sticks and lighting some candles, he explains to the Lord why they want to build the bridge, and promises to send the pig and chickens to him. He also asks the Lord not to let anybody damage the bridge.

Afterwards they go to the bridge site, make the offerings and

Afterwards they go to the bridge site, make the offerings and begin to build the bridge. They eat there as well. This type of bridge is built over a stream, a little way outside the village. If there isn't a bridge the soul wouldn't be able to get back, and the boy would die. This bridge is called *doa chor dteh* in Hmong.

The Lahu, Lisu and Yao also conduct soul-calling bridge ceremonies. One distinctive feature of the Lahu Sheh Leh bridge ritual is the almost constant playing of the musical gourd pipes during the ceremony. The low drone tone is thought to ascend to the heavens all the way to G'ui sha, the principal Lahu god. A distinctive feature of the Yao bridge ceremony is the slaughter and cutting into five pieces of a pig. These then are reformed into the shape of a pig and placed at the end of the bridge closest to the village as an offering to the sky spirit. Another feature is the burning of letters written by the presiding priest prior to the ceremony: one to the spirit of the sky, one to the ancestors and another to the soul which has departed. The action of burning is thought to send the letters on their way to the realm of the ancestors.

In all these soul-calling ceremonies, if everything has gone according to plan, the soul should again be dwelling in the body of the patient, thus ensuring almost immediate recovery.

16 – Anonymous—Hmong

In the following account from a Hmong village, a young man who prefers to remain anonymous, describes the binding of his younger brother's soul to a tree. This was performed to hinder the soul from wandering off and coming to harm. Our anonymous informer also speaks of the clash which ensued later (1990) when a Thai Buddhist monk attempted to fell the tree for timber.

The Good 'Tree Lord'

You see that big old tree over there [pointing across a mango orchard]. That's the one. That's where my parents tied my younger brother's soul so the tree spirit could look after it. You see, when my brother was young, when he was about five or six years old, he was always sickly, always thin and weak. My father tried everything. He made offerings to the spirits and took my brother to the hospital and to the local health-care clinic. After going to the hospital there was a slight improvement, but he was still in pain every day, and always in a different place. It wasn't anything really serious, he was just sickly all the time.

My mother tried everything as well. She sometimes got medicine for him, and initially his condition would improve. But then it would worsen again. Finally she decided to find a very powerful shaman. She knew he'd be able to find out what the problem was. She wanted to get the whole picture, so she invited a really powerful shaman to come and examine my brother. She asked him to divine her son's health.

He discovered one of my brother's souls didn't want to stay in his body, but instead wanted to wander off all over the place. That's why he was ill all the time. The shaman told us we'd have to take the soul and give it to the 'Lord of the tree' to take care of.

You know, there are special spirits living in some trees, good spirits who are far more powerful than a person's wandering soul. If the Lord of the tree would look after my brother's soul, my brother wouldn't be ill any more. He'd be able to eat properly, and sleep well. After hearing this my mother pleaded with the shaman to help her son and do whatever was necessary to save him.

He told her to get a chicken to sacrifice to the Lord who lives in the tree. He also told her to get some white thread ready to tie the soul to the tree. But first he had to call the soul. Once he had the soul back he took my brother to the tree and repeated some incantations to the spirit. After this the long piece of thread was slowly wound round the trunk of the tree in order to bind my brother's soul in.

Even now the string is still there, although the tree is much bigger now. You can see it from here. See, over there behind the mango trees [pointing], that's the one. These days my brother is very healthy. He goes to school in Chiang Saen and stays at one of the temples with the monks. You see, it's since giving his wandering soul to the tree to look after that he's been healthy and strong. Now he's growing quickly, he's much taller than most other boys his age.

And then with obvious anger he speaks of the attempt by a Thai monk to fell the tree despite being fully aware of the tree's importance to the Hmong family.

Do you know, last year the monk from the temple wanted to cut down the tree, the same tree where we put my brother's soul. Oh, oh, that monk. Can you imagine what would have happened if the tree had been a long way from our house? He would have chopped up my brother!

We were so lucky that day. My other brother Ter heard the chain saw and went over to have a look. He saw a Thai bloke over there. He was the one the monk sometimes hires. Then Ter heard the engine start and went to have a closer look. Shit, the Thai was just about to cut my brother's soul. Ter quickly ran up to him and stopped him, telling him he couldn't have that particular tree. He told him to wait until I got there, saying I'd sort it out. But that day I wasn't at home, I had gone to see some relatives at Tung Sai village [a Hmong village to the south of Kiew Khan].

What did the Thai do? He went back to the temple to tell the monk. And Ter came back home. He thought that now the monk knew why we wanted the tree left everything would be alright.

But an hour later the Thai returned, following behind the monk. They didn't come across the fields, the short way, but instead walked right through the village and straight past our house. They didn't care who saw them. They were carrying the chain saw, and they went straight to the tree.

My mother saw them and went to get Ter. Ter rushed up to them, but the monk ignored him and continued walking along the track to the tree. Ter passed them and blocked the path with his body. The monk just pushed him aside, saying 'I have to build my temple, and I'm going to fell that tree. I've got special permission to cut trees from the Forestry Department. I can cut any tree I like. Nobody can stop me.'

Ter and my mother asked him very politely not to cut it. But he wouldn't listen. He was very rude to my brother. Then Ter ordered our little brother to go and fetch our father, who was working in the fields nearby. My father came, and he, my brother Ter, and my mother tried to reason with the monk. They explained about my brother's soul being kept in the tree. But the monk just said it wasn't his problem.

There was nothing my father could do. He had to speak politely to the monk because he's the only monk we've got in the village. He asked him at least to wait until I got there because I might have a solution to the problem. He also said I might be able to find another good tree for the monk; a tree to replace the one with my brother's soul in it. The monk agreed to wait until twelve noon, but no later.

But it was already eleven, he probably thought I'd get back too late to do anything. But Ter hired a pick-up truck from the village to go and collect me from Tung Sai. It cost four hundred baht for the round trip. I arrived back just after twelve and waited in the house. Ha! Why should I go and wait for him at the tree! No, I thought, he could come to me. But then I heard the saw. He obviously hadn't realised I was back.

I rushed over and tried to be friendly. I explained about my brother's soul and asked him not to cut down the tree. My father and Ter also tried talking to him again. But the monk was angry and started cursing me. He knew very well that this tree was important to us. He knew the tree was the guardian of my younger brother's soul. But he wouldn't listen.

At this point in the telling of the account, our informant began finding it difficult to disguise his obvious hatred of the monk.

I stayed cool. It was he that was angry. Ha! He thinks he's such an important monk. Ha! He thinks he can do whatever he likes. He said he was going to fell it and that if anything happened to my younger brother, if my brother died because the tree holding his soul had been felled, he, the monk, would pay us 10,000 baht. Shit, I was angry.

Now I couldn't keep calm. I had tried to reason with him, but he wouldn't listen. He just acted the powerful man, the man with money. He thought he could buy anything with money. Bastard. So I told him 'OK, my brother is an ordinary person. His head is only worth 10,000 baht. You're a monk, so your head should be a bit more expensive. I want to buy your head for 50,000 baht. That's a real good price for you. I'll pay you your 50,000 now. OK? Fifty thousand's a lot for a bastard like you.'

Then I called out to Ter to go and get a gun and ask my father to bring 50,000 baht in cash. Ter ran home and a little while later returned with my father, the money and the gun. Then I held the gun up and could have shot the bastard any time I liked.

Did he try and run?

No, he didn't run. He saw I was really angry and meant business so he kept quiet. He didn't say anything to me but shouted to his man to take the saw back to the temple. Then just before he left he told me he was going to inform the police that I had an unlicensed gun. I replied 'Go on, I'm waiting'.

Then my father told him to be careful, for if the police came to the village they'd see all the wood he's been cutting. They'll see that he's been destroying the forest. Then the monk left. And so my brother's soul was safe.

The tree still stands (late 1993).

17 – Najeu Selee – Hmong

Najeu Selee is a thirty-three year old Hmong mother of two living in Kiew Khan. She was born in Laos, but fled from the civil war there with the rest of her family in the seventies. She lived for a number of years in the refugee camp at Chiang Kham in Phayao Province, from where her parents and brothers and sisters have since migrated to the United States. She alone has remained in Thailand, having run away from the camp to set up home with her boyfriend – now husband – Laoteer.

Despite having no relatives of her own in the village, she has many friends and is held in a certain esteem by the other women for her skill with the embroidery needle and her ability for making 'superior' – Thai-style – shirt patterns. She alone in the village continues to employ dressmaking techniques once taught to village women by a group of Thai Buddhist nuns who lived for a number of months in a forest retreat close to the village more than eight years ago.

Identification Marks for Wandering Souls

The souls of young children are thought particularly susceptible to wandering off while the child is asleep, and the Hmong have a number of simple devices to ensure that a wandering soul may easily find its way back to the host body.

Sometimes it happens that you want to go somewhere, but the baby is asleep. When it's sleeping its wandering soul might be off somewhere. If you were to dress your baby so you could take him with you, then when the soul comes back it's possible it might not recognise the infant any more. It'll think it's a different child. This is because when the soul left, the baby was without clothes. But when it returned, the baby was wearing a shirt. When this happens the soul won't go back into the baby, and the baby will die. Therefore, if the baby is still asleep the mother must always make a mark on him before dressing him. We use dirt, or soot from the fire. This way the returning soul will recognise its body.

There's another type of mark we use, but this isn't for the wandering soul. It's used to stop spirits pestering our children.

See, my son's got one. We always make it on the forehead. It's to stop spirits bothering him when I take him to the fields. It's important to do because we live in the jungle where there are lots of spirits. We can't see them, but they can see us. Whenever I take my baby somewhere I have to make sure he's got his mark. We use soot from the cooking pot. Some people use dirt from their feet.

We also make little tassels on their caps. See, my boy's got one as well. Actually, it's usually these tassels that we have for protection. Only those people who haven't got one for their baby rely on the mark on the forehead. I've made the mark to be extra careful. When the spirits see the tassel or the mark they think it's something the shaman has done, and they are frightened of it. Of course, when they are frightened they won't do anything bad, and the children are safe. We only have to do it for babies and very young children.

A Hmong from Jin Haw Country

The following story was related to us by Najeu after the visit to the village of a wandering – and prosperous – fortune teller. The man was Hmong, and professed to be from 'the land of the Jin Haw', which we take to be China: the Jin Haw being a Chinese people from Yunnan. Though he came with wondrous tales of far-off places: telling stories of giants, missing American pilots and Hmong customs unknown to the Hmong in Thailand, his speciality was reading palms, and for this service he charged each enquirer ten baht. His expertise was much in demand during the two days he remained in the village, and at peak times – before eight a.m. and after five p.m. – excited crowds gathered at the headman's house, with most people being only too happy to part with their dirty, crumpled ten baht notes in exchange for a reading from such a master.

Oh, I've forgotten his name, but I know he was Hmong, and he had just come from Laos. He said he had come to Thailand to see some Americans at the refugee camp at Ban Vinai [Loei Province]. He wanted to tell them about an American pilot who was living with the Hmong in Laos. The pilot had lived with them for many, many years. He had crashed his plane during the big war with the

Vietnamese. After the crash he had walked to a nearby Hmong village and there had received help from the headman. Eventually he had married the headman's daughter and they had a child. He has no papers, no identification card or anything like that, so he can't leave Laos.

The American government is today still investigating crash-sites in Indo-China in an effort to recover the remains of their pilots and crewmen. In Laos alone there are more than five hundred American military personnel (mainly air crew) still listed as missing in action (MIA). Much of the attention is centred on interviewing refugees from Laos – now in Thailand – in an attempt to obtain POW/MIA information. People living in the region are aware of this continuing search, and many are under the false belief that payments are made by the US authorities for information concerning the whereabouts of prisoners of war and the location of crash sites and/or human remains. Not surprisingly this has led to a small cottage industry in fake ID documents, to reports of airmen supposedly still held captive, and the existence of, yes, you've guessed it, professional bone sellers.

The man I met is a friend of the American. He said the American had promised to help him get a visa to go to the United States. But first he had to help the American get out of Laos. He said the pilot had promised to take his whole family to the States.

He told me he'd already been to the camp and met the officials from America. They were very happy to see him, and very happy to hear about their pilot in Laos. They'd said they'd get papers for all of them to go to the United States. But it would take time, they said.

I was once offered two sets of Russian skeletons by a Hmong man from Laos. We were standing in the back of a speeding pick-up truck – this being the local taxi. Shouting to be heard above the wind, he said he had shot them two years previously, at a place not too far from the border. Was I at all interested? Russians were reported to have been over there a few years ago: KGB some say. I declined his offer. Should there perhaps be a warning to tourists visiting Laos? – 'Beware of the bone-sellers. They may be after YOU!'

This man lives with other Hmong in Jin Haw country. There are many Hmong there. He also told us of a land further north. There are also Hmong up there too. But they aren't like us. He told us funny stories about them, about head-fighting. He said he had travelled a long way from his district, and had crossed two mighty rivers—the Red and the Yellow. Then he had come to a Hmong village. The Hmong there spoke the same Hmong language he did, and they had the same spirits, but the women there wore white skirts and had their hair long.

When he arrived in the village he was taken to the headman's house. The headman welcomed him at the door. But before he could enter the house he was asked if he knew their customs. He was told he had to take off his shirt and trousers and fight with three different men from the headman's household. But it wasn't your normal sort of fighting. No, they had to fight each other just using their heads!

First he had to fight with the headman. If he won he could sleep with any woman in the household for three nights. But if he lost he had to give five bottles of rice liquor to the headman, and then fight the headman's son. He had to pay a fine of five bottles of rice liquor every time he lost a fight. If he lost all three fights he wouldn't be allowed to touch any woman in the village. There was an alternative to fighting though. If he wanted he could buy the headman fifteen bottles of liquor straight off, and then he'd be allowed to meet any woman he liked in the village.

He paid for the whisky and met many nice women. You know, in 'head fighting' you have to bang your head against your opponent's head. You can't use your hands or legs. If anybody gets hurt they stop immediately. And they have to fight naked.

You wouldn't believe it, the whole village was built underground. Not like our village at all. And the houses were smaller than normal Hmong houses.

We understand Jin Haw country to be in southwestern China, probably Yunnan. Crossing the red river (the Hongha? which rises in Yunnan), and then the Yellow (Hwang Ho?), would take him north through China towards Mongolia. Interestingly, Mongolia is one of the three areas some anthropologists consider may have been the original homeland of the Hmong — the others are Tibet and Siberia. Could there be a connection? Is

Najeu Selee

there a tradition of head-butting (not Mongolian wrestling) in northern China or Mongolia?

He also told us about six very large animal skulls that he had once seen in the land of the Jin Haw. Each was big enough for six people to stand on at the same time. Nobody knows what type of animal they came from. There were no other bones nearby, just these six giant skulls. They were lying in a circle, and no grass or plants were growing where they were standing. He said he had a photograph of them, but I forgot to ask him to show it to me.

And she tells of his palm-reading skills:

Oh, he told us many things. He was a very clever man. He knew so many things. And he could tell people's fortunes. He could see if they were going to be rich one-day. Many, many people went over to see him. We had to pay ten baht for him to read out palms. He said my sons will grow up to be strong, and they will marry and have many children. He said we'd be poor for a long while yet though. Our financial position would only improve when my sons are older.

And about Nachai's Nayua [Nachai's eldest daughter], he said she will marry, and the man will be quite old, and he will already have four children. His first wife will have died. He will have a house and be comfortably off. He warned Nayua not to marry a young man, for if she does she will end up getting divorced, and will then be on her own again. She wasn't happy to hear this. You know, Najia, she only wants a young handsome man for her husband. She'll never get one. She's too old.

Many people went to see him. After Kiew Khan he was going to go to Huai Haan.

18 – Napur Muangjai – Lahu

Napur Muangjai is a fifteen year old Lahu Shi woman from the Lahu-Lisu village of Ja-pu'er. She boards at a Thai government school in Mae Chan and only returns home to the village during some weekends and for the school holidays. Her school is a special school for hilltribe children from poor families, and one of the rules is that all students have to spend their free time – including weekends – working in the school's vegetable gardens to help pay for their keep. Napur is bright and very articulate, and has the appearance and mannerisms of a well brought-up Thai schoolgirl. Her Thai name is Siriporn.

Chicken-bone Divination and Soul-calling

Elders know all about divination. The usual way is by looking at chicken bones. They examine the tiny holes found in the bones. I don't know how they read them, but I know they boil the chicken for a long time, remove the meat, and then with a knife they scrape the bone to reveal the little holes. It's usually the thigh bone they use. The bones have to be in perfect condition, they can't be cracked or damaged in any way. Once they've found the holes they insert into each a small piece of wood. They do this to every single hole. It's the household head who does it.

Then he takes the bone with the wooden slivers still in place to the village priest for him to have a look at. The priest explains everything. He will tell them what the bones indicate concerning the subject in question. If the holes show something bad, he will tell them. Then he'll let them know what they need to do to improve matters. People often consult the bones, especially when someone is ill, or when someone has to undertake some sort of business.

One result of a divination ritual may be that an apparently healthy person is found to be missing a soul. When this occurs a soul-calling ritual may be performed, as Napur explains:

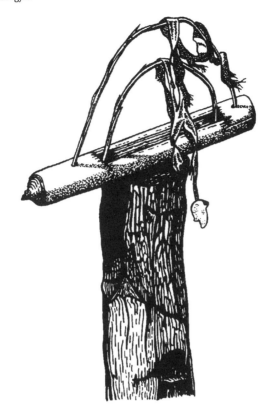

Lahu soul-calling offering post

There are a number of ways to call back a soul. Whenever a child's soul has fallen, say, in the fields, we have to call it back. For instance, a child may go to the river to play and be frightened by something. When he's frightened his soul may leave him. And then later, maybe when he's back home, he may fall sick. If he tells his parents where he's been that day and what he'd got up to, they'd realise what had happened. They'd go to the spot and place a soul-calling offering somewhere nearby. This helps to call back the soul. Then later they'd tie string around the boy's wrists to keep the returned soul in place.

Lahu Holy Days

The Lahu observe holy days at full moon and new moon each month. The observance of the holy days differ slightly according to sub-group. However, the general outlines are similar. Observation usually starts the evening before, when a woman from each household takes water to the village temple and pours it into a common vessel. This act demonstrates the unity of the village. Then under the direction of the wife of the sala *— a spirit specialist concerned with healing — the women wash the hands of the villagers to cleanse them from sins committed since the previous holy day. That same evening someone from each household takes some uncooked rice to the house of the village priest and pours it into a basket. The following morning the wife of the priest adds her share of the rice into the basket and then cooks all of it. Later that day the priest will take some of this now cooked rice to the temple and offer it to* G'ui sha *— the Lahu supreme being.*

Napur describes a holy day in her village.

Today we are asking for blessings. You see that everyone is carrying kettles of water. Everyone has their own kettle. We pour the water over the hands, feet and heads of the elders in the village. We pay particular attention to Khun [Mr] Ja-pu'er, the founder of the village. Actually, usually we don't pour the water over their heads, we just pour some into their hands and they let it drip over their heads. Old people get cold easily, so we first tell them to remove their shirts if they don't want to get them wet. Then we politely ask if we may pour the water over them. We pour it slowly over their shoulders and backs.

By doing this we are asking for forgiveness for any wrongs we may have done them since the last time we performed this ritual. We are saying sorry for being rude to them, or for ignoring their advice, or for having been naughty. And at the same time they bless us, saying something like 'live well and have a long life'. Khun Ja-pu'er, or any other elder, will say this as the water is being poured over him.

The water we use is special water that we get from the water source very early in the morning, at about three or four o'clock. This is before anyone has used the water for anything. We keep it in a separate kettle ready for the ceremony. The young pour the water over the elders, and in return the elders give us their blessings. We do this on every holy day, and also at the New Year festival. Today is the holy day for eating 'new rice'.

Most Lahu groups observe three main holy days during the year, when work in the fields ceases for two days, rather than the usual one day. The first occurs after they have burned their fields and before they plant their rice (April); the second is held at the time of the maize harvest (August-September); and the third is held just before the rice harvest (October-November). 'New rice' is the very first batch of rice harvested each year. All three of these special holy days are borrowed from the Tai peoples, and are observed primarily by those Lahu subgroups most influenced by Tai Buddhism.

Seeing some unusual objects standing in a bowl of water on the veranda of Napur's house we asked whether these objects had any religious significance.

Oh, those, we make them to take to the temple on our holy days. It's a bit like taking incense sticks, candles and flowers to a Buddhist temple, except we Lahu take these things and some other stuff to a Lahu temple. Thais have their special days four times a month, that's one every week. We have ours just twice a month.

The Lahu temple is the ritual centre of the village. All Lahu groups, bar the Lahu Sheh Leh, have a tradition of temple building. Depending on the individual subgroup the temple is referred to as the 'palace house' or 'blessing house'. These temples, which are dedicated to G'ui sha, are generally located at the higher end of the village, a little set apart from the other buildings. They may be built raised on piles – as in Ja-pu'er village – or built on the ground, and do not look that dissimilar from the houses in the village. A small village, or any village with no resident priest, is unlikely to boast a temple, in which case the ritual focal point of the village may be a shrine dedicated to the spirit of the locality (see Janoo, Losing the Old Ways).

During our holy days every household in the village makes two of those from especially absorbent wood. We call them *ku-ti*, they symbolise flowers. We make them in the morning and then leave

Lahu **Ku-ti** *temple offering*

them standing in a bowl of water during the day so they swell up a bit. We also make little sticks about eight centimetres long, onto which we put tufts of cotton wool. And we prepare an open-topped basket containing either two or four silver bracelets, some beeswax candles, a ball of white string, some stones and some vegetables. We usually use whatever we normally plant in the fields, such as cucumber, sweet potato, chilli and egg plant. And every basket also contains some white material, which is a flag.

At about three or four o'clock in the afternoon we carry our baskets to the village temple and place them on the floor in front of the altar. The flags we hang up against the walls. Then we return home. After supper we return to the temple to hear what the priest has to say. He says something about every family in the village. He tells us which families need to call in a shaman to rectify something, and warns those families which he has discovered are going to get some bad luck in the near future. And he tells us which families have done nothing wrong and stand in good stead with the spirits. All this usually takes about two hours.

We leave everything there for the night. In the morning we collect the silver bracelets, as well as the baskets, but leave most of the other things, such as the carvings, the stones, vegetables and flags. We do this on the second day of the two-day holy day.

We go to the temple on all holy days, and can do no work on these days. Usually holy days are single days, twice a month. But three times a year we have special two-day holy days. Today is the second day of the 'new rice' holy day. The rice in the fields is just about ready. The very first areas are now being harvested.

We were sitting with Napur's mother and younger sister on the large veranda of their house. Attached to a bamboo lattice-work above the open door were perhaps twenty or so flimsy star-shaped bamboo taboo devices – also known as a spirit guards. Lahu refer to them as leh-o.

You see the rope tied around my house, and those spirit guards above the door, they are *leh-o* to fight off evil spirits, to keep them out of the house. The priest told us to have this done during the previous holy day. He warned us there was some misfortune coming our way. The shaman did it for us. It's to frighten off the bad spirits, to make them leave the house and not come back. Once they had been fought off we put the rope up to stop them returning. When this is done the family cannot leave the house for three days. We leave the rope there forever, or until it breaks and falls apart naturally. We only take them down if we want to do another one. The shaman also tied string around our necks, and said a prayer to keep our souls safely inside our bodies.

You know my grandfather, Khun Ja-pu'er, and my grandmother, they have loads of strings around their necks. There's so much, it's almost like rope now. That's why my grandfather has had such a long life. He's over ninety and still very strong. He can still work in the fields. He likes to keep busy. Most people in the village like to have this done. They keep the strings all their lives. I had it done when I was about seven or eight, I can't remember when exactly. When I went to school in the village I still had it around my neck. But then I had to take it off when I went to school in the town. It was too embarrassing to wear it at school. So I took it off and gave it to my mother to look after for me.

We asked Napur whether there was any conflict in being a Lahu woman living in a Thai town.

When I am school I don't think much about the village, or about Lahu culture. I'm too busy studying. I tend to forget about life in the village. But when I come home I return to being a Lahu girl, just like all the other women. I live exactly like everyone else when I'm here, and follow our ways completely. I'd feel bad if I didn't live according to our traditions. I wouldn't feel so save, so secure.

The sending of selected tribal children (those who show an aptitude for studying) to special schools, where all lessons are held in Thai, where they learn Thai history and geography and, above all, respect for the Thai nation and its institutions, is one of the cornerstones of the government's **Thai-isation** *programme. This long-term programme, whereby the government aims to integrate the minority hilltribe peoples into mainstream Thai society (more for reasons of chauvinism than for consideration of their needs) is seen by many as constituting one of the principal threats ranged against traditional ways of life in the northern hills.*

The building of roads through formerly remote regions, the provision of health care, the despatch of mobile family planning teams, the establishment of police posts in tribal villages, the introduction of improved farming methods (including opium-substitution crops), and the granting of Thai identification documents which permit travel and work nationwide (to all who can prove to have lived in Thailand for a required length of time), are all part and parcel of this programme of assimilation: a programme which will, by its very nature, invariably – and intentionally – result in the destruction of much of the traditional culture of the tribal peoples of northern Thailand.

Solitary Chicks, Disappearing Pigs: Bad Death and Ghosts

The lengthy and elaborate rituals associated with death are among the most complex and intricate of all rituals of the tribal peoples of northern Thailand. They have as their ultimate aim the safe despatch of the soul of the deceased to the land of the ancestors. They are also essential for the soul's eventual reincarnation into the living world. Full mortuary rites, however, are not performed for people who have suffered so-called 'bad deaths'.

What constitutes a 'bad death' differs slightly from tribe to tribe. Generally a 'bad death' is one that results from an accident – particularly if bloody – or other unusual circumstance. The Lahu rate death from stabbing, shooting, attack by wild animals, childbirth, drowning and lightning strike as 'bad'. People who have suffered 'bad deaths' are thought to become malicious spirits, condemned to remain on the face of the earth. These fearful spirits try to bring about similar bloody ends to those about them that they themselves have suffered. Such spirits, which include vampires, are thus among the most feared of the malicious spirits that infest the world of the living. As a precaution against these spirits of bad death, the bodies of those unfortunates who have suffered 'terrible deaths' are disposed of as quickly as possible. The same is done with the stillborn, and babies who die within a few days of birth. Such children lack souls, since they have not undergone the appropriate soul-calling and naming rituals, and therefore funeral rites cannot be performed for them.

We asked Napur to tell us something of the 'undead'.

If Lahu people die when they are pregnant they are buried straight away. The family then have to make spirit guards for inside the house and over the door. The ones over the door are very important. And when the burial party leaves the grave they have to walk over a fire and then wash their hands and head from a bucket of water standing on the track. They have to do this before returning to the village. It's to stop having bad dreams at night, to stop the spirits from disturbing them. The spirit resulting from a deceased pregnant woman is particularly evil.

Any site where a person has suffered a bad death tends to generate evil spirit or ghost sightings in a local community. In Ja-pu'er village there is one such place.

I've never seen a ghost. But that's because I don't like to go anywhere outside the village at night. However, young boys from the village have seen spirits and ghosts. They've seen them when they are walking back to the village after watching an open-air movie in one of the nearby Thai villages. It's after midnight when they come back. Sometimes they have seen a light suspended over the track in front of them, but when they get closer all they see is a branch lying across the path. At other times they have seen a cat cross in front of them. There is one particular place where they often see spirits. It's on a small hill where they have to get off their bicycles and push for a while. Sometimes at this place they've seen a single little chicken, a chick, walking along. It makes them really frightened.

At other times men from our village have been driving along in their trucks when they have suddenly seen a wild pig on the road in front. Of course they try and run it down. But they never hit it. No, that's wrong, they do hit it, they hear the knock and feel it. But when they stop and run back to pick it up thinking how lucky they have been to get a pig they can eat for free, they've always found there's nothing there, not even any blood. Whenever this happens they run back to the truck as fast as they can and rush home frightened.

And then Napur told us of another eerie place; the site of a pregnant woman's death.

There's another place where they always see spirits. It's where a pregnant woman once died. She was Lahu. When I was younger, whenever a pregnant woman died she would be buried at the spot where she died. They wouldn't take her back to the village, but bury her straight away. It's a very bad way to die. We'd build a sort of gate and conduct a special ritual to stop the evil spirit from coming to the village. People are always seeing ghosts at those places. All Lahu are terrified of such a spirit.

There's one place like that here. You know how children take cows and buffalo out to graze every day. Well, when it's really hot in the middle of the day, after eating their rice they lie down to rest and sleep. Well, sometimes they go near this place, and when they wake up after their nap they still feel tired and drowsy. Then later at night when they are at home asleep they have very bad dreams. And in the morning they are sick. Whenever this happens their mothers have to call back their souls. They use a raw egg. Once the soul is back, the child and the soul are taken to the village priest for him to bind the soul to the child's body. He ties white string around their wrists. This sort of thing happens quite often when people hang around those places.

Recently a Lahu Shi woman living in the Lahu enclave in Kiew Khan died after suffering a short illness. The woman, who was eight months pregnant and in her late twenties, had been suffering from a fever, and at times, severe pain. Her husband and parents had been reluctant to take the poor woman to hospital due to the expense this would incur – they are opium addicts and live in extreme poverty. After nine days all movement in her womb ceased. Three days later the woman herself died.

Such a death is a calamity, not only for the family concerned, but for the entire village as well. Fearing that having suffered a bad death her spirit would return as a much feared meh *spirit (Lahu bad death spirit), her parents pleaded with friends and neighbours – myself included – for a volunteer to come forward to cut open their daughter's body and remove the dead baby. They wanted at least to be able to bury their daughter without her body being too misshapened. Such action, it was thought, would placate her injured soul to some extent.*

Perhaps understandably, no-one at first could be found to perform this rather ghoulish operation. I certainly did not feel able to help. Eventually, and after much pleading, they found a Hmong man, a Christian, who was willing to perform this grisly task for a large fee (the other Lahu families clubbed together to raise the money), and the body was hastily consigned to the burial ground just outside the village.

Before conducting the burial the village people had first constructed a spirit gate across the track leading to the burial ground. This was to stop her spirit returning to the village. It was built from bamboo encased in reeds and plastered from top to bottom with numerous bamboo taboo devices. As the burial party returned to the village they passed through the gate, thus leaving the evil spirit behind them.

19 - Narong Gangyang—Karen

Narong Gangyang is a twenty-nine year old Karen man living in the large, long-established and fairly prosperous lowland Karen village of Ban Huai Sak, which lies to the south-east of Chiang Saen, a few kilometres north of Ban Doi Karen village. Narong is married with two children, both of whom, like their parents, speak excellent Thai. As with the vast majority of the inhabitants of Haui Sak, Narong and his wife work on the land, farming paddy rice, maize, garlic, soy bean, cabbages and other assorted vegetables. Their house is elevated on thick supporting posts, has walls of timber plankng, and a roof of timber shingles.

The Karen Afterworld

The Karen believe their essential souls journey to the afterworld known as **phlyng** *to become disembodied spirits. Here they live a life that mirrors an earthly existence: they build houses, till the fields, raise children and die. After this second death they travel to another spirit world called* **xaa***. From* **xaa** *they will be reborn again as humans.*

However, not everyone is so fortunate to have their vital souls travel to the land of the ancestors. For example, the souls of infants and people that do not receive a proper burial are not permitted to enter **phlyng***, but are condemned to wander the earth in ghostly form. Souls of those who have died violent deaths (bad deaths) are also barred from entering* **phlyng***, and instead become vampires that attack other men's souls, causing mortal diseases. Also forbidden entry to the afterworld are those souls of wicked men and unjust rulers, who are doomed to wander the earth harassing the souls of mortal men.*

In the following short interview conducted one morning before he left for the fields, we asked Narong of his understanding of the afterlife.

INTERVIEWER: Can you tell me something about a person's souls?

NARONG: Eh, what do you mean? What do you want to know? You should talk to the priest, or to one of the elders. They know about these things.

INTERVIEWER: Can you tell me anything? Anything at all? How many souls does each person have?

NARONG: Oh, everybody has thirty-two. I'm Red Karen, in Red Karen we call souls *la-sow-si kee ya*. But in Pwo Karen we call it *tshia-si kee ya*.

INTERVIEWER: How many of these souls are essential to life?

NARONG: There are six very important ones. These are found in the head, heart, mouth, hand, feet and eyes. These are very, very important, and must stay in the body. They keep you healthy. If any of these do leave you'd feel unwell.

INTERVIEWER: What do you do if the vital souls leave the body?

NARONG: Call them back.

INTERVIEWER: And if they don't come back?

NARONG: If they don't come back you'll die.

INTERVIEWER: What happens to the souls when a person dies?

NARONG: They go up to the afterworld.... If a person has led a good life the souls can go straight to heaven. But if the person has done bad things, such as stealing, committing murder or adultery, then the souls can't go up there.

Neither can a person's souls go up to heaven if he thinks too much about his fields and his earthly belongings, or even about his wife and children. The souls of a person who is worrying about these things when he dies, go straight into these objects. If a person has always done good when alive, if he has always been honest and fair, and always been a nice person, then when he dies he can go up top.

INTERVIEWER: What about people who have suffered bad deaths?

NARONG: Oh, I don't know.

INTERVIEWER: Where do their souls go? You don't mind me asking do you?

NARONG: No, I don't mind. Those souls don't go up to heaven. They stay down here.

INTERVIEWER: What happens to them?

NARONG: They go to the forests and become ghosts, bad ghosts. People have to be careful at night, or any time they are in the forest. There's one that bites people, and kills them.

INTERVIEWER: Which one is this?
NARONG: We call it *na*. It's very dangerous. These sort always attack children at night.

The Karen rate na *(vampires) as constituting the chief evil spirit that afflicts them.* Na *devour humans at night, or take possession of individuals who then become malignant influences in society. According to the Karen, such individuals are under the delusion that humans are rats, and hence seek to devour them.* Na *are also thought capable of causing blindness and disease, and most dangerous of all, of destroying a person's* k'la, *or vital quality, through which all animate and inanimate beings are endowed with life. In former days death by beheading was imposed on anyone suspected to have been possessed by a vampire.*

INTERVIEWER: What is the Karen word for 'to go to the afterworld'?
NARONG: *Mo-khor.*
INTERVIEWER: Can you describe what the afterworld looks like?
NARONG: Oh, ha! ha! ha! How can I tell you what it looks like? I've never been there, I'm still alive. Nobody knows what it looks like.
INTERVIEWER: But do you have any idea at all what it may be like?
NARONG: No, I don't know...I suppose it's...something like down here.

20 - Nayua Sewa—Hmong

Nayua is about twenty-eight or twenty-nine years old and is Nachai's eldest daughter. She is a clever, articulate woman with strong views on marriage and the role of women in society. Despite much pressure from her family to marry before she is 'too old to find a husband' – which local men say is already the case – she seems determined to remain single until her ideal man comes along. This apparent disinterest in finding a husband – and thus securing a bride price – has occasionally led her father and brothers to threaten to eject her from the family home. Her usual response to such a threat is simply: 'Do what you want, why should I care.'

Hungry Ghosts

When food and other offerings are not forthcoming from their descendants, the deceased do not go to the 'beyond' to be reborn, but instead their spirits remain on the earth as so-called 'hungry ghosts'. Living in forested areas close to villages, they are regarded as being constantly on the lookout for people to attack in order to capture souls which can then be held to ransom against the payment of food offerings. A belief in 'hungry ghosts' is found in all cultures in northern Thailand.

In the following account Nayua recalls an incident in which she believes she almost came face to face with a 'hungry ghost' intent on capturing her soul.

When I was a girl we lived on Doi Luang mountain. I used to help my mother by working in the fields and looking after my little brother Do. In those days I was always terrified of spirits and ghosts because our village was really small and was located right in the middle of the jungle. Whenever I had to go anywhere I'd always make sure I had someone to go with me. I'd never go anywhere alone.

At night we'd stay at home sitting in the dark inside the house. It would always be dark because we couldn't light a fire in case the spirits in the jungle saw the light and came to investigate. We could use our torches at night, but we'd have to be careful. We couldn't cook anything after dark because they would smell the cooking oil, or they'd smell the fish or meat. For sure, if they'd smelt anything they'd come to eat in our house. Spirits are always hungry.

You know, if spirits come to your house to share your food, then you yourself become half spirit. You'd be half spirit and half human. To avoid this we'd always cook before it got dark. I'd stop work in the late afternoon and go home to prepare a meal which we'd eat before dark. If I was ever left alone at home for the night I'd be terrified the whole time.

One day a group of us girls agreed to help a friend in her fields. The fields were quite a long way from the village, so we decided to go together in a group. But before I could go I had to feed the pigs and tidy up the house. The other girls waited for me outside. But after a while they got fed up waiting and went on ahead. I told them I'd catch them up later.

As it had taken me quite a time to finish my jobs I tried to make up lost time by walking fast. I'd thought they'd probably be waiting for me somewhere about half way. As I got close to the spot where I thought they'd be I called out the name of my best friend. I shouted out that I was nearly there, and heard someone shout back telling me they were still waiting.

As I got closer I could hear them chatting. But when I got to the place where I expected them to be I couldn't see anybody. At first I was frightened. Then I realised they must be playing a joke on me. They were probably hiding somewhere behind the bushes. So, I called out again, telling them to come out and stop being silly. I heard one of them giggle. Now I was getting cross. It was getting late and they were still playing games. I called out again, but they still wouldn't show themselves, so I decided to leave them to it, and continued walking to the fields.

I walked quickly because I was cross with them and because I wanted to get to the fields before them so I could complain about them wasting time. But as I approached the fields they were all there, working. Confused, I asked them how they'd managed to get there before me, and why I hadn't seen them overtake me. But they didn't know what I was on about and thought I was angry with them for not waiting. My best friend said they'd walked slowly all the way thinking I'd catch up.

I told them I'd heard them talking and giggling behind the bushes. I said I knew they'd been hiding from me, and asked them again how they had managed to get there before me. But they replied they hadn't waited but had carried on walking slowly all the way to the fields. I told them again about the talking and giggling I had heard, and that someone had shouted out to me. But they wouldn't believe me. They said it was nothing to do with them and I was just fooling around trying to frighten them.

I thought they were doing the same with me, just playing around. But while we were talking one of my father's friends came by. He was a shaman and told us to shut up. He said he'd find out who was right and who was wrong. He then went off to cut some bamboo. On returning, he sliced the bamboo in half while chanting a spell through the bamboo to the ground. Then he sat thinking for a while.

We are not sure what the man was doing here. On asking Nayua she simply replied that he was asking the spirits for information. Possibly he was asking for help from the spirit which owned the locality – the local 'Lord of the Land.'

Afterwards he explained what it was all about. He said a long time ago a woman had died in that place where I had heard the voices. He said her ghost had nothing to eat and was very hungry and so, whenever anybody walked past alone, she tried to tell that person she wanted something to eat. He said it'd be dangerous if I didn't give her something because she'd take away my soul to force me to make an offering.

You see, now she knew me I'd have to give something. He said I should get my parents to kill a chicken, cook it, and offer it to the spirit of the woman. If I didn't do it within three days I'd fall sick.

So we killed a chicken and gave it to the shaman to make the offering. He took it to the spot where I'd heard the voices and offered it to the spirit of the woman. It was all very, very frightening for me. When you live in a small village in the jungle you have to be so very careful all the time.

Magic to Save Little Jeu

In 1992 Nayua gave birth to a healthy baby boy which she named Jeu. She smothered him with affection, and the ever-smiling little baby quickly put on weight and appeared to be in the best of health. And then suddenly when he was seven months his health began to deteriorate. His skin developed a yellow tinge and he rapidly lost weight. He had been poorly for a number of weeks when by chance a shaman called in on Nayua. Seeing the sick infant she immediately warned Nayua that something was wrong with the baby's soul. The shaman examined Jeu, paying particular attention to the tiny veins on the backs of his ears, and eventually informed Nayua that her baby was unwell because his soul had left him and was now in the womb of another woman in the village. She established that Jeu's soul had been away for about a month. However, she thought she might be able to call it back, but if successful, the other woman's unborn child would subsequently die: either it would be stillborn, or the mother would miscarry.

Fearing for her own child if no prompt action were taken, Nayua pleaded with the shaman to help her. A chicken for the sacrifice was procured, and one evening the shaman came to the house to conduct the ceremony. The proceedings were closed to all but the immediate family.

Auntie told me I had to get a small chicken, then kill it and cut it in half. Half was for Jeu to eat, and the other half for Auntie. She really wanted to help Jeu, she said she'd try her best.

We asked about the ritual.

What did we do? Well, before we killed the chicken we did all the usual things, the usual preparations. When Auntie came we lit the incense sticks and beeswax candles to invite the spirits to come to her. And then she rode off into the Otherworld chanting. She used her special language which I don't understand.

Later I tied one end of a piece of string to the chicken and the other end to Jeu's finger. The chicken was by the door, facing out. Jeu sat on the bench facing the altar. Then Auntie said a spell and cut the string near the chicken. She slowly pulled the string to Jeu and wound it round his wrist while calling out for the soul to return home. Then we killed the chicken, cut it in half and put it in boiling water. Half I kept for Jeu to eat, and half I gave to Auntie. For two days we had to keep Jeu in the house and bar visitors from entering.

That's all there was to it. Now he's feeling better and eating properly. It's been two weeks, I feel he's much happier now. He's safe, I don't need to worry any more.

At the time of writing the other woman still carries her unborn child. As far as we know she is unaware of the ritual carried out by the shaman on Nayua's behalf.

A Messenger of Death

The following interview with Nayua was conducted after speaking with another man in the village about a malicious spirit which takes the form of an evil, death-bringing black bird. She would not mention the spirit by name, but indicated the evil bird in question was, in fact, the dreaded Poosu *spirit (see Jonglao Selee, Poosu).*

We have known Nayua well for more than five years and are on very intimate terms with her. This was the first occasion she had been reluctant to talk to us on any spirit-related subject.

INTERVIEWER: Nayua, did you hear a strange bird singing in the jungle this morning? I ask you because Fat Uncle [Laopia] said he heard it. You get up early, so you must have heard it too?

NAYUA: Yes, I heard it. Just one, then it stopped. Why? Why do you ask?

INTERVIEWER: I want to know about it. Next time you hear it would you try and remember its song. I'd like to know what it sounds like. And if you would show me roughly where the sound comes from, because I want to see where it nests.

NAYUA: [speaking quickly to her sister] Don't tell them Nabai, don't say anything. And don't you ever listen to it. [turning back to the interviewer] Why do you ask these strange things? Why are you always asking about spirits? It's not nice. It's especially not nice talking about bad spirits. You shouldn't talk about those birds.

INTERVIEWER: Alright, don't tell me. But could you just wake me when you hear it the next time?

NAYUA: It's not my business to get you up in the morning. And I'm not going to listen to it just so I can tell you what it sounds like. This bird is no good, it's evil. Nobody listens to it. Everybody in the village is frightened of it. People don't talk about it, it's unlucky. Even just to think about it is unlucky.

INTERVIEWER: It's just a bird, isn't it?

NAYUA: ...

INTERVIEWER: It can't be that bad.

NAYUA: I'll tell you how bad it is. It's very, very unlucky if this bird calls three times in a row. We believe it's a spirit, an evil spirit. If you hear it three times it's a warning from the spirits that someone in the village is gong to die.

INTERVIEWER: Die?

NAYUA: Yes. it could be anybody. If anyone hears it three times, somebody will die. So, if people hear it they must forget it straight away and not listen for it again. No way can they go telling other people, or waking up other people to listen.

INTERVIEWER: But why can't you wake up other people to listen?

NAYUA: I just told you. People can't, it's unlucky. If I or Nabai were to hear it and then wake you up to listen, you may die because the bird will be calling you. Or if you were sleeping and you suddenly wake up and hear it, and then wake Jon, and he hears it, then he'll die. The noise the bird makes is it calling your soul, your 'inner self', to follow it. On the third hearing someone has to die. Please, don't ask again.

And we didn't.

21 – Jonglao Selee – Hmong

Jonglao is the headman of Kiew Khan. He is 29 years old, married and has one child, a son. He is a close friend, and is a frequent visitor to our house.

Poosu

Poosu is an evil spirit which the Hmong say takes the form of an eagle and delights in causing all kinds of accidents. Gashes and other wounds made by an axe or knife when clearing fields are often attributed to 'the evil Poosu'. Some Hmong refer to this spirit has the 'spirit of fire and blood', because most accidents suffered by the Hmong involve these two entities. Trying to elicit information about this particular evil spirit from the Hmong has proved very difficult. Most people we asked were extremely reluctant to talk on the subject, telling us that just the act of thinking about such a spirit would be asking for trouble.

Sitting inside his house, Jonglao spoke to us when there were few other people about.

There's a particular type of evil bird. It's quite big, and it's black. We don't hear it often; there aren't many of them around. I've never seen one, other than in a book. The wingspan is more than one metre. It's a very bad omen if you hear or see this bird. They can sometimes be heard very early in the morning, or occasionally during the day. It lives in the forest, deep in the forest, and they eat animals. They can take a wild chicken easily, or even a small dog.

Oh, you know, whenever I hear it I come over all strange, with goose pimples all over my arms. I remember I heard it once when I was a young boy and asked my father about it. It's an unusual sound, you see. But he got really angry when I asked him and told me to shut up and not to ask again. All he would say was that it lived in very tall trees deep in the forest. I knew all the old people in the village didn't like to hear it, so I tried to ask my father again. He wouldn't say anything, other than to order me to let him know at once if I ever saw a big black bird fly into the village.

Later, when I was older, I asked a shaman about it. He told me whenever this bird flies into the village he has to kill a pig and send the pig's soul to frighten off the bird's spirit. The only other thing I know about this bird is that if some of the older people hear it when they are walking through the forest to their fields, they return to the village for at least three days. I don't know anything else, and that's the truth.

In many parts of the world certain birds have been seen to be bringers of misfortune and death. Large black birds have long been considered particularly ominous. In the Gospelles of Dystaues *(1507 - in Opie & Tatem) the reader is informed that should a man or woman fall sick, and a raven come and cry upon the patient's chamber, it is a sign that the sufferer shall die of the sickness. The ravens acute sense of smell was thought to bring it to the site of a coming death, and thus whenever such a bird was seen, an omen of death was read. Even during the early years of the present century it was widely believed in the British Isles that a crow's caw three times heard was an omen of death.*

'Have You Ever Seen a Spirit Walking down the Mountain?'

The question of the title was asked of Jonglao by a Thai anthropologist who regularly stays with us. Originally coming to the village as a member of a development team from Bangkok, Anucha became somewhat disillusioned by the development proposals for Kiew Khan and resigned his post in favour of concentrating more fully on furthering his anthropological studies.

ANUCHA: Have you ever seen a spirit walking down the mountain? What do they look like? Do they wear Hmong jackets? Do they smoke pipes?

JONGLAO: I don't know, I've never seen one [laughing]. Neither has my mother. It's not really important whether a person has seen one or not. Why do you want to know?

ANUCHA: But how do you imagine they look?

JONGLAO: Well, what I dream—and what my mother dreams and talks about in the morning—is that the mountain spirit attacks me because I've done something wrong, like I've cut down a tree, or I've said something wrong, like 'sod the mountain spirit'. I never actually see the mountain spirit in the dream, but I do hear it. I hear a sound coming from behind a bush. I part the bush and what I see is an old man sitting there who died in the village a long time ago.

ANUCHA: And he's the mountain spirit?

JONGLAO: Oh, it's difficult to explain. You don't understand. I can't explain...I know, you tell me something. Which came first, the chicken or the egg? Go on, tell me. I want to know.

ANUCHA: Ha! ha! It's a cycle, but the egg must have come first. First the egg, then the chick, then another egg.

JONGLAO: So where did the first egg come from?

ANUCHA: From the chicken.

JONGLAO: Where did the chicken come from?

ANUCHA: From the egg.

JONGLAO: Well, that's the same thing then. I also can't explain. If you were to tell me the chicken came from an egg, but that the egg came from a cow, well, then I too could explain to you about spirits.

Jonglao thus suggests he could only offer a rational explanation of his beliefs concerning spirits by falsifying such beliefs simply to suit an easy explanation.

ANUCHA: I'm only asking because I want to finish my PhD thesis in ten months. I've been to some villages in Chiang Mai Province. I spent a whole month over there, but didn't get any information about spirits. Then I went to a Lahu village near Chiang Rai for fourteen days, but still didn't get anything. And I've been here now four or five times. It's all cost me quite a lot, you know. If I go back to Bangkok empty handed I won't get my doctorate.

JONGLAO: Well, why don't you go to China where our people come from. You could ask the very old people there, maybe they could explain to you about spirits. You could examine the ancient books the Chinese have.

ANUCHA: But I can't speak or read Chinese. I won't be able to finish my degree. I want to surprise my teachers. My professor is a woman; she has studied hilltribe spirits and wants to know what they really look like [laughing]. I have to find out for her.

Unfortunately, Jonglao was unable to help further.

22 – Nasuo Selee – Hmong

Nasuo is a petite twenty year old Hmong woman living in Kiew Khan village. She speaks very good Thai and for a long time entertained hopes of marrying a Thai (to increase her family's wealth and status). She also once hinted she wouldn't be too adverse to marrying my brother (who has lived with us from time to time), believing, and hoping, she'd be the very first Hmong woman ever to marry a Westerner (in Thailand, possibly, but there must surely be mixed couples in the United States). She has put aside these hopes since getting pregnant and marrying a local man.

Taken Away by the Spirit of the Rainbow

A few years ago Nasuo's younger sister died in a tragic accident while playing in a shallow pond close to the village. Most people in the village blame the 'spirit of the rainbow' for the death, as Nasuo explains:

My sister was twelve years old when she died. That was five years ago. She died when the rainbow spirit took her away. Everybody in the family agrees this is what happened to her. You see, the day before she died someone saw the rainbow spirit come down to the pond near the temple. That's where she died.

That pond used to be ours. It was on our land. My dad dug it and filled it with fish. But now it's a part of the temple. The water was only about one metre deep. Children looking after their cows and water buffaloes nearby would go there every day to swim and play in the water. My sister also went there – almost every day. And then one day she went there and drowned.

The day before it happened Uncle Laoneng – who also had a fish pond nearby – saw the rainbow spirit drinking from my father's pond. Laoneng said the rainbow spirit's head was in our pond, and it's tail reached over the hills towards Chiang Khong town. And the very next day my sister and her friends went to play in the water, and she drowned right in front of their eyes. So it had to be the rainbow spirit that took her.

According to Hmong mythology the rainbow spirit is a supernatural being who inhabits the Hmong Otherworld. This being, called Zai Laug, *is an ancient dragon – the oldest of all the dragons no less – who takes the form of the rainbow. He is thought to control the waters which surround the flat Earth, as well as controlling the rains. Often large bodies of water, such as pools, ponds and lakes are said to be inhabited by water dragons who should not be disturbed.*
We asked Nasuo whether her sister could swim.

Oh yes, she learnt to swim in that pond. Oh, Najia, Jon, ever since she died my family has been so very unlucky. Maybe it's because we didn't offer enough pigs to the spirits. In the past we were poor. Most of us children were young, so there weren't many hands to work in the fields. We didn't have pigs to kill. It was only very rarely that we could kill a pig for the spirits.

You see for a long time we only had two pigs, a sow and a hog. We wanted to keep them to breed. If we had killed one of them we wouldn't have got any more. So we kept them, fed them well and got lots of piglets. And from those piglets we got more piglets.

I think if we could have sacrificed more pigs to the spirits we would've been luckier. Nowadays we kill one almost every week – usually just a small one. For something important we'll kill a big one. Now, because we've got pigs for the spirits, we know the shaman can help us if something is wrong.

And then she told us of an event prior to her sister's death which in her eyes was the real cause of the drowning – the reason why the rainbow spirit came to claim her – just days later.

Five days before my sister died she had gone to the fields to help my mum. Her job was to look after our little brother while he slept in the field house. But while she was meant to be watching him she too fell asleep. She was under a mosquito net, but one of her arms was sticking out from under the net. When my mum returned to the field house for lunch she saw a small snake lying across my sister's arm. The snake was sleeping there!

My mum didn't know what to do. She didn't know where it had come from or how long it had been there. She was afraid to wake my sister with the snake still lying on her arm, so she first frightened off the snake and then woke her. My sister didn't know anything about the snake, of course. She hadn't realised it had been there.

My mum didn't call the shaman to investigate this happening. She just left it. The snake must have been a spirit. There were many spirits in those days. Ask my grandmother about them, she'll tell you.

Thus it is thought the snake had been sent by the spirits to warn them of something amiss — possibly something the family had neglected to do. Normally they should have consulted a shaman who would then have investigated the matter and provided the remedy: an offering to a spirit. Because the mother ignored the warning, or omen, the spirits (we don't know which) retaliated by making off with the girl's soul, which resulted in her death by drowning.

Had the snake been poisonous?
'Yes, it was a small green viper.'
And did it bite her sister?
'No,'
Was she sure?
'Yes.'

23 – Najia Selee – Hmong

Najia Selee is twenty years old, married, and has one young son. She is considered in Kiew Khan to be extremely beautiful, and her husband, Jonglao, who since 1991 has been the headman, is thought particularly fortunate to have found such a woman.

Najia attends the Thai language evening classes in the village, and has taken well to her new position as 'mother of the village'. As such, she is expected to set a good example, and when not busy in the fields regularly gives advice to women on simple health matters. She also encourages parents to send their children to the village school (some mothers prefer to keep them working in the fields) and, when coerced (usually by Suphawan), helps her husband in entertaining visiting officials and dignitaries.

'Snake Splash', and the Rainbow-tooth Cure

Last year Najia went down with a mysterious illness, one of the symptoms of which was a dark spreading rash over her chest and back – a condition called 'snake splash' in the village. Najia tells us of her frightening experience.

I tried the medicine from the hospital, but it didn't help at all. The blemishes were still getting worse by the day. My mother-in-law asked a shaman to come over and have a look at them. I told him all the symptoms, how I felt hot where the marks were, really hot like a burn, but how they didn't itch at all. And that my whole body ached, and that I was running a high temperature.

Eventually he said a spirit must have called to me sometime when I was in the jungle, and because I hadn't paid any attention to it, had retaliated by causing the strange spreading blemishes over my body. He told me this type of sickness is very rare these days.

Forests and jungles are the domain of spirits and ghosts. Many Hmong when walking through forests take special care not to attract the attention of these spirits, for fear they may provoke them into attack (this may have been Nayua's mistake – see Hungry Ghosts). For this reason Hmong never sing to each other – or themselves – when walking along a forest path. It is even considered risky to raise one's voice too loudly in such places. A 'calling' from such a spirit usually entails the victim suffering a minor illness. As Najia implies, failure to make an offering once a spirit has 'called' one, would normally result in the grieved spirit causing that person to suffer a major illness by way of retaliation.

We asked how Najia's condition had started.

One day after coming home from the fields my body started to ache all over. My back, my head and all my bones were aching. I went to have a cold shower to help clear my head, but afterwards I felt really cold and my throat was dry. I didn't feel like talking, so after eating I didn't sit by the fire with the others, but went straight to bed.

That night I sleep very, very well and the next morning got up late. That morning I had a bad fever, but thought it must have been because I had been in the sun all day the day before. But anyway, I decided to stay at home and rest.

The following day the red marks appeared on my chest. The skin was hot, as though it were burning. At first I thought there must have been a poisonous caterpillar, or something, inside my shirt. But there was nothing there.

The marks were really red, I had never seen anything like it before. I went to my mother to show her and tell her about it. She thought it looked odd, but still regarded it as a normal sort of illness and so helped me by drawing blood to my forehead.

We asked Najia to elaborate further on the various methods employed by villagers to alleviate fevers and headaches.

We draw the blood to our foreheads, thus causing a raw welt to rise. This helps when you are suffering from a headache, or when there is something wrong with your blood. We heat a coin and then put it against the forehead and cover it with a china cup. You must know all about it: everybody does it. Other ways? Well, we pinch the skin between two fingers [pressure-point medicine]. This helps if your blood pressure is down. It helps get the blood moving.

Herbal remedies?

Oh yes, we use herbs from the jungle. But I don't really know much about them. One I do know about though is 'cat's whiskers'. We grind it to powder and then add cooking fat. Then we rub it on the patient's sole. When we are finished we wrap the foot in some material and then put a plastic bag over it. This is done to reduce a person's temperature.

And did the heated-coin-on-the-forehead remedy do the trick?

No, it didn't help. The red marks were getting bigger and bigger. They were spreading onto my breasts, and then after a few days they spread around one side to my back. Then I got my husband to have a look; he has some medical knowledge. He was very worried when he saw it. He thought the 'snake splash' was really unusual. He said we'd have to go to hospital and let a doctor see it.

The doctor said there was no medicine that could cure it. He said all we could do was to kill all the germs that were already there, and then keep it clean. He gave me some paracetamol for the headaches.

This rash would thus seem to be some sort of viral infection, one that is immune to the workings of normal anti-biotics.

We were all really frightened. This illness is dangerous. It starts at one place and then spreads around the body. And when it completely encircles you, you die. So my mother-in-law called in a shaman.

She asked the shaman to use herbal medicines to cure it. But he said there's no medicine for this problem. He told us there's only one thing that can help. Only one thing that can actually cure it. But he said he wasn't sure if he could get hold of any of it. The only thing that could help, he said, were the teeth from a rainbow. He told us only spiritual means could cure my condition.

You know, we often see the rainbow spirit near the village. It's head is near Chiang Khong, drinking water from the Mekong river, and it's tail reaches over to the hills near the village. Only a tooth from the rainbow spirit could help me.

The shaman warned us it would be difficult to find a tooth because people these days don't keep old things like they used to in former days. He said rainbow teeth were particularly rare because the illness they're used for — my illness — is now so unusual. But he thought maybe someone had kept one.

My husband asked the whole village over the village public address system whether there was anybody with one of these special teeth. And uncle Sombao came over with one. He is a diviner, and he knows a lot about herbal medicine, too. The tooth used to be his grandfather's. It had been handed down to uncle Sombao by his father. It was very worn because it's been used a lot in the past.

We asked Najia how the shaman had used the 'rainbow tooth' to cure her.

He ground the tooth against a stone, and then poured water over it to wash the powder into a cup. Then he rubbed the water containing the powder onto the blemishes. It felt really cold when they were doing it. The burning sensation stopped almost immediately. And since then I've been feeling better every day. It's been three days now. The marks have stopped growing, and even started to disappear. It should be completely better after a few more days.

A Thai teacher in the village has a similar rash on his face. He does not believe in the 'rainbow tooth cure' and prefers to pin his hopes on medicines prescribed to him by the large state hospital in Chiang Rai. His disfiguring rash is with him to this day, whereas Najia has been totally cured.

And the tooth? Unfortunately, I did not see it myself. Suphawan did, however. She describes it as six centimetres long, two centimetres wide and about three deep. It was heavy and cold to the touch, and was translucent, with small, bubble-like inclusions. One side had been worn smooth from use, the remainer showed a rough texture. And that is all we know of it, other than its provenance: the mountains, possibly a mountain stream. Any guesses?

Could there be a connection here with the wondrous tales of 'snake stones' found in writings down through the centuries? Such stones were thought to be created out of the hissing and blowing of a great company of snakes, gathered together on Midsummer-Eve.

Writing at the very end of the seventeenth century, E. Lhwyd relates (in Camden's Britannia 1772 ed.) how the snakes would congregate in great companies and through the joining of heads and much hissing, a kind of bubble would be formed around the head of one of them, which the rest would then blow on till it came off at the tail. The bubble would then immediately harden to resemble a glass ring. According to Lhwyd, the finder of such a ring 'shall prosper'.

Another writer, Marie Trevelyan, describes (in her book Folk-Lore and Folk-Stories of Wales, 1909) one such snake stone, or 'Maen Magi', as being of a soft pink shade blended with lilac, with tints resembling those of opal. She adds that the 'bead' is extremely cold to the touch and that according to the owner, if rubbed against the affected part, is a never-failing cure for inflammation of the eyes, ulceration of the eye-lids, and for sties.

Serpents and rainbows? A magic charm derived from 'the viscous slime which exudes from their [the snakes] mouths' (Pliny: Natural History), and a 'tooth' of a rainbow with magic curing properties — for rainbow read dragon. Serpent and dragon, slime ball and tooth. A connection perhaps?

24 – Laojia - Do - Yeh — Hmong

In the following interview with three young Hmong men from Kiew Khan, an horrific accident is seen as a direct consequence of a family's disrespect for a shaman's prophesy.

A Shaman's Prophesy Ignored

One fateful November night three years ago, while on a hunting trip in an area of thick jungle close to the Laotian border, eighty kilometres south of Chiang Khong, a party of four young men mistakenly crossed the unmarked Thai-Laos border, and two of their number were injured – one fatally – by a booby-trapped mine.

Laojia speaks first. He is twenty-four years old and was a member of the hunting party that night. (The interview was conducted nine months after the harrowing incident.)

LAOJIA: This year nobody will be going over there to plant cabbages. Everybody is really frightened of that part of the border. I will never forget what happened there that time. It's still fresh in my mind. My eyes can still see it all. It was the worst thing that's happened to me in my life. Even now, I'm afraid when I hear the sound of a gun shot.

Sometimes when I'm in bed at night I can still hear Laodoa moaning in agony, and I wake up shaking and covered in sweat. His death was a real shock for me. We were of the same clan. We were friends. If Laodoa and his younger brothers hadn't gone to Huai Haan to plant cabbages this awful thing might never have happened.

Nachai's nineteen year old son Do joins in. He was a neighbour and close friend of the deceased.

DO: Oh, that's not right. It was his time to die, to finish his life. Just before it happened he had come home to replenish his rice supplies. His mother asked him to stay for a few days before going back to the fields. She wanted to consult the shaman about the omens for the family's future. So he delayed his return by a few days.

The shaman came to their house and using his divining horns looked into their future. He discovered there was something wrong. He checked twice to make certain and got the same result both times. The horns showed that someone in the family was going to die. It was a very bad omen. He told the family everything.

Of course, they were all very frightened. Laodoa's father asked the shaman to make sure. He asked him to try and help them if he was certain there was something wrong. So the shaman went into a trance and journeyed to the Otherworld. Here he asked the bad spirit, the one who was going to make someone in the family die, whether he would accept a cow or water buffalo instead. The shaman offered the bad spirit anything he wanted as long as he didn't take a person. And the spirit agreed. The shaman then told Laodoa's father what must be done. They were to sacrifice a large animal to the spirit.

However, according to Do, someone in the household objected to losing such a valuable animal and no sacrifice was performed.

Then three days later one of their buffaloes dropped dead for no apparent reason. It hadn't been ill. Really, it just keeled over and died. See, it was just as the shaman had said. One of their animals had to die. The spirit hadn't specified which animal he wanted, and in the end he took the buffalo. None of this is made up, it's all true. That particular shaman is very good. If he predicts something, it's sure to turn out that way. He never gets it wrong.

The buffalo that died was a big, strong one. A healthy one. The family were just about to sell it for ten thousand baht when it died. Two of Laodoa's brothers took the meat from the butchered carcass to sell at Ban Rai, Mae Kham and Ban Paca [Thai villages]. They didn't want to waste any.

Really, this family is very stingy, they thought it would be a waste to share out the meat with their neighbours. They are so tight-fisted. The shaman had told them to sacrifice an animal, and not to eat the meat. He said they could give it out to their neighbours, but mustn't eat any themselves whatsoever. But they didn't listen to him. They didn't kill one, so the spirit had had to take one himself. And they didn't share out the meat, but sold it to Thais. And then what was left over from the village markets they brought back home and ate it themselves.

Laodoa also ate some of it. You see! They took the misfortune from the meat. They believe in spirits, but not a hundred percent. They believe, but they don't always do the right thing. They have a lot of misfortune because all they ever think about is money. Money, money, money. And what's more, Laodoa's brother lied to the Thais about the meat. He said somebody with a grudge against the family had shot the buffalo. For sure, if the Thais had known how it had really died nobody would have bought any of it.

We asked Do whether he thought Laodoa's death a few days later was at all connected with this episode.

If he hadn't eaten any, if none of them had, and they hadn't sold it, then the accident wouldn't have happened and Laodoa wouldn't have died. They ate it because they thought the spirit had already taken the buffalo's soul. They thought they could dispose of the meat however they liked. They ignored the shaman.

We then asked Laojia to tell us of that fateful night in the jungle.

LAOJIA: Laodoa had been back in the fields for twelve days before that night. Laodoa, myself and two others, Seng and Gi, decided to go hunting. Seng and Gi were close relatives of Laodoa's from Huai Haan. It was their idea to go hunting. Laodoa's younger brother Laoma tried to stop Doa [Laodoa] going: he was frightened to sleep alone in the field house. He grabbed hold of Doa's shirt, but Doa just took it off and gave it to him saying, 'If you want me to stay you can have my shirt instead'. He took another shirt, ordered his brother to lock the door, and we left.

We normally hunt fairly close to the fields. There are still many animals in the area around Huai Haan village—wild pig, deer, leopard, armadillos, and even bear sometimes. You know, when we are staying in the fields we usually don't need to spend any money on food because we always bag something hunting.

We take lamps when we go at night. They're the ones you can fix onto your heads, leaving both hands free for the guns. The night Doa died we had first tried our luck near the fields, but there wasn't anything about, not even forest rats. The others wanted to call it a night and return to the field hut, but I wanted to carry on.

We walked to the stream which forms the actual border with Laos. Our fields are right on the border, you know. The stream is a good place for hunting. We sat down and waited very quietly for some animals to come down to drink. It's a great place for hunting, but also very dangerous because of the booby-traps put there by the Laotian army to stop cross-border smuggling. Earlier we had agreed not to cross the border because someone from Huai Haan had warned us about new traps and anti-personnel mines put their by the Laotians. The Laotians always let the villagers know when they've mined an area.

Certain stretches of the border between Laos and Thailand are notorious for the ease in which heroin traffickers and gun runners (particularly ethnic Chinese, Yao and Hmong) can cross between Laos and Thailand with apparent impunity. The mining of the border opposite Huai Haan is a measure undertaken by the Laotians to plug one such gap.

We knew it was dangerous, but that night it was very dark and we crossed over the border by mistake. No animals had come down to the stream, so we had started walking back to the fields. We looked very carefully to make sure we were following the right track. We were being extra careful. We thought we were on the right path, but we weren't. We had crossed over by mistake and only realised later.

Four of us were walking along the trail. Seng and Gi were in front. Laodoa was number three, and I was in the rear. It was strange that the two in front went past alright, and it was Laodoa, the third person, who tripped the wire.

We were walking along, very relaxed because we thought we were on the Thai side. We were careful to follow what we thought was the right path. But we weren't watching our footsteps.

Oh, it was terrible. We had no idea what was about to happen. I remember it was very quiet just before, and then the bomb exploded—bang—and everyone jumped and dived for cover.

Everyone must have been very frightened and shocked. I was terrified. I thought I was going to die. The explosion was really loud and echoed around the mountains.

I heard someone screaming, and stood up to go and see what had happened. But my leg was hurting. I pointed my lamp down to it. 'Ahh,' I thought, 'I'm going to die, I've walked on a mine.' It was covered in blood. It was gushing out like water from a tap.

I was so frightened, but didn't scream. I think I must have been too shocked to scream. When I saw my leg I forgot about the other person screaming. I didn't know what to do. It hurt badly, and blood was everywhere. I shouted out to my friends for help. 'Oh, help me, help me, I've stepped on a mine, I'm going to die.'

My lamp was still on my head. I turned towards the others and saw them in a group struggling with someone. There was a lot of moaning. I heard someone call out 'Help me, help quickly, I've been hit in the neck. I'm bleeding a lot. And my stomach. Oh, help me, help me.' I didn't realise it was Doa. I tried to walk over to them, but couldn't manage, and nobody came to help me. It was only about four or five metres, but it seemed a lot further.

Then someone came to me and told me to be strong. He said he'd take me to hospital. Then Gi told me it was Doa who had been badly hurt, and that he was losing a lot of blood from a neck wound. He also said his legs had been blown to bits. He said I shouldn't worry too much because he and Seng were unharmed and could carry us back to the village. And then we could go to hospital.

I forced myself to stop moaning and told myself I wasn't going to die in the jungle. I tried to ignore the pain by thinking of my wife and parents. Then I prayed to God [Laojia is a Christian] to ask him to help me and to save my life.

He then described the frightful journey in which he and Laodoa were carried through the jungle back towards the village.

Gi carried me, and Seng carried Doa. It was dark and very difficult going. I'm tall, and Doa is big, so it was difficult for them to carry us. Doa was quieter now. He was talking all the time, but only quietly. Sometimes he called out to his parents, or to his younger sister. Gi kept telling me to be strong, saying I wasn't too badly injured. Probably Seng said the same to Doa. They both kept telling us we weren't going to die.

Then Doa stopped moaning and was very quiet. I asked Gi about him. Gi shouted out to Seng, but Seng was talking to Doa telling him to be strong and saying they were going as fast as they could. Seng called out that Doa was still breathing, and that he must be in a lot of pain so they should hurry. Oh, it was a terrible time.

Eventually we reached a track used by pick-ups to collect the maize after the harvest. They decided to leave Doa and me there while one of them ran on to the village to get a car. They thought it would be better than walking all the way.

But I suggested we should keep going while one ran on ahead to get help. I thought I could manage to walk on my own, and the other one could carry Doa. If I couldn't keep up they could go on ahead. Then Seng said Doa's breathing was getting weaker and he couldn't leave him here. Gi and I told him we weren't going to leave Doa, but that Gi would continue carrying him, but that he, Seng, should run on first to get help. But again Seng said Doa was getting weaker and he wouldn't leave him.

The three of us called to Doa to be strong and not leave us alone. We were four together, we said. But he couldn't speak. Then we realised he had stopped breathing.

It was a shock for us; we all cried. We stayed there quite some time. We didn't look at our watches, but I think it must have been early in the morning. After a while we decided to leave his body there and go to the village for help. We told Doa's dead body to wait for us while we go and get his parents and sister. Then Seng and Gi carried me to the village. It was getting light as we approached. We called out to them to get the car ready to take me to hospital. We told them of Doa's death, and someone went to tell Doa's relatives in the village. His relatives came with me on the truck to the hospital and then went on to Kiew Khan to tell his parents the bad news.

Yeh was staying in the nearby Hmong village of Huai Haan at the time of the accident. He has been sitting with us listening to Laojia's story and now recounts how the death, which occurred in the jungle at night (the domain of the spirits), and was the result of a bloody accident, and thus

Laojia - Do - Yeh

considered 'bad' in the extreme, was further exasperated by the location of the accident – in remote jungle close to the Laotian border one hundred kilometres from the deceased's home. It was considered imperative for Laodoa's father to take charge of the body before a fellow clansman of the same lineage living in Huai Haan took the body inside his house, thus accepting responsibility for the funeral.

YEH: I was at Huai Haan village that night. It was a real shock for me when I heard Doa had been killed. I found it difficult to believe. I walked with a few friends into the jungle to the body. Doa was my friend, it was terrible when I saw him. We waited with the body for a while. We weren't sure what to do. If we took the body back to the village we'd have to take it into the house of one of Doa's relatives. But that would have complicated matters for his parents.

In Hmong culture a person's relatives are of the same clan. This means they conduct all the rituals in the same way. So Laodoa's body could be taken into a relative's house, and it wouldn't be a problem with their house spirits. But then the wake and the funeral would have to be held at that house. This would make it difficult for all his relatives in Kiew Khan. His grandmother is getting very old, she wouldn't have been able to go. And nearly all the families in Kiew Khan are Selee, the same as Laodoa. They would all have had to go to Huai Haan.

Of course his parents would want to take Doa home with them. If we'd taken him inside another house, they'd still be able to take the body out of the house, but this would involve first sacrificing a pig to the household spirits. This takes time and is a lot of extra trouble. So we waited with the body for some time before taking it back to the village.

The sun was high in the sky. Doa's relatives from Huai Haan said it was getting too hot outside and we'd have to get his body inside soon. So we cut some bamboo and made a stretcher and carried his body to the village. It was a long walk. We arrived at the village and headed for the house of one of his relatives. We were just five seconds away from taking Doa inside when the pickup from Kiew Khan arrived bringing his parents to collect him.

The driver sounded his horn to make us stop. Oh, if they'd come only seconds later it would have been too late, his body would have been inside and they'd have had to make all the offerings to the house spirit to retrieve him. They were just in time.

As soon as the car came to a halt everybody spilled out wailing and crying. They crowded around the body holding on to him. It was very upsetting to witness. A while later we put the body in the back of the truck and left for Kiew Khan.

On the way we had to stop quite a few times at police checkpoints. At most they didn't realise we were carrying a dead body. They saw Laodoa and thought he was seriously injured and told us to hurry to hospital. But at one checkpoint just before Chiang Khong the police saw that Doa was dead and asked to see the papers giving us permission to move a dead body. Of course we didn't have any.

They told us it was illegal to transport the body without authorisation and demanded 700 baht. Laodoa's parents wouldn't pay. They told the police they had no money. They explained they had just lost a son and were very upset, and asked why they should pay the seven hundred baht. Then everybody in the truck started wailing and making a lot of noise to embarrass the police. We told them we weren't going to pay and if they kept us there too long the body would start smelling. After we'd been there for about twenty minutes the policeman told us to go away.

There were a lot of people waiting for us when we reached Kiew Khan. Guns were fired into the air as we carried the body into the house; then the wailing got under way properly. He was kept for three days in the house. A cow, a pig and some chickens were killed. And then Doa was buried. After thirteen days his parents killed another big pig and offered it to his soul, the one that remains with the body in the grave.

We asked Yeh to describe the funeral.

Oh, it's difficult to know what to say, there were many things.

We asked where in the house had they put the body?

It was put on a bier in front of the spirit altar. First the brothers washed Laodoa's body, and then the special burial clothes were put on him. Everything had to be new. One man chanted the incantation to guide Doa's soul to the land of the ancestors, others fired off shots. There was a lot of spirit money hanging from the roof, and paper gold ingots lining the wall.

The burial clothes are made beforehand and laid aside specially for the occasion. The Hmong consider it essential for the deceased to wear new clothes before undertaking the long journey to the ancestor's village.

Everyone had something different to do. Some made the coffin, and some offered food and whisky to the body. Others fired off their muskets. Laojan played the mouth organ, and Laoseng beat the drum.

The firing of three shots each time the corpse is 'fed' is thought to frighten away any wild spirits of the forest which may seek to attack the departing soul or his household at this time. The ceremonial drum, or death drum, is a special drum only used during funerals. Afterwards it is taken apart, only to be reassembled when death strikes again in the village.

Many, many people came to see him. Some came from Huai Haan, others from Hmong Gahn village. Hundreds came. Everyone was crying and very sad. A pig and some chickens were sacrificed, and offerings were made to the ancestors and the spirits. A bottle of whisky, a cooked chicken, a boiled egg, a knife and some other things were placed by Laodoa's head. The chicken was to guide him to the ancestors.

The high point of the proceedings is reached when the presiding elder instructs the soul of the deceased on which path to take to reach the land of the ancestors. These instructions are chanted as part of the 'opening of the way' incantation. Its purpose is to guide the soul through the many hazards and ordeals of the Otherworld back to the village of his ancestors, where he will dwell for a while before being reincarnated into the living world of man. The words of the incantation describe the creation of the world and the origins of mankind, the flood and the first drought. It also recreates backwards through time the historical journey of the Hmong from a country probably to the north of China, to which the deceased must return before being reborn. On the way the soul of the deceased must pick up his 'birth shirt' — placenta — which he will wear during the long journey.

More and more people kept coming. Laodoa's brothers came from their schools in the lowlands. They were really upset, it was a great shock for them to see his dead body. Everyone was distraught. Laodoa was a good person, he had many friends. He wasn't married, he wanted to wait until he was twenty-five before getting married. He thought by doing this his children would be cleverer.

After three days he was taken out and buried. He wasn't interned at the normal place, but far away from the village. It was the same place where his younger sister had been buried. She's the one that drowned. It's now nine months since he died. His mother is still very upset. She misses him every day. She's lost two grown-up children. First a daughter, and now a son.

Normally the family of the deceased will wait until all the arrangements are ready and then choose an auspicious day for the burial. As Laodoa had suffered a 'bad death' the burial took place after only three days. The body was taken out of the house and placed on a wooden carrying frame. A cow was then sacrificed close by. Just before four in the afternoon the funeral procession consisting of family members left the house for the burial site, a remote spot well away from the village. The coffin was placed into the grave and the body carefully lowered into it. After the lid had been put firmly in place, the grave was filled with earth and a cairn of stones built over it.

25 – Boonchu—Hmong

A Tale of Dark Deeds

In Kiew Khan there have been numerous ghost sightings in the vicinity of a Thai Buddhist temple (more correctly, a forest monastery) which is located on a forested hillside just outside the village. Not only did a young girl drown in a nearby pond – her death being attributed to the 'rainbow spirit' (see Nasuo Selee) – but we have been told of murder committed there in days gone by, on almost the exact spot on which the temple has since been built.

A terrifying sighting of a ghost by one of four novice monks living at the temple recently went the rounds of the village. This sighting resulted in all four boys – children from the village – wanting to leave the temple, and for a few nights kept many of the villagers (including Suphawan) huddled around their house fires, reluctant to venture out into the dark.

In the interview below, conducted only hours after the sighting, Boonchu, the young boy who saw the ghost, recounts his frightening, and rather baffling, experience. A neighbour, who sits with us while we talk with Boonchu, offers some background information on dark deeds committed at that place ten years before.

INTERVIEWER: What's this, you've seen a ghost? Where? When?
BOONCHU: This morning, very early. It was at the temple. Oh, it was ugly. It had a really ugly deformed hand. It was all burnt and cracked. The abbot doesn't believe me. He thinks I'm making it up.
INTERVIEWER: Where did you see it? Where at the temple?
BOONCHU: By the main door.
INTERVIEWER: Did you see the face?
BOONCHU: No, just the hand and arm. I was so frightened.
INTERVIEWER: [to neighbour] Really, he saw a ghost at the temple? Did anybody else see it?
NEIGHBOUR: No, just him. He was about to unlock the main door. It was still dark. He pointed his torch towards the padlock and saw the hand holding the lock.

BOONCHU: It was all black with the skin cracked. And the fingers had really long nails. There was a piece of black cloth wrapped around the wrist. And I could see a leg through the grill. It was wearing black trousers, Hmong trousers. When I saw it I was so frightened I couldn't speak. Then I screamed and ran upstairs to the monk and my friends.

NEIGHBOUR: The abbot doesn't believe him, he thinks Boonchu is pretending.

INTERVIEWER: Is that right Boonchu? What did the abbot say?

BOONCHU: He said I was trying to frighten the others. He was angry with me. But it's true, I saw it. The arm had no shirt on, and the hand was holding the padlock. It was trying to get in. I told the abbot to go and have a look for himself. But he wouldn't go, he said it was only his grandfather, and we shouldn't worry about it. But then he made us go back to bed. He ordered us to sleep in his room. And he came in with us and locked his door with a big padlock, and wouldn't let us out until it was light outside. I think he was really scared as well.

After breakfast I went to school and told my teacher [who is a Thai border policeman] and my dad all about it. The teacher thinks I'm making it up because I want to leave the temple. He just laughed at me. My dad went to see him and told him I wasn't making it up just to leave the temple because I'm going to leave in two weeks time anyway. The abbot has already given us permission to leave. He's going to India on his pilgrimage tomorrow. I can leave as soon as he gets back. He's going to fly from Bangkok. My dad and brother, and loads of others are going to sleep at the temple every night until he returns. They're going to look after us.

NEIGHBOUR: I don't think it was a ghost. It was probably someone trying to break in to steal something. If the person had long fingernails then it was probably an opium addict.

Burnt residue can be gouged out of the bowl of an opium pipe with a fingernail.

BOONCHU: I'm not lying. The hand was terrible, it can't have been human. And all the nails were long, not just one. It was really ugly, all black and deformed. It must've been a ghost.

INTERVIEWER: Maybe it was a ghost, people are always seeing them over there by the temple.

NEIGHBOUR: Er, yes, well I suppose he may be right, there are ghosts over there. You know [lowering his voice confidentially], before the temple was built someone was shot over there. More than one in fact. That's where Neng was living when his son was shot. There used to be houses over there. Later they came over to this side to be with the rest of the village. Something very bad happened over there.

And then our friend and neighbour, whose identity we prefer to keep secret, as we do also of Neng (not his real name), told the story of the temple-site killings.

Neng had a very bad son who used to gamble a lot. He'd steal from people in the village to finance his gambling. He wasn't Neng's real son, just his stepson. His wife was already pregnant when he married her. She gave birth one month after getting married. He never liked this son. Then one day his son suddenly died from a mysterious illness. Nobody knew much about it at the time.

INTERVIEWER: What sort of illness?

NEIGHBOUR: Oh, Najia, he said it was a mysterious illness... And then during the wake something even worse happened. While the body was lying inside the house some Thai road builders who were working on the road nearby called in to view it. They were government employees, not just hired labourers. When they saw all the silver which had been placed on top of the body they decided it would be easy to steal it. So they robbed the family.

There were three of them, and they all had guns. During the robbery Neng's real son, who was fourteen years old, tried to run away to alert the neighbours. And the Thais shot him dead. Then the three men, carrying the silver with them, fled towards Ban Rai [nearby Thai village].

Many men came running to the house when they heard the shots. A group of them went off in pursuit of the Thais. On the road near the bridge by Laogwa's fields they found one of them. The others had shot him and left him to die. But he didn't die, and he told us the names of the other two thieves. His friends had shot him because they wanted a bigger share of the spoils.

INTERVIEWER: What happened? Were they caught?

NEIGHBOUR: The border police were told what had happened and they sent a message by radio to all the villages in the area to be on the look out for the two fugitives. Eventually the two were caught trying to board a boat at Bon Kong village. They were trying to flee across the Mekong to Laos. They had wanted to hide out over the border. They were sent to prison in Chiang Rai. Both were from Lampang Province; they weren't local men.

We know what Neng had done. He's left the village now. This all happened more than ten years ago. But you see don't you, his stepson died, and then his own son was killed. And the Thais who killed his son then tried to kill each other. See, it's a circle. And now there are ghosts at the temple.

Our informant, however, and perhaps rather surprisingly, lays the blame for so much ghostly activity in the vicinity of the temple squarely with the monk.

Two people have died at the place where the monk built his temple. Both suffered a bad death. And before the monk built his temple he didn't apologise to the 'Lord of the Land' for disturbing the land. Most Buddhist monks usually do this, but this one didn't. Neither did he ask the spirits of the dead for their permission to build there. He didn't do anything at all. And another thing, usually monks pray to the spirits every morning, but this monk, who is Chinese, doesn't. That's why people often see ghosts near the temple. It's his fault.

26 - Malee Selee—Hmong

Malee is a thirteen year old Hmong girl from Kiew Khan. Along with Nabai (one of Nachai's daughters), she has recently left the village to work in a large Chinese-run shop in the market town of Mae Chan. She is one of six or seven young people to leave the village this year in search of work. This is a new development in Kiew Khan; in the previous five years there have been barely three or four who have left for the towns – all except one have since returned. Greater contact with outsiders, particularly with developers and missionaries, and a recent boost in the issuing of Thai identification documents to hilltribe people (as part of the government's program to integrate highlanders into Thai society) are the primary factors behind this development.

Ghost Sighting

Malee, too, has seen a ghost in the vicinity of the temple (see Boonchu, A Tale of Dark Deeds). She describes her experience.

I saw a ghost not long ago. It was in the forest near the temple. I had gone there to look for firewood with Nabai and my sister. It was winter and nearly dark. We were carrying the wood back towards the village when I noticed a chilli plant by the side of the track. I stopped to pick some chillis while the others carried on walking.

I didn't rush because we were already near the village. When I had collected enough I continued walking. The others were some way in front. Then I saw a woman carrying a baby walking in front of me. And suddenly she disappeared and I couldn't see her anywhere. I hurried and caught up with Nabai and my sister and asked them if they had seen the woman behind them. But they said they hadn't. Then I realised I had seen a ghost and burst into tears.

When I arrived back home I told my parents what I had seen. I was very frightened. My father said a woman must have died and been buried there sometime in the past. Other people had seen a spirit-woman near the temple, so my father thought it must have been the same one. He told me not to worry because he'd do something to make the spirit frightened of me.

The following day he invited the shaman over to our house. He killed a chicken and offered it to the household spirits. Then he told my mother to cut a figure out of some white cloth and sew it onto the back of my shirt. While she was doing this he repeated some spells.

It was to make me look different. So, if the ghost sees me again it won't recognise me because the back of my shirt will look different. The ghost will think I'm somebody else. And it will frighten the ghosts. I think I'm safe from her now. I don't mind if she sees me.

These simple figures, which are usually twelve to fifteen centimetres high, are commonly seen on the backs of Hmong children's shirts. A similar deception was practised in England until fairly recent times. According to tradition, if one were to turn an article of one's clothing inside out, witches and other evil influences would be frightened off.

We asked Malee why it was only she who saw the ghost and not the other two girls.

It must be because I was alone for a while, because I was the person walking behind the others. That's why I saw the ghost.

Malee's mother, who has been sitting quietly in the background, has the last words.

No, no, it's nothing to do with being the first or last person. You saw the ghost because your soul-force is weak. That's why you saw it.

Incidentally, it was Malee's father who killed Suphawan's cat, believing it to be a vampire.

27 – Nachai Sewa – Hmong

We return to Nachai Sewa, our Hmong neighbour and practising shaman, for three further narratives: an account of a strange spirit once found in her cousin's house, the story of a local woman who is thought to have married a weretiger, and lastly, a cautionary tale of a man who dabbled in the supernatural, only to find himself locked into the body of a tiger.

Worldly Goods

In the following account Nachai tells of a spirit with strange eyes and a hairy monkey-like body which once took up residence in her cousin's house.

My cousin in Tung Sai village is a silversmith. Before he came to Thailand he lived in Laos. His children were very young when he lived over there. They lived in a small village in an area of thick forest. For a time there was a spirit living with him in his house which was making his children cry every night.

How did he know there was a spirit in his house?

At first he didn't know; it wasn't until the shaman told him that he realised. It all started with him finding something unusual in his fields. There were two things; he wasn't sure what they were. One looked like a big silver bracelet, and the other was an old knife. He took them back home with him.

After finding these things his children began crying every night. At first he didn't realise there was a spirit behind the crying. He used herbal medicines to try and stop them crying. But nothing worked. Then he noticed something unusual. The family dog, which always slept by the fireplace, made a whining noise whenever the children were crying. It was the same sort of noise a dog makes when it sees a spirit. You know, a dog barks at a spirit in a different way that it barks at a person. It makes a noise similar to that made by two dogs when they are playing together.

Thinking there was something strange going on he went to the shaman and asked him to come to his house. When the shaman called in to see for himself what the problem might be he saw the knife and the strange bracelet. He asked about them and heard they were from the fields. Straight away he realised what the problem might be. He told my cousin that those two things probably belonged to a spirit. And that this spirit must be one of those that likes to own things, and likes to look after it's possessions.

He told him these spirits often take the form of a white rooster, a wild one that lives in the fields, or a white rabbit. And that they originate from people who bury their belongings and say something like 'When I die I will come to look after my things, no matter where they are'. He said the spirit must have followed him home. And it was the spirit which, by playing with them in their sleep, was making the children cry.

My cousin asked the shaman to help him get rid of the spirit. But the shaman was busy and could only promise to come back in three days time. So he had to wait. While waiting he got thinking about the dog. It was lazy, and was always just eating and sleeping and not doing anything for the family. So he decided to give it away and get a new one. He got himself a very aggressive hunting dog.

This new dog also slept in the house next to the fire. The first night it was there it started barking and barking, as though there were two dogs fighting each other. My cousin woke up, but was too tired to go over and hit the dog, so he tried to ignore the commotion and went back to sleep.

And then early the next morning the frightening discovery was made.

The following morning his eldest daughter got up to get the fire ready for the rice when she suddenly noticed a pool of blood near the fireplace. She directed her torch at it, and then quickly shone her torch around the room. She saw a dead animal covered in blood.

Quickly she woke her father and the rest of the family. They all looked at it. It was a really weird animal, nobody had ever seen one like it before. Its body, arms and head were all hairy like a monkey, but its eyes were standing vertically in their sockets.

Everybody was terrified, so my cousin took it outside and burnt it straight away. And from that night his children stopped crying.

The shaman later told him the weird animal was the spirit. It had gone to live in the animal's body, probably a monkey's body, and the dog must have seen the spirit-animal and killed it, making the spirit leave.

Bansia Married a Weretiger

Stories of weretigers – evil spirits which take the form of a tiger and are able to possess a victim – are common in Kiew Khan, as they are in other Hmong villages of our acquaintance. One story of particular interest to us is that of a woman named Bansia who is thought to have 'married a weretiger' after her death in 1987.

Bansia, who was thirty when she died, was crushed to death by a falling tree while she was in her fields collecting vegetables. This is reported to be a rather common way to die in hilltribe areas, as the practice of burning the undergrowth to make fields, invariably leaves some large trees weakened by partial burning. These trees then fall with little warning. Bansia and her friend Nasuo were unfortunately standing next to such a tree when it came crashing down. Nasuo fell between two large boulders and was saved. Bansia was not so lucky.

We were in Nachai's house, sitting around the dying embers of the log fire.

'You really want to know?' she asked.

'Yes, of course we want to know.'

'Well, she married a weretiger.'

'Come again?'

'Bansia, she became a weretiger's wife.'

The younger children were already asleep on the bamboo sleeping platform. Five little bundles under three threadbare grey blankets.

'You remember Bansia don't you?' she asked.

Four years before, we had called in during the wake to view the body and pay our condolences to the family. While men sat outside playing cards and drinking rice liquor, women were gathered inside the house, periodically 'feeding the corpse' – that is making food offerings to the deceased. We had stayed just ten or fifteen minutes, and remember being *particularly saddened by the shocked, totally lifeless faces of Bansia's three young children. We also recall there was some confusion as to which burial custom to follow for, in a bid to change their fortune, Bansia and her family had converted to Christianity just a week before the accident. With the tragedy coming so soon after abandoning the spirits her husband had at first been unsure of his convictions. In the end he decided to stick with his new faith, however, and the following day Bansia had been given a Christian burial.*

'You mean the Bansia who died a few years ago?'

'Yes, Bansia who died in her fields when the tree fell on her.'

Nachai's eldest daughter Nayua noisily upturned the small wooden eating table, letting the food scraps fall onto the hard earthen floor. She watched a mangy-looking dog slobber over them for a few moments before delivering a well-aimed kick that sent it squealing out of the house and into the darkness outside.

'You said you wanted to know about weretigers,' continued Nachai, ignoring her daughter's disapproving look, 'well, after Bansia died, a weretiger took her body and married her.'

'Married her?' For an instant a picture of a typical English church wedding came unexpectedly to mind, the bride, dressed in white, holding out her third finger to a hairy, salivating werewolf.

'Yes,' Nachai said matter-of-factly, 'she now lives in the mountains near Huai Haan.'

Our interest aroused, Nachai then told us of the two mysterious men living near the Hmong village of Huai Haan, one of whom is thought to have been the weretiger husband of the dead Bansia.

Many people in the village think it was the spirits that caused that tree to fall on Bansia and kill her. And they think a weretiger has now taken her body. I'll tell you why.

Back then, when it happened, two men went to Huai Haan village to ask for some gunpowder. They said they were living in their fields on the mountainside near the village. But nobody had ever seen them before. They were Hmong. They said they wanted the gunpowder because one of them had a new wife who was ill. They said they had just got the wife from Kiew Khan and her name was Bansia. She was badly injured. They wanted to put the gunpowder on her injury to try and heal it. All this happened just a few days after Bansia died.

The woman with the injury had the same name as Bansia, and she was meant to come from Kiew Khan. You know, Bansia is quite an unusual name for a Hmong woman, it's not a common name at all. So when a few days later some people from Huai Haan happened to be in Kiew Khan they asked about Bansia.

They didn't know she had died. They asked whether she had divorced her husband and married someone living near Huai Haan. They explained they were asking because of the two men who had come to their village asking for gunpowder for a woman from Kiew Khan named Bansia.

Of course, they were then told the bad news, that Bansia had died four or five days earlier when a tree had fallen on her. Everybody thought it strange that at just the same time she had died the men from the mountain had gone down to Huai Haan to ask for medicines to treat an injured woman. And that this woman was meant to be from Kiew Khan and was called Bansia. Nobody knew anything about another Bansia from Kiew Khan getting married.

So now everyone thinks those two men must have been weretigers. They must have taken her body from the grave.

And then Nachai rounds of the short account with what could be her own fabricated addition to the story, or alternatively, that of the woman named Nasuo (who incidentally is not the same Nasuo of the 'rainbow spirit' story).

And I'll tell you something. Nasuo who was with Bansia in the fields when it happened says that just before she died Bansia said without thinking, 'When I die I'm going to be a tiger's wife.' The villagers think the spirits were angry with her because she had become a Christian. That's why she died.

The Tiger-Man

In addition to weretigers, we have also heard many stories concerning men who wish to become tigers, usually in an effort to boost their hunting prowess. These tiger-men can be distinguished from the weretigers in that no possession by a malevolent spirit is involved, and the resulting tiger does not normally prey on others. Nachai tells of one such tiger-man from the far-off past.

In the past people had more knowledge of certain special spells than we do today. There is one story of a Hmong man who lived in his fields on a mountainside who could transform himself into a tiger.

In those days they didn't know how to make guns or gunpowder, so when they went hunting all they had were crossbows. It's difficult to kill a large animal, like a deer or wild pig, with one of these. But the man on the mountainside knew the right spells and could make himself turn into a tiger to make it easier for him to hunt.

What he did was to make a basket from bamboo while chanting a spell. With this basket he could turn himself into a tiger. All he had to do was put it over his head and say the right spells. Of course, he had to keep it well away from the children.

So, whenever he wanted to go hunting he'd put the basket over his head and become a tiger. Then when he returned from the jungle his wife would knock the basket off his head using a long bamboo pole. Then the tiger would become a man again.

However, one-day his wife's younger sister came to visit them. She wanted to stay the night. They didn't have any nice food for her, so early the next morning the man went out to hunt wild boar — as a tiger. He went without telling his wife. When she got up and couldn't find him, she thought he must have gone off behind a bush somewhere to go to the toilet, and she left the house to go to the fields to look for vegetables. That morning it took her a long time to find enough vegetables to take home, so she was out a long time.

While his wife was still away the husband returned with a dead pig in his jaws. His wife's younger sister didn't know anything about her brother-in-law being able to turn himself into a tiger, so when she saw the tiger she screamed and shut the door quickly and locked herself in. She was terrified and couldn't bear to watch the tiger prowling about outside. Of course, she didn't know about the basket.

When the tiger-man realised his wife wasn't there he sat down and waited for her to return. It was a long time before his wife came back from the fields. She saw the tiger waiting there and went to get the pole, and knocked the basket off the tiger's head. But there was something wrong. The tiger didn't change back to normal, it stayed a tiger. Her husband had been a tiger for too long, and now he had to remain one for ever.

They were both very upset. Of course, a tiger and a human can't live together in the same house, so her husband had to go and live a tiger's life in the jungle with the wild tigers.

A very similar story is found in Thai folklore, as well as in other folk traditions of the region.

28 – Abu Merlaygu – Akha

Abu Merlaygu is twenty-four years old and married with two young children. He lives in the traditional Loimi Akha village of Mae Tur, a settlement of thirty-four houses situated in a beautiful mountain setting just a few kilometres north of Mae Salong.

Abu's Tale

One evening, having already spoken with his father, brother, younger sister Mee-dor, and his niece, a pretty fifteen year old called Mee-ba, we broached the subject of tigers and weretigers with Abu. He told us a tale of an Akha man who once lived in the village. Originally from Tibet, the man had supernatural powers, including the ability to change himself into a tiger. This is Abu's tale:

We Akha have this sort of thing. There used to be a man with the power to turn himself into a tiger living in our village. He was an Akha man from Tibet. He travelled from Tibet to Burma, and from there on to Thailand. He only lived in Mae Tur for a short while before moving on to Paca Sup Jai village on the other side of Mae Salong. He had family there.

He was here for two or three years. You know, he was really something. A knife couldn't cut him; it was impossible to stab him. Sometimes he'd take on four or five other men, and he'd always win. He was very fast, and a very clever fighter.

The shaman from our village knew him from Tibet. According to the shaman this man would often be challenged to a bout. People would want to start a fight to test themselves against him. Sometimes he'd fight a hundred men at once, but he'd never want any help. He always wanted to fight them alone. And he'd always only use a knife. Whenever there was a really big crowd against him he'd just fall down and become a tiger, and the people against him would see the tiger and try and flee. He never once lost a fight.

Where had the man learnt this useful ability?

Tibet. He had a master there, in the mountains. He studied there to become invincible against wounds. When he first arrived in the village he came to see my big brother, because my brother's the headman. He told my brother about his travels, about leaving Tibet and travelling through Burma. He told us he'd often been attacked, and had had to fight off robbers many times.

From Burma he had crossed over into Thailand. First he went to Hoor Mae Kham village; that's a big village nearer the border. There's not only Akha there, there's also Meo [Hmong]. Then he came here. And now he's at Paca Sup Jai village. He's been around here for a few years now. Sometimes I see him at the morning market in Mae Salong. He's about forty years old.

Does he work in the fields? Is he a spirit specialist of some sort?

Yes, he has rice fields, but he also performs rituals. He knows many spells and incantations. He doesn't only become a tiger, he can also turn himself into a cat. People have seen him when he's a cat.

One man was walking behind him once on their way to the fields. He was very talkative and they were chatting as they went. Then he asked the man from Tibet something, but received no reply, and when he looked up all he saw was a cat walking along in front of him.

This tale shares certain similarities with some of the Thai and Chinese folk tales often shown on local televisions. Master teachers in the high Tibetan mountains and unarmed combat against fearful odds, with men falling to the ground and rolling over to become tigers, typically play a major part in these action adventure yarns, and it is possible that Abu's tale has been influenced by them. Certainly groups of gaping hilltribe youths can often be seen crowded around flickering screens in the open-fronted shops and street restaurants of the nearby Chinese-populated town of Mae Salong.

Chasing Out the Spirits

Having earlier in the day seen a bundle of painted wooden sword-like objects lying to one side of one of the village gates, we asked Abu to explain their meaning.

Oh, they're for the 'chasing out' ritual. We do this at the end of the wet season. Only the young men of the village take part—fourteen or fifteen year-olds. A whole band of them come together. Each one carries a short sword and, shouting as they go, they enter every house in the village to frighten off any bad spirits. Some also carry guns and shoot up into the air.

The Akha consider the monsoon season, when much of the work in the fields is suspended, as being the spirits' dry season: a time when spirits are likely to be out and about, working in their own fields, courting and getting married, just as their human counterparts do in their own dry season. The Akha therefore are particularly wary of encountering spirits at this time of the year. The playing of musical instruments, for instance, is forbidden during the rainy season, lest the musical notes attract the spirits.

The village priest is in charge; he's the leader of the band of youths. He carries an extra long sword. They're only wooden, but we pretend they're real. We make them really sharp, though. The priest leads us into every house. We thump our feet and make as much noise as possible: firing off guns, screaming, shouting, anything. Then once we've done the entire village we take the swords and stick them in the ground next to the spirit gate.

Having apparently exhausted that subject for the time being, we turned to the question of divination. The Akha are great believers in omens obtained from pig livers. We asked Abu to tell us something of this practice.

Reading a pig's liver is nothing special. When we kill a pig, we check its liver to see the omens for the family, to see whether good or bad is on the way.

Wooden swords used in the Akha 'chasing out' ritual

Who does it? It's the elders. I don't know how they read them; I can't do it. Often it's the diviner who does it. Sometimes after examining a liver they see a problem and the family have to sacrifice a chicken to the spirits. This then improves the reading, it improves their future. That's all there is to it. It's nothing much really.

We asked him whether he 'believes' in the spirits.

I've always believed fully in the spirits, from the time of my birth, right on until now. I, my parents, and my grandparents, all believe one hundred percent in the spirits. We have done so for all our lives.

And has he ever seen a spirit?

Oh, me [laughing], no, I've never seen a spirit, not even one. But I've heard people say they've seen them over there [pointing to the jungle]. My father has told me spirits can see us, but we can't see them. You see, spirits don't have a body, they're…bodiless.

29 – Laoheu Selee—Hmong

Laoheu Selee is a thirty-eight year old father of five from Kiew Khan. He is a Christian convert and regularly attends the Seventh Day Adventist church meetings in the village. He is also a part-time recruit at the village police post, where he works alongside Laopia and Laoleuer.

Tiger or Weretiger?

Laoheu recounts the mysterious goings-on in the vicinity of his fields following the death of a Lahu woman.

Two years ago we had some fields over the other side of the hill near Haui Tu and Huai Sa villages. There were two Lahu families living close by. They were Lahu from Laos. One of the women was very sickly for a long time. Sometimes she'd be alright for a while, and then without warning she'd be back to being bad again. Her husband used to come over to our field hut to ask for medicines. And now and again I'd pop over to see how she was. She never got better.

Once when I went over there I saw that her parents had tied her legs to a post in the house. I asked why they'd done this. They told me she was sometimes very weak and would sleep all the time, but at other times when she wasn't sick she'd be very strong, and want to get up and walk in the jungle. She'd have wide staring eyes and be foaming at the mouth, and walk on all fours like an animal.

Eventually she died and her husband and parents buried her. They put her at the junction in the track, the one that leads to Huai Tu. The morning after the burial some people were walking to their fields from Huai tu when they came across tiger tracks on the ground. The prints lead straight from the Lahu house to the grave. They were really big prints, the size of a bowl. And that night-the night after she was buried-her husband dreamt that his dead wife didn't want to be buried where they had put her, but preterred to be burled on the track to Huai Sai So the next day they dug her up and reburied her at the other place.

The night after the second burial there was very heavy rain. In the morning the skies were clear and the people from Haui Tu went to their fields. On the way they saw more tracks, this time leading from the original grave site to the new place, near the turning to Huai Sa village. Now, with the signs so obvious, they were sure she had become a weretiger after her death.

We asked Laoheu whether he thought she may really have become a weretiger.

I believe in spirits, but I'm not frightened of them because I'm a Seventh Day Adventist. I've sometimes seen tiger prints near our fields. The Lahu over there are sure they've been made by the woman who died.

This story of Laoheu's was of particular interest to us, as there had been rumours in the village two years before of a tiger roaming the nearby hills. Tiger tracks had been found near the White Lahu village of Huai Sa, and Lahu villagers staying the night in their fields had reported hearing tiger-like roars in the immediate vicinity. Traps lined with bamboo stakes were dug, and hunters armed with muskets, shotguns and US carbines had scoured the area for weeks trying to locate the prized, and much-feared, feline. But there were no sightings, and eventually the excitement of hunting tiger in the area – for the first time in twenty years – died a natural death; but not before a Hmong farmer had fallen into one of the camouflaged pits and been hospitalised for three days with deep puncture wounds to his legs. For more than two years we had heard nothing more of the mysterious tiger – or tigers. Not until Laoheu told us his story of a Lahu woman's transformation into a weretiger.

30 – Laoleuer Sewa – Hmong

Laoleuer Sewa is forty-six years old and is the husband of Nachai and the father of Nayua. He is a friendly, intelligent man with a reputation in the village for being an 'able talker'. As a result he is often asked by friends and relatives to help in bride price negotiations. He is employed at the police post in the village, earning nine hundred baht for a fifteen day month. When not at the post he normally spends his days – and nights – watching over his small herd of cows which the family keep in their fields high up in the hills. He shares a small field house with two other families, and evenings are usually spent sitting around a log fire talking of crops, the weather, land disputes, debts, hunting, women, problems with Thais, and dreams of a better future.

A Strange Family from Laos

Exhausted and grimy we filed slowly across the darkened field heading towards the trail which cuts through the narrow belt of dense tropical undergrowth just below my own house. I turned to the man behind me.
 'Leuer,' I said anxiously, 'the wind's getting stronger.'
 'Don't worry,' he panted, a wry smile coming to his drained, dog-tired face, 'we know what we're doing.'
 'How did it start then?'
 Someone had miscalculated when burning his fields the night before. Unnoticed, the fire had continued to smoulder throughout the day, before finally igniting again into flame with the onset of the evening winds.
 'We're mountain farmers', the man in front said matter-of-factly. 'This is the way we clear our fields every year.' Carrying a home-made powder musket, Leuer's friend Laodeng had come out this night as hunter rather than fire-fighter, and even now his eyes constantly searched the scrub on both sides, hoping for one last chance of making a kill before returning to the village. He looked over his shoulder.
 'Still,' he said, 'even if the village did burn, you'd be alright. You're rich aren't you, you could easily build another house. And one for me too.' His small wizened face creased up in laughter.
 Behind me I heard Leuer giggle.

Our group of seven had been just one of many out that March night in 1991, trying to halt the approaching belt of fire. Working on sixty degree slopes, in the dark, and choked by dense clouds of ash-laden smoke, we had spent more than three hours desperately cutting and clearing a number of narrow fire breaks across two hillsides just a kilometre from the highly combustible village. Though confusion had reigned in places, with some groups initially attacking the fire head-on, only to be forced back time and time again by the fast moving flames, until they, too, were forced to accept the folly of resisting the onslaught without proper defences, in most places the line held and, sapped of their strength, the flames had been quickly beaten into submission. Leaving a dozen or so men and women to stand guard over the last few patches of fire, the majority – us included – had headed for home, but only having first promised to stay awake for the rest of the night in case events took a turn for the worse.

'Leuer,' I called out quietly as we approached the police post on the edge of the village, 'what else did they do?'

'Who?'

'The strange parents in Laos?'

'Oh, them. They did many unusual things. Strange things. My friend saw it all.'

At one point during the night, while sitting perched behind a clump of young bamboo on a steep hillside, resting from the smoke and heat of the fire below, Leuer had pointed out a man from a neighbouring village, and then started to tell us a strange story concerning this man's family.

According to Leuer, the man's parents possessed unusual powers, and once when they had been living in Laos, in a bid to frighten away a suitor who was showing too much interest in their daughter, they had actually turned themselves into two one-metre long lizards. And that was not all. There were other unusual goings-on in that household, Leuer had whispered, things which other people couldn't explain.

Unfortunately, before Leuer could explain further, a localised flare-up in the fire had brought the tale to a premature end. Later that night, however, in the early hours of the morning, while sitting around a log fire in the kitchen of the police post, Leuer had told us his story.

My friend told me about them. He lived in the same village over in Laos. This was before he came to Thailand. This family were really strange. There were two sons and a daughter; the daughter was very, very pretty. A real beauty, she was. A lot of the boys in the village were attracted to her. But there was something odd about them, something mysterious. The people in the village thought they may have been possessed by spirits, but nobody could be one hundred percent certain.

Of course, with the woman being so beautiful men would visit her every night. My friend liked her, and used to go to see her often. Naturally, any man that went would have had to wait until late at night until her parents had fallen asleep.

One winter's day my friend went to see her and was sitting with her by the fireplace, chatting with her while she embroidered a new jacket. It was late and the room was quite dark. Suddenly he noticed two big lizards lying by the fireside within inches of the family's dog. No kidding, he saw them with his very own eyes. They were just lying there watching him and the woman.

The woman was just as surprised as he was to see them there. Neither of them knew where they had come from, they hadn't been there earlier. But what was really weird was that they were there with the dog. Normally when a dog sees a strange animal, like a lizard, it would bark a lot. But it didn't make a sound, it just lay there, quietly watching them. It was as though the dog thought the lizards were people, people it knew.

They weren't tied up, so it was unlikely her parents had got them. Lizards live in holes in big trees, and they're normally frightened of dogs and people. But these two weren't frightened at all. My friend concluded they must therefore be her parents. He thought the woman's parents may have been worried that he might sleep with their daughter, and so had become lizards to frighten him away. Realising this he left and didn't sleep with her that night.

Did he ever return to court her favours?

No, never again. Really, this family were odd. They were never friendly with their neighbours. And sometimes at night people living close to them would hear a tiger's growl nearby, but strangely the dogs wouldn't start barking. And a few times they even saw tiger tracks right in front of their house. Everybody suspected the parents of being possessed.

And then one day the woman's mother died. She had been ill and had stayed inside the house for some time. Sometimes when neighbours called in to see how she was, they'd look at her on the bed and for an instant think they were looking at a tiger. And then it would be her again.

We asked Leuer if he knew the mother's name.

Yes, I know it, but I can't tell you. She was from a big clan, and her daughter and that son are now living in Hmong Gahn village [just down the road from Kiew Khan]. They'd be very angry if they were to find out I'd been talking about their mother. The father is already dead. The son's a blacksmith. That's all I can say.

Leuer continues the story:

After the parents died the strange happenings ceased and people stopped talking about them. My friend moved to Thailand and forgot all about them. But then one day an old man came to my friend's village in Thailand. He was a shaman, and had lived in that village in Laos. He had often been consulted and asked to perform rituals by that strange family. He told my friend he thought the parents had been possessed. In his opinion the parents had been possessed after taking over some fields previously abandoned by the Khamu.

The Khamu, who prefer to be called Lao Theung, *are one of the principal tribal groups of northern Laos. There are about eight thousand living in Thailand, mainly in Nan Province. There is one Khamu village on the valley floor just below Kiew Khan. Relations with the local Hmong are good.*

If Khamu die outside their houses they have to be buried straight away. So if they die in their fields they have to be buried in those fields, and then the fields are abandoned. And because it's done so quickly, no offerings are made to their spirits. So, of course, the spirits are hungry and wait for someone to come along. And the newcomers wouldn't realise the danger, they wouldn't know anything about a person's death there in the past.

In those days in Laos—and in Thailand—there was always plenty of land. We'd clear land to make our fields, and then a few years later move on to a new area. The land wasn't crowded. There wasn't anybody buying and selling land like they do now here in Thailand. However, sometimes Hmong would take over old land if the soil was still in good condition. This is what the strange family must have done. The shaman from Laos thought a Khamu spirit must have followed them home.

Strange things used to happen in their house. Nobody in the family had any idea what it was all about. The son, the one now in Hmong Gahn, was talking about it once. Sometimes when his family returned home from the fields they'd find fresh fish from the river left in a bowl in the house. Of course they'd think a friend must have left them there, but when they'd ask around, nobody would know anything about them. At other times they'd shut the door and go to the fields to work, and when they returned for lunch and opened the rice pot there'd be some rice missing. Somebody had eaten their rice. Things like that happened to them often.

And the explanation for all these strange goings-on:

Later, the shaman said it was a spirit from the Khamu fields doing these things. And because they had eaten rice from the same bowl as the spirit—the spirit's leftovers—they too had become spirits, or rather, half-spirits, like being possessed. People shouldn't eat anything a spirit has left. After the spirit had done this it probably went away to be born again as a human.

So, that's why so many strange things were happening. Now they are both dead, and the son and the daughter live near here.

31 – Laosong Selee—Hmong

Laosong is a burly twenty-four year old Hmong man living in Kiew Khan. He is married and has four children, all of whom are girls. One child is his daughter from a previous marriage, and two are his wife's children, also from a previous marriage. Laosong rarely works in the fields. His elder brother runs a daily pick-up truck service to Chiang Khong, taking people and goods to and from the fruit and vegetable market, and Laosong usually goes along, partly for the ride, and partly as his brother's assistant. His services are particularly needed during the monsoon season when, with the road turning into a river of mud, his great strength – and the use of the wheel chains – is often called upon to keep the vehicle moving.

Death Spell

In Hmong villages we have encountered a number of instances of death spells being placed upon chosen victims (see Laopia Selee, A Curse on a Woman-hater). The Hmong have traditionally made great use of placing death spells on people, particularly on habitual thieves, as a sort of trial by ordeal. One such method was to place a spell on a glass of water and then offer the glass to the accused thief to drink from. If innocent the accused was thought to gain good health and much luck from the draught; if guilty, he or she would be expected to die. Whether or not the accused would accept the trial, having first been informed of the likely consequences, naturally indicated to the 'judges' the guilt or innocence of the suspect. Another method was to place a death spell on a small white chicken, then to kill the chicken by cutting it's throat, cook it, and order the accused to eat the meat. If guilty, the suspect would die.

The following account from Laosong illustrates the perceived effectiveness of Hmong death spells. He tells of his father-in-law's death from a spell actually intended for the victim's daughter – Laosong's wife.

My mother-in-law wants us to move in with her so we can help her in her fields. But I don't want to. She's very old and her husband is dead. He died before I married his daughter. They've had a lot of problems in their family. I'm fed up with it all. I'm fed up with her too, my wife, that is. She's so lazy, everyone knows it. When I married her she already had two daughters. Her first husband had left her.

Why did I marry her? Well, she had those two daughters, and I also had one. I thought if we lived together things would work out. And now we have another daughter, that's four altogether. Our problem isn't anything special, it's just a problem with the housework. She won't do it.

My mother and my brother's wife don't like my wife. It's because she's so lazy, and because she steals from the neighbours. She takes vegetables and kitchen things. She even steals from my mother. My mother wouldn't mind so much if only her bad daughter-in-law would sometimes help out in the fields, or help feed the pigs in the morning, or cook for the family so that at the end of a hard day they could sit down and eat, and not have to think about cooking for the whole family. The rest of the family have to work hard, but my wife does nothing.

It is true, the rest of Laosong's family do work hard, extremely hard, and by village standards are very wealthy, owning a pick-up truck, more than ten head of buffalo, many pigs, ducks, chickens and, not least of all, a good many acres of productive land.

I keep ordering her to help my mother, but all she says is that it's not her job to help my mother. Before I married her I had no idea she was like this. She comes from Hoor Mae Kham village near Mae Salong. I had only seen her a few times before I married her. Afterwards the people over there told me all about her. Everybody told me how bad she was. Her brother's wife even told me how my new wife had caused her own father's death.

We asked whether his wife had killed her father.

No, she didn't kill him. But it was because of her he died. Her sister-in-law told me all about it. Her sister-in-law, who's called Leejer, and her brother, Laodeng, built a house next to the family house. They had two children. One day while they were in the fields my wife—my future wife—stole Leejer's silver jewellery.

Laodeng knew for sure who had taken the silver because my wife was the only person who knew where they kept the key to the wooden box. They asked her to return it, but she said she didn't know anything about it. So Laodeng asked his father to order her to return the silver. But his father liked his daughter and always sided with her in disputes. He said she hadn't taken it. When Laodeng told his wife what his father had said she was angry and went to her own father to tell him about it. It was her parents who had given the silver neck ring to her husband when they had got married.

Leejer's parents were very unhappy about it all. They wanted the silver back. But there was nothing Laodeng could do to get it back from his younger sister, especially as the father supported the daughter, and not the son. So, Leejer's parents decided that as their daughter's husband couldn't do anything to help, they had no choice but to try something for themselves.

Thus they called in a shaman. Shamans are not normally considered to be practitioners of black magic – they are not 'wizards'. However, from the accounts of our informants it would appear that some shamans can, and do, dabble in spells for the benefit of one group over another. An example we have already encountered is when the shaman recalled little Jeu's errant soul from the womb of another woman, as told by Nayua in 'Magic to Save Little Jeu'.

They went to a very powerful shaman and asked him to help them. Shortly afterwards the shaman got some water, just ordinary stream water, and said a spell over it. Then they gave the water to my wife – the suspected thief – to drink, saying that if she hadn't stolen the silver the water would make her healthy and very lucky in the future, but if she had taken the neck ring the water would kill her. She refused to drink it. But then her father said he'd drink it because he knew his daughter hadn't stolen anything. And she let him drink it. The spell worked. What the shaman had predicted was true. After drinking the water he fell ill and two months later he died.

They had taken him to hospital. But there was nothing the doctors could do for him. He didn't recover. With her father dead my future wife had to look after her mother. Then I started going to see her, and took her away. No one told me then how bad she was.

Now she and I have a child together so it's difficult for me to leave her. I keep telling her to stop stealing, but she won't listen. She enjoys stealing. I don't know what to do with her now. I'll probably have to leave her soon.

There's nothing else I can do. She's so lazy. She doesn't like working in the fields. Even when we have nothing to eat: no rice, no vegetables, nothing, she still won't work. She's lazy, she prefers to take food from the neighbours.

We asked Laosong whether it might not help if he were sometimes to accompany his wife to the fields to work, in order to encourage her.

Me! Work with her? Why? She's a Hmong wife, I've paid for her to work for me. A Hmong woman has to work, not the man.

32 – Nabai Sewa – Hmong

Nabai Sewa is a fifteen year old Hmong woman from Kiew Khan. She is an intelligent, articulate girl with a wicked sense of humour who, until very recently, had set her sights on gaining a decent high school education. Her only realistic chance was to win a place at a Christian school. In an effort to boost her chances of acceptance, for a number of months she willingly adopted the stance of a Christian convert, staunchly avoiding all contact with traditional Hmong religious practices, much to the dismay of her family. She initially tried for a place at a Seventh Day Adventist college in Chiang Mai which offers free education to hilltribe students and poor lowlanders. Having been rejected, she then tried at a Catholic college. However, here, too, she failed to find a place and, having tried her best, she has now given up in despair. Recently she left the village to work in a large Chinese-run grocers in Mae Chan.

A Curse on Nadoa's Babies

In an interview conducted just two weeks before she left for Mae Chan, Nabai tells of the death spell laid upon the unborn children of one of our neighbours. The name of the woman concerned has been changed to preserve her anonymity.

You know how bad she is, everyone in the village knows. Shall I tell you something. In the past, two of her children died just after birth. One was four days old, and the other five days. Both were boys. The shaman made them die to teach Nadoa a lesson. Both of the boys had been healthy and shouldn't have died. The shaman did it because of Nadoa's stealing.

She used to steal all the time, but nobody could accuse her because her parents were quite wealthy. People were wary of causing trouble with her family. She knew people couldn't do much about it, and her parents never told her to stop. Really I think they were proud of their daughter.

She'd steal from the shops in Chiang Khong. She'd take mirrors, jewellery, talcum powder, towels, anything at all. She'd even take umbrellas. Once a shopkeeper caught her. But nothing came of it because she had enough money on her to pay. When the man asked her whether she was going to steal the things she'd already put in her basket, she just said she was going to pay for everything once she'd finished looking around his shop. He knew she was Hmong, and probably thought she was honest. But really, oh, you wouldn't believe it, some Hmong are always stealing from the shops in the town. Once when she was quite young she even stole a watch from her uncle.

Many shopkeepers in Chiang Khong have asked us how we can possibly live with the Hmong, thinking the highlanders surely steal from us all the time. Well, happily they don't. Instances of theft do occur in the community, but then this should only be expected in a community of a thousand people. Chickens sometimes go missing, as do pieces of embroidered clothing from washing lines and vegetables from fields. But that is all. Admittedly, some Hmong, however, do consider Thais as fair game, and would not hesitate to walk off with a water buffalo if they thought they could get away with it.

It was because of her stealing that the shaman took her babies. I'll tell you about it. Nadoa had sold some of her embroidery to her grandmother to raise some money because one of her children, the little one, was unwell. She wanted to take her little daughter to hospital.

Her maternal grandmother was also unwell at the time, but she still wanted to help Nadoa. So when Nadoa asked for three hundred baht for the embroidery her grandmother gave her five hundred, even though it was really only worth about one hundred. Her grandmother felt sorry for her and wanted to help. The embroidery was nothing special, just bits and pieces ready to go on a new jacket.

Two weeks later the old woman asked one of her daughters to make a new jacket using the embroidered pieces from Nadoa. But when the grandmother went to get the pieces, she couldn't find them in the chest. Also missing was an embroidered belt, a sash and an apron that she herself had made many years ago when she was young.

Normally nobody else would know where the key was hidden, but the old lady remembered Nadoa had been nearby when she'd put away the embroidered pieces. Nadoa had seen her take the key from under the sleeping platform.

She went over to Nadoa's house and asked her about it. But all Nadoa would say was that she had no idea what her grandmother was going on about. The grandmother wasn't angry, she even said Nadoa could keep her pieces and had only to return the old embroidery that the grandmother herself had made.

But still Nadoa said she knew nothing about them. Then the granny asked Nadoa's husband to get her to return the things. But still Nadoa repeated she knew nothing.

Then, foolishly, Nadoa raised the stakes.

Nadoa said if nobody believed her she'd swear by the spirits she hadn't stolen anything. She'd swear she was innocent. There was nothing anybody could do, so they had to forget all about it.

Her family, though upset about Nadoa stealing from them, naturally did not want any harm to come to her, and so ignored her challenge. But later, after discovering the articles of clothing with their distinctive embroidery patterns had been sold to people from another village, Nadoa's grandparents finally decided something drastic had to be done.

But about a month later some people from the village saw the missing embroidery. They found out it had been sold to some Hmong people from another village. Nadoa had sold it! The grandmother came to hear of it and was really angry.

Her husband at that time was still a practising shaman; he decided he had to do something. He summoned Nadoa's husband to discuss it with him. Nadoa's husband knew his wife was very bad and was always stealing from people. He admitted to being very embarrassed by his wife's actions.

The old shaman knew he had to do something, but first he tried talking it over with Nadoa. He asked her to own up to the stealing. But she wouldn't. So, he asked her to swear by the sky spirit and some other powerful spirits that she was innocent. He promised if she was innocent, the spirits would send her good fortune, but if she were guilty, she'd receive misfortune.

He warned her he'd ask the spirits to kill her new-born babies if she were guilty—including the one she was carrying inside her at the time. Nadoa agreed to swear, saying it didn't matter because she knew she was innocent.

The sky spirit is the dreaded Ntxwj Nyug, *one of the two 'lords' of the Otherworld.*

The grandfather almost believed her, but he wanted to be certain, so he went through with it. He lit some incense sticks and called up the spirits to come and listen to what Nadoa had to say. Then he told her what to say.

She had to say, 'If I've stolen the embroidery from my grandmother, the spirits can kill the baby I'm now carrying and also all my future babies.' This she said, but then added, right at the end, that if she was innocent, the spirits should make her grandmother die.

Four months later Nadoa gave birth to a strong, healthy baby boy. He died five days later. The following year she gave birth to another boy, and he, too, died just a few days later. Realising her folly, Nadoa approached her mother.

Her husband was of course very unhappy. They both wanted to have a son. And she realised her mistake in making that oath by the spirits. She went to her mother, who had by this time taken over being a shaman from the grandfather, and asked her to help her, to help save her babies. So her mother went to the grandfather to ask for permission to stop the deaths.

It was difficult for the old man to refuse, after all they were of the same family. So her mother arranged it with the spirits, and after that Nadoa was allowed to keep her babies. Only those two boys died, since then she's had three more, all boys, and all healthy.

We asked Nabai whether she knew of any cases where an oath had been made by a guilty person, and yet nothing untoward had happened as a consequence. No, she replied, she didn't. 'If a person is guilty, something will happen. But nobody knows when.'

33 – Amer Merlaygu – Akha

Amer Merlaygu is the headman of the Loimi Akha village of Mae Tur. He is married and has eight children, five of whom still live at home. His house is a traditional elevated Akha house, complete with large open veranda and low sloping roofs. The interior is divided into two main sections – a men's section, and a women's section. A shoulder-high partition separates the two. Each section is divided into a sleeping area and an area for work and other activities. The ancestral altar, which is the focus of all ceremonies (relating to the ancestors), and which tends to lend a certain aura of sacredness to every Akha house, is hung in the sleeping area of the women's section. Ten people live in the house: Amer and his wife, their five children, Amer's aged parents and his younger sister Me-do. His son Abu, who spoke earlier on the subject of tiger-men, lives nearby.

Rice Rituals

Life without rice is almost unimaginable to most tribal farmers, and as one might expect, its cultivation is steeped in ritual, with the so-called 'rice rituals' constituting a significant proportion of all ceremonies held in hilltribe communities every year. This is particularly true of the Akha.

In the following interview, which was conducted one winter's night sitting around a roaring house-fire in the men's section of the house, Amer describes some of these Akha rice rituals, from the ceremonial first planting, through the growing season, and culminating in the annual ritual harvest.

Some people don't follow the traditions properly when planting rice, but most of us do, however. Usually we first have to build a house for the rice spirit. Then before we can plant the field properly we first plant some rice for good luck. This special rice we plant around the spirit house. This rice is very important, the success of the whole field depends on it.

According to Akha tradition rice is under the care of two separate spirit entities, both of which are compounds of a male and female spirit: the 'rice spirit', also known as the 'rice owner', and the 'field spirit', sometimes referred to as the 'field owner'. Of these two important spirit couples the rice owner seems to receive the most attention.

Each household builds a temporary shrine – or spirit house – for the use of the rice owner during the growing season in at least one of its rice fields. Constructed from sticks and grass thatch, this small structure is placed upslope from the family's field house.

Before we can plant the seeds we first have to do something with them. We take them to the village water source to purify them. We kill two chickens for the spirits. Then we take the seeds to the fields. After we have planted this first rice we can then go ahead and plant the whole field. This 'first planting' is so important. I really can't over-emphasise how important. If you do it wrong at this stage, or if you don't do it at all, then you'll be in for trouble later.

The ceremonial first planting, held at the onset of the wet season in May, is the first of the yearly sequence of rice rituals. The priest sacrifices a hen and cock in one of his fields as an offering to the rice owner. He then places some sticky rice on the ground upslope of the spirit's shrine as an offering to his ancestors. A further offering is then made to the rice owner by burning the tail feathers of the two birds – the resulting odour is the offering. The oblations now complete, the priest proceeds to plant rice seeds – which have been purified in a pre-dawn ceremony at the village water source – in nine holes in the ground in the vicinity, and slightly upslope, of the shrine. Some seeds are left in a bamboo section which is hung from the shrine. The following day the priest's assistants use some of these seeds for their own fields, after which each household in the village carries out their own ceremonial planting, using their own seeds.

A while after the first planting, when the rice shoots have already grown up a bit, we have to do something to protect the rice. Every family makes offerings to the spirit who owns the rice – the rice owner.

Offerings to the rice owner are made during the growing season to ensure a healthy and abundant crop. Each family does this independently. Two chickens are killed (one cock and one hen). Blood from the hen is smeared over the basket used to transport them to the fields. The blood-smeared basket is then attached to a stake which has been driven into the ground upslope of the spirit's shrine. It is considered important for the mouth of the basket to point towards the east, this being the direction associated with the sun. The Akha consider the male sun spirit, and the female rain spirit, to be essential to the growing rice.

We also have to do something with the white grubs that are in the fields. They eat the roots of the rice. We get some of them from the field and wrap them very tightly in leaves. Then we wedge them into a notch at the top of a stake which we've stuck into the ground near the spirit gate. This is to stop the other grubs from eating the roots of our rice crop.

There are a number of rituals carried out by the Akha which may be classed as rice rituals, but which some Akha suggest should rather be thought of as field offerings. One of these is 'catching grubs', as described by Amer above. This is usually held a month after the fields have been planted. Each family catches white grubs in their fields which they then take to a stake which has been driven into the ground – often in the vicinity of the village gate. The grubs are rolled in leaves and wedged into a notch at the top of the stake. This is so the root-eating grubs will be unable to 'see' the roots of the rice plants and thus will not be in a position to damage the growing rice. A similar ritual is performed when the rice crop is approaching ripeness. This is called 'catching grasshoppers'.

And later, just before the harvest, we go to catch grasshoppers from the fields. We get them from the area around the spirit house. If we can't find any we just take some soil instead and pretend it's a grasshopper.

We take them to the spirit gate and put them into another notch in the stake. This time at the bottom because grasshoppers eat the head of the rice. You see, we have to make sure they are well away from the heads of the rice stalks. The grubs eat the roots, and so we place them at the top of the stake. We held 'catching grasshoppers' just three days ago. We left them there for one night. The following morning we got up very early and made rice cakes. Then we ate 'new rice'. Today is a rest day.

Traditionally one grasshopper is separated from the rest and taken home to be 'blinded' by being steamed over the women's hearth in a container of sticky rice before being placed together with the others on the stake. Both these rituals are carried out primarily as symbolic pest control measures. It will be interesting to see whether they survive the introduction of chemical pesticides – a development that is surely on the way.

There are also a number of field offerings held when specific rice plant forms considered to be particularly auspicious are found. The 'great rice head offering' is held when an especially full ear of rice is discovered in a field in which a shrine is located. This type of ear is thought to have been planted by Apoe Miyeh.

Other less frequent forms honoured include 'walking rice head', which grows like a vine, the 'plentiful rice head', which is a large rice head, and the 'corn-like rice head', which resembles an ear of corn. All the above, which may be found in the fields or in a rice store, are considered a blessing on the family concerned.

We also have to thank the spirits when the rice is perfect, such as when it's very straight, or if the rice heads are extra large. Whenever the rice is perfect we make field offerings. Our elders tell us these things. Our ancestors have always done them. I can't tell you exactly why we do what we do, all I can say is that this is what has always been done. These are the ways of our ancestors.

The ceremonial harvest is held in late November or early December. It is referred to as 'plucking rice ears'. The harvest is initiated by a man specially selected for the task by the village priest and who goes under the name of 'village good day chosen person' (Kammerer 1986).

Once all the harvested and threshed rice has been carried back to the village the 'dismantling of the rice owner's house' ritual is performed. Three stalks of rice purposely left uncut in the vicinity of the spirit house are harvested and placed inside a shoulder bag. The rice spirit is thought to enter the same bag. The spirit is then invited to take up temporary residence in a simple structure built in the yard of the family house. The spirit house in the field is then dismantled.

The final ritual in the cycle is performed after the new year festival. This is known as 'storing rice seeds for first planting'. It may be held any time from the middle of January to early March. The recently harvested rice seeds, which until now had been kept in a container hanging from the

Akha rice spirit 'house'

Amer Merlaygu

structure in the yard, are first purified to ensure that neither rodents, birds nor spirits interfere with their health and fruitfulness during the next growing season, then they are put into a gourd and placed in the ancestor basket kept below the ancestral altar in the family's house. Here they remain until the next ceremonial first planting.

Animal-name Day Omens

Many hilltribe communities follow the Chinese pattern of using a twelve day week with each day being named after an animal. These names are usually the same, and in the same order, as the names of the years in the 12-year cycle. The Akha week is as follows: (The fifth day and fifth year are named 'forgotten', after a mythical, unknown animal)

1	nyo	*(buffalo)*	7	yaw	*(goat)*
2	k'a la	*(tiger)*	8	myo	*(monkey)*
3	tah la	*(mule)*	9	za	*(chicken)*
4	lah	*(rabbit)*	10	kui	*(dog)*
5	sheh	*(forgotten)*	11	za	*(pig)*
6	mah	*(horse)*	12	ho	*(rodent)*

The Akha pay particular attention to these days, associating the omens for each day with the characteristics of the animal in question. Amer offers some examples:

Monkey Day is no good for threshing rice. If we were to thresh rice on Monkey Day, it wouldn't matter how much we threshed, it just wouldn't be enough to last the whole year. Really, Monkey Day is a bad day for almost everything. Chicken Day is a particularly good day for harvesting. And Goat Day and Tiger Day are definitely no good for field burning. They are both bad days for burning.

We live in the mountains, in the forests and jungles. Whatever we do, we first have to consult the spirits to make sure the day is auspicious for the activity in question. For instance, if we were to burn fields on those days, on Tiger or Goat Day, the burning wouldn't go well. It'll burn a little bit here, a little bit there. We'd end up with a field burnt in the same pattern as a tiger's skin, in strips, or in blotches like a goat.

We have to be careful with the days, especially with anything to do with rice. We have to follow the ways of our ancestors in everything. There's no other way.

The Akha also consider it bad to begin a wedding on Pig Day, or to hold ancestor offerings on a Dog Day. Failure to take note of the day's omens is likely to lead to hardships and troubles with the spirits. For example, to fell a tree on an inauspicious day is thought to anger the 'Lord of Land and Water'.

34 – Jantong Muangdee—Karen

Jantong Muangdee is sixty-three years old and is a widower with two daughters. He was born in Ban Doi, but for many years lived in the nearby Karen village of Huai Sak. After the sudden death of his young wife he had intended to enter the Buddhist monkhood. However, partly due to his family responsibilities, he never took the necessary steps and now, in is old age, regrets his earlier lack of conviction. He has since returned to his natal village and currently lives next-door to one of his younger sisters.

Rice Planting and Village Shrine

In the following account Jantong outlines some of the steps taken to ensure a successful paddy rice harvest. The cultivation of paddy rice requires flat fields (due to the irrigation) and is therefore largely restricted to lowland dwelling communities.

Spirits play an important part in our lives. The houses, fields, trees, animals, everything, all of it is closely tied in with the spirits. For instance, with planting rice the first thing we have to do is wait for an auspicious day to plant the rice seeds. We have to ask the spirits for a good day. We ask the spirits to look after the seeds, to keep ants, insects and birds away from them. Then we plant just one corner of the field. This is the special corner. You see, with rice, the spirits are so important.

The first corner of the field planted is referred to as the 'spirit's corner'. It is here the 'soul' of the rice is thought to dwell. Yes, rice, too, has a soul.

Then after about twenty-five days or a month the new rice shoots are thinned out. This has to be done on an auspicious day—you can't just choose any old day, it has to be a lucky day, a day the spirits agree with. Those shoots taken out are then replanted over one quarter of the paddy field. Then we wait for another month before once again thinning out and replanting for a third time. This time over the whole field.

It is vital to commence each planting on a good day. Even if you are only able to plant a few seeds or shoots that day, and do the rest later, it doesn't matter. What is important is that you start on a good day.

Just before the third planting we ask the spirits to take care of the entire field for the rest of the growing season. Then we make a bamboo star-shaped taboo sign which we attach to a post and then place in the ground at the place where we first planted the rice grains. This is the spirit's corner. We also put a banana and some flowers on the shelf on the post, as an offering for the spirits.

This method of planting paddy rice mirrors almost exactly the traditional practice of the Thais and other lowland dwelling Tai peoples in the region: the Tai of southwestern China, the ethnic Lao, and the Shans of Burma.

We look after the rice during the growing season. Then we harvest it. The harvested rice from the first area planted is kept separate from the rest of the rice. This rice that has come from the spirit's area we keep at the very bottom of the rice store. This is the rice's soul. At the end of the harvest, when the whole field has been harvested, we sacrifice a chicken and, together with some sweets and pudding, make an offering to the spirits, that is, to the 'Lord of Land and Water'. Then it is all over until the following planting season.

The 'Lord of Land and Water' is the most important spiritual force in Karen lives. Every traditional Karen village will have a shrine to this Lord, usually located a little way out of the village on a slight rise. Generally a simple structure of bamboo or hardwood planks containing an unadorned altar, it is to this shrine that the village priest leads the men of the village twice yearly to perform a ritual ensuring an abundant rice crop and a healthy and, perhaps above all, harmonious village. Jantong outlines the ritual activities of these twice yearly offerings:

In our village we still have a special shrine dedicated to the spirit who looks after the village. We call this shrine the *pee siow ban*. Twice a year men from every family in the village make offerings at the shrine. Each family takes some whisky and a chicken. The whisky we make ourselves. Sometimes a group of four or five families get together to distil it. Any family without any has to give a large tin of rice to the priest instead.

Rice liquor is used in most Karen ceremonies. Tradition dictates that each household must distil whisky from their own rice for ceremonial use – a custom which certainly irritates the official Thai whisky distillers.

Once everyone has gathered over there with their whisky and chickens we tell the Lord we have come to make offerings to him. We ask him to take care of us, to make everyone happy and content, and to look after all our livestock. And also to keep thieves and other bad people away from the village. Then we kill the chickens and throw them into the pot. Every family brings their own cooking pots and firewood.

When the chickens are nearly ready we make twelve banana-leaf bowls. Five are for the female spirits; five for the male ones. Then the men dish up the rice and chicken into ten of the bowls. One of the remaining two bowls is filled just with rice, the other just with chicken. And then, together with the whisky, the bowls are placed on the altar. Once the offerings have been made the priest eats from the bowls. And after that everyone joins in. Only the men of the village take part in this ritual. The women eat later when the men bring some of the food home for them.

Normally during this ceremony we should shut off our village from the rest of the world for a few days. This is what they do in Haui Sak. In the past we could this in Ban Doi too, but now the government won't let us. They've built a road right through the village. Now we can't close the road.

The road passes right through the middle of Ban Doi. However, it bypasses Ban Huai Sak, the nearby Karen village where Jantong lived for many years, and so here the villagers are still able to put up the taboo signs when necessary, thereby forbidding entry to the village. During one excursion to Huai Sak we came across one such taboo-plastered barrier. It had been erected across the main track leading into Huai Sak. Stopping directly in front of it, we were quickly approached by a group of youths who politely, yet forcefully, requested us to observe the restriction and come back another day. This we did, of course.

In the old days we'd shut the village by putting up taboo signs on all the tracks and paths leading into the village. We'd put a big barrier across the main track. People knew they couldn't enter. If anyone did enter we'd fine them two baht. Always two baht. Even if it was a large group of ten or twenty, we'd still only be able to fine them two baht. This is what our traditions dictate. We can't change it. The money was for salt. We'd buy salt and share it equally among the villagers. In the past you'd get quite a lot with two baht, even a whole sack full. Nowadays you'd just get a handful.

Of course, it'd be impossible to ask people now, what with the road passing right through the village. There's far too much traffic. Now we shut off every house instead.

35 – Nai-wun—Yao

Nai-wun is a fourteen year old girl from the Yao village of Padua, a large settlement located astride a paved road in mountains to the west of Mae Chan. This road, which leads from Mae Chan up into the hills to Mae Salong, is heavily used by tourists travelling on 1-day guided tours out of Chiang Rai and Chiang Mai. As a result of this traffic there is now a bustling tourist market in the settlement's main thoroughfare, with stalls piled high with tacky tourist-orientated merchandise brought in from outside.

Tourist Market

Nai-wun goes to school in Chiang Saen and speaks fluent Thai – she even knows a few words of English and French. We met her during the school holidays. Along with two friends, she was manning her mother's stall at the lower end of the village. Being the low season, there were few tourists about, and she happily found time to talk to us.

NAI-WUN: [in English] Hello, you want buy one, Sir?
INTERVIEWER: You speak English! Where did you learn to speak English? Is there a school in the village?
NAI-WUN: [speaking Thai] I learnt it at school. But not here in the village; I go to school in Chiang Saen. The school here is only for very young children, just for the first three years. I go to the temple school in Chiang Saen. Was my English correct? Did I say it right? I'm in the second year [of high school]. I learn English at school, but can only speak a few words.
INTERVIEWER: At least you can practise on the tourists. Do many come here?
NAI-WUN: Hundreds! Like now, it's still the rainy season, but tourists are coming all the time. Even now there are three minibuses parked up there on the road. And it's still early in the day. Are you tourists?

We explain our interest in Yao culture, and tell her briefly of our life in Kiew Khan. She agrees to talk to us about her village.

NAI-WUN: It's now the school holidays. I've come to help my mother sell things to the tourists. I always come home to help my mother during the school holidays. I've taught her a few words in English, too.

Sometimes there are so many mini-buses on the road, there's no room for any more. Loads of Westerners walk down from the main road to look at the stalls. Some just look, some come to buy. It gets really crowded.

The Thai Tourism Office estimates there are now in excess of 100,000 tourists going into the northern hills annually. The primary draw is the image of tribes entertaining a way of life which contrasts sharply with modern Western urban civilisation.

Nearly all visitors have false expectations forced upon them by a tourism industry which describes the hill peoples as being 'untouched by civilisation', 'remote and unspoilt', 'almost unknown', 'primitive' and 'prehistoric'. Many a tourist has thus been disappointed at seeing radios, printed T-shirts, pick-up trucks, bottled soft drinks and other signs of the industrial age in otherwise traditional villages.

Tourists wishing to visit tribal villages have a number of options open to them. A growing number will choose a 1-day sightseeing tour. Booked at their hotel (or with their tour company), they will travel by comfortable air-conditioned mini-bus, stop off at two or three different villages, perhaps spending thirty minutes at each, where they will take photographs, hand out sweets to children and peer into people's houses. Having 'done' the tribes, they will then lunch at a comfortable town restaurant, and perhaps take in a hot spring, an elephant show, or a temple or two before returning to their hotels. It is in villages which receive a steady stream of such visitors that Padua-like tourist markets are likely to develop.

Another option for the tourist is to go on an organised trek. Guided treks are relatively cheap, fairly strenuous, and tend to appeal to younger, independent travellers hoping to experience the tribes and the Golden Triangle in a more down-to-earth fashion. A typical excursion booked out of Chiang Mai normally lasts from three to five days, involving four or five hours walking each day, perhaps visiting four or five villages in total. Nights are passed in the village, either in a standard village house, or in a hut specially constructed for trekking parties.

There are usually no formal arrangements between the trekking agency and the village. Obtaining food and lodging depends on the guide's trustworthiness, persuasiveness and personal connections – hilltribe guides tend to be more readily welcomed and trusted than Thai guides; the trekkers themselves have very little direct contact with the villagers. Increasingly, elephant rides, bamboo raft trips and the chance to see opium fields are included in schedules. Though trekking organisations promote the tribes as living in remote locations, and as being hardly ever visited by outsiders, in truth, many formerly isolated villages receive a steady stream of visitors, so much so that the hills have, in places, taken on the appearance of a giant open-air museum – or zoo!

A third option is for individuals to hire motorbikes or jeeps and tour the hills unescorted. Although trail bikes can reach even the remotest villages in Thailand, the absence of detailed maps tends to restrict unaccompanied adventure-seekers to areas close to known routes. Typically, independent travellers do not attempt to find lodging in tribal villages, preferring instead to stay overnight in lowland towns on their route.

INTERVIEWER: Is business good?

NAI-WUN: Yes, very good. The best time to sell is during the winter. That's our busy time. Sometimes if we are lucky we can sell a big thing for four or five thousand baht. We make a lot on expensive things. The day we sell something like that we are very happy. But business is usually quite good any time. We live off the profit.

INTERVIEWER: Where do the souvenirs originate from?

NAI-WUN: We get our stock from various places. The big Burmese wall hangings come from Burma. The lacquer boxes and the jade jewellery we get from Mae Sai. And the wood carvings come from Kamphaeng Phet. A man brings the carvings here and leaves them for us to sell. We don't have to pay for anything until after it's sold. No matter how much we sell it for, we can keep the profit. He tells us what he wants, then we raise the price for the tourists. Sometimes we get a lot extra, other times it's not so much. For instance, we might pay him 100 for a carving, then we'd charge 130 or 150. So we always make something. Some of the Yao clothes we sell we make here in the village, and some we get from Mae Sai. The fake silver comes from Mae Sai.

INTERVIEWER: What do you think of the tourists who come here? Are they friendly? What do you think of their dress?

NAI-WUN: Oh, they're usually friendly, although sometimes they do get angry and start shouting when they're bargaining. You get both types.

INTERVIEWER: And their clothes?

NAI-WUN: Um, I don't really know.

INTERVIEWER: I mean, do you think they wear nice clothes? Do they dress politely? You know, they dress very differently from Yao and Thais, especially the women. Does it disturb you that some of them dress immodestly? [This is a common complaint of the Thais.]

NAI-WUN: Well, at first I was shocked and didn't like it, but now I've got used to it and think it's normal. Sometimes the old women do look strange; they're fat and can't walk properly [she's laughing]. And many women do dress impolitely, showing too much of their body. We Yao cover most of our bodies. But anyway, we get used to it.

INTERVIEWER: What are the Japanese like?

NAI-WUN: Oh, they spend a lot, they pay high prices. But they don't come often. Most of the tourists are Westerners or Chinese. We are very happy when the Japanese come.

INTERVIEWER: Padua is a developed village with electricity, with a good road nearby and with lots of tourists coming to buy souvenirs and take photographs of the people here. Are the villagers happy how it is?

NAI-WUN: Yes, of course.

INTERVIEWER: We ask because we've heard that some people in other villages get tired of having Westerners photograph them all day. They don't like the disturbance. What do you think about it?

NAI-WUN: The people here are glad that the tourists come to see them. Every family in the village has a stall, some even have two. They don't mind if tourists film them, they're happy about it. Sometimes when a tourist has finished filming he gives us some money—maybe ten or twenty baht a person. He pays us to be on the film. It's very good for the village if more and more tourists keep coming.

There is a pause in the conversation while we all watch a German tourist on the other side of the street as he haggles over the price of a costumed doll. The asking price is 180 baht. He beats the old Yao lady down to 140 baht and hands her two one hundred baht notes. She takes the money, examines them, and then breaks out into loud squeals of laughter. 'Dollar, dollar', she insists. The German becomes flustered. 'One hundred and eighty dollars? Dollars you say?' He can't believe his ears and quickly hands back the doll. A younger woman now intercedes on the old lady's behalf. '180 baht, pay dollar.' He now understands, displays his open wallet crammed full with Thai notes, and repeats 'Baht, baht'. The two women agree to take baht and he hands over another two notes before walking off, apparently happy with his purchase.

Nai-wun laughs. Not only has the tourist paid twice over, but he paid the original asking price and didn't even wait for his change — 400 baht for a doll which probably cost the old woman barely twenty.

INTERVIEWER: Do the people in your village still adhere to the traditional beliefs? Do you still believe in the Yao spirits?

NAI-WUN: Yes, of course. Our lives are the same as they have always been — nothing changes. We still keep our own ways, the traditional ways of our people. Everything is just the same as before. There are no Christian families here, not even one.

INTERVIEWER: Doesn't the presence of so many tourists interfere with normal Yao life?

NAI-WUN: Business is business and nothing to do with being Yao or not; they are different things. Whenever we have to hold a ritual for the spirits we just close the shop for a day. It's no problem at all.

While tourism initially may not adversely effect the traditional belief system of a community, it can certainly have a marked impact on a village economy. Four typical stages of contact between village and tourist have been identified:

1) At first tribespeople are frightened of the Westerners who suddenly appear in their midst. After guides have quickly pacified villagers and assured them the strange white-skinned people are not dangerous, highlanders typically shower their strange guests with traditional hospitality. At this early stage the tourists are as much a curiosity as are the villagers for the tourists.

2) As the frequency of the visits increases, the traditional hospitality once so graciously offered gradually falls by the wayside as group after group of non-communicative strangers eventually leaves the locals with a passive indifference to them.

3) Taught by the tourists to expect sweets and coins, sometimes in return for allowing their photograph to be taken, villagers, particularly the children, soon start to beg, while others, realising the demand for their traditional crafts, begin hawking souvenirs.

4) Finally, receiving tourists in their village becomes a regular phenomenon, and supplying the wants of these visitors becomes an important branch of the local economy – often at the expense of agricultural pursuits. The selling of crafts directly to the tourists tends to be the biggest money-spinner; income from hosting, guiding, putting on dance shows and begging usually remains relatively insignificant.

In many instances tourism merely creates a false economy, and contributes very little of lasting value. Needless to say, within a single region different villages may exist at different stages of this development simultaneously. Lao Shi Guai village (Yao), for instance, is at the indifference stage, while Huai Sa (Lahu) is currently at the primary stage, and Padua is, of course, at the end stage. Not all villages necessarily progress through to the fourth level. Road accessibility is typically the deciding factor.

Kiew Khan at present is just hovering at the indifference stage. Despite the continued bad state of the road, 1991 saw the arrival of the first convoy of tourist mini-buses in the village. There have been many others since, but nowhere near as many as there will be once the road is completed.

Perhaps the ultimate 'end-stage' tribal village in Thailand is Doi Pui, a Blue Hmong village in the hills overlooking Chiang Mai. In this, the nearest hilltribe village to the city, there are streets with purpose-built shops, restaurants and cafes, impromptu opium-smoking shows and flower gardens where, for a fee, visitors may take photographs of Hmong children specially dressed up in traditional costumes. Many of the Hmong women and children selling crafts in the Chiang Mai Night Bazaar are from this village.

NAI-WUN: Oh, can you call those Westerners over – in English. Tell them to come and buy something.

This we do. They saunter over, glance over the table, which admittedly has less displayed than many of the others, ask the price of a cheap factory-made Yao cap, grunt at Nai-wun's reply and, without a word, amble off.

36 – Lortee – Lahu

Lortee is a forty-eight year old Lahu Hpu (the 'H' is silent) woman living in the Lahu village of Huai Sa. This large village of eighty-four households, situated close to the Mekong river twenty kilometres to the north-west of Chiang Khong, has a mixed population of Lahu belonging to four sub-groups: Lahu Hpu, Lahu Shi, Lahu Nyi and Lahu Na. The Hpu are in the majority.

The first settlers to Huai Sa were refugees from across the river in Laos, who were settled there by the Thai government – two neat rows of houses bordering the main street testify to the former official involvement. In more recent times further groups of Lahu have settled in the village, locating their houses in traditional clusters on low hills on two sides of the village. Approximately half of the village profess to being Christians – Catholics, with the remainder adhering to the traditional Lahu beliefs and customs. There is a small school run by Thais in the village, and a police post, also manned by Thais.

Lortee has lived in Huai Sa since the mid-seventies. She was born in Laos and came to Thailand as a refugee. Her husband died five years ago, leaving behind five daughters from an earlier marriage for Lortee to take charge of. I first met her in 1990, when she welcomed two 'white Indians' to the village by sending her daughter over to the village seat with some drinking water (the Hmong would never do this, being far more reticent with strangers). She later joined us, and after our thanking her for the water (in Thai), asked for the English translation of water. The following thirty minutes were then spent, much to the hilarity of the assembled children, with her attempts to pronounce the 'ter' of 'water'. The 'wa' was no problem whatsoever.

Lahu New Year

Lahu ceremonial life revolves around the annual New Year celebration. The time set for the festival varies from year to year, and from village to village. Some Lahu follow the dates of Chinese New Year, although most set it according to other criteria. It is usually held at a time in the year when the agricultural workload is at its lightest, as no one is allowed to work in the fields at this time. A cluster of Lahu villages will tend to celebrate New Year at the same time; this facilitates the interaction between them during the celebration. Preparations start months in advance, as the women must make new clothes for each member of the family. The festival is an important time for courtship, therefore particular attention is paid to the outfits of the young people of marriageable age.

Walker (1970) has identified five important themes to the Lahu New Year festival: village solidarity (the sharing of rice cakes), inter-village solidarity (interaction between villages during the festivals), equality of the villages and of the households (the ritual bathing of villagers), harmony of the sexes (male and female themes recur throughout the festivities), and the dependence of the village community on the spirit world (offerings are made inside the house and at a special 'Year tree').

Hoping to be able to identify some of these themes we asked Lortee to tell us something of the New Year celebrations in her village.

We all enjoy ourselves at New Year. We stop our work in the fields and everybody dresses up. We eat chicken and pork and dance around the Hk'aw-dur [the 'H' is silent]. A Hk'aw-dur is a big bamboo post which we stand up in the centre of the village. Girls and boys dance around it to the accompaniment of the musical pipes. Anyone can join in. A spirit shelf is attached to the post. This is where we place rice cakes and flowers.

The rice cakes are special New Year rice cakes. We call them hk'aw-buk in Lahu Hpu. We make them from sticky rice. First we steam the rice and then pound it. We add sesame seeds and then form it into thick round pieces. We keep them in banana leaves, this way they last for the whole New Year celebrations.

The Hk'aw-dur ('Year tree'), which is normally a long bamboo stalk complete with foliage and encased in four shorter bamboo posts, represents the 'Tree of Life' which the Lahu see in the shadows of the lunar landscape. They believe that if they possessed even just a tiny part of that tree they would be immortal (Lewis 1984:199).

Every morning after breakfast during the celebrations, one man from the village goes around to every house carrying a big basket. His name is Ja-gor, and he's followed by lots of children and young people. As he goes from house to house he plays pipes and

Lahu 'Year tree'

dances. At every house he is given some rice cakes. It is already late afternoon by the time he has been around the whole village. He then goes to the 'Year tree' and places all the cakes on the spirit shelf. Then at night anybody who wants can go and dance around the 'Year tree'.

The dancing is often to the accompaniment of a musical gourd pipe, though drums, gongs, and cymbals are used by some. Groups from other villages nearby typically form dance groups and call in on other villages, bringing offerings to the headmen. This shows mutual support between villages. Boys and men also spend many hours during the festival playing top-spinning, in which hard-wood spinning tops are sent careering into an opponent's top – and anybody's ankles that happen to get in the way! Young unmarried men and women play a game of catch with black cloth balls made by the girls. Though it can be played just for fun, its ulterior purpose is to introduce the players to members of the opposite sex, and it is often the precursor to more serious courting.

We asked whether Ja-gor recites anything as he places the cakes onto the spirit shelf.

Er, yes, he says something to the spirit we call Jor-wor-lu [village guardian]. He offers the rice cakes to Jor-wor-lu, and Jor-wor-lu comes to take them. If any families don't make this offering to Jor-wor-lu, they won't get enough to eat from their fields the following year. There wouldn't be enough rain on their fields. Jor-wor-lu is a good spirit who helps people.

A friend of Lortee's who has been listening, a man named Ta-bor, now adds his piece.

When Ja-gor offers the cakes to the spirit a priest gives blessings to all the people. We leave the cakes there until the end of the celebrations. Then they are collected and taken to the headman's house. Here they are cooked, together with a head of a pig which had also been left on the spirit altar in the middle of the village. We also add some skin from the sacrificed pig. It's all fried together and then distributed to every family in the village.

We asked Lortee whether people in her village bathe the elders with 'new water'.

Yes, we do this. We use 'new water' to bathe the elders. The water comes from the normal water source, the same place we always get our water from. But for the 'new water' we have to go very early in the morning, before anybody uses the water. Every family in the village does this. We keep the water in a kettle or bottle, or any other container. Then the young people of the village visit all the old people taking the water with them. They take the water to wash the hands of the old people. In return the elders bless them and say, 'Oh, I wish you a long life, as long as the river is long, and health and much happiness'. We say this because a river flows a great distance. *I-ka-seu-wey* is what we call it. *Seu* is 'new' in Lahu, and *wey* is 'to get' or 'to take'. And *I-ka* is 'water'. So *I-ka-seu-wey* means 'to get new water'.

The drawing of 'new water' is an important part of the festivities. According to Lewis, young people make a game of seeing who can reach the water source first when the new year arrives. Lahu believe 'new water' begins to flow with the coming of the new year. Using the 'new water' a female representative goes from house to house washing the hands and feet of the household head and his wife in a ritual very similar to that performed during the Lahu holy days (see Napur Muangjai, Lahu Holy Days). Later in the day parents are bathed by their adult children, and elders held in high esteem are bathed by the young people of the village, as outlined above by Lortee.

After four or five hectic days of making ancestor offerings, bathing the elders, feasting, dancing, spinning tops, firing off guns, throwing balls and visiting friends in other villages, the annual festival is over for another year. A new year has dawned, and with it new hope for a bright and prosperous future.

37 – Laobor Seyang – Hmong

Laobor Seyang is a gregarious, outward-going twenty-eight year old from Kiew Khan. He is married and has four young children. Recently Laobor has been plagued by misfortune. One April night in 1991 (just three weeks after the big fire scare in March) his neighbour's house caught fire. The flames quickly spread to his own house which rapidly burnt to the ground. Laobor and his wife lost almost everything they had: bedding, clothes, hunting musket, cooking utensils and all other household possessions – even his wife's silver neck ring had been badly damaged.

To make matters worse, cartridges, and certain other materials kept in their bedroom exploded during the fire, badly wounding in the foot a young boy who had been helping to fight the flames. Laobor was held responsible for this accident, and was blamed by the villagers for not warning them of the possible danger. Strangely, and perhaps perversely so, he may have been right to keep quiet. For if he had spoken up earlier, the chances are nobody would have been willing to risk life and limb trying to put out the fire, and half the village would likely have been lost.

Unfortunately for Laobor, misfortune struck again four months later when Thai forestry officials made a surprise raid on the village and confiscated the stack of neatly sawn planks he had prepared in readiness for rebuilding his house (logging in the area is illegal). Despite this further set-back, he still entertains hopes of being able to accumulate enough timber one-day to rebuild his former family home. Until such a time, however, he and his family are obliged to live in a small, cramped, one-room hut.

Sending Away the Old Year's Misfortune

Perhaps thinking of his own unlucky year, Laobor told us of the ritual performed on the first day of the Hmong New Year festival: a ritual which aims to 'send away the bad influences of the old year'.

As it's the New Year we do something to bring us good fortune. The cock we sacrifice takes away all the evil and misfortune that's left over from the old year. Every family must hold this ritual.

Usually families band together in lineage groups, with maybe two, three or four families in each group.

We start the preparations in the late afternoon of the first day of the new year. We get a bamboo pole or big sapling, and stick it into the ground outside the house. This is where the ritual will be held. Then we make a grass rope and tie both ends to the pole, one end to the top, the other at the bottom. Some families also make little grass rope crowns for the children to wear on their heads. And we also have to get hold of a cock. It has to be one with a lot of red feathers — a red cock. And then we prepare our muskets and other guns.

A cock, particularly one with pronounced red markings, is seen by the Hmong as a sort of heavenly messenger. A Hmong myth tells of a semi-legendary heroic figure called 'The Heavenly Archer'. He fashioned the first crossbow out of iron and copper and fired it at each of the nine suns that passed over the world. He shot eight of them clean out of the sky, causing drought and death. The last sun was so frightened she (Lady Sun) disappeared and would not re-emerge until she heard the crowing of a cock, the head of which, struck by the first rays, ever afterwards bore a red plume. This is why the cock is seen as a heavenly herald, and why, incidentally, the sun will not appear until after the cock's crow in the morning.

When everything is ready someone from the lineage head's household calls the other families together. We start by firing a single shot into the air. Then one of those gathered, usually the lineage head — an old man, recites an incantation to drive away all evil and bad influences, and to invite good fortune, health and happiness.

You see, we throw out the old and bad, and bring in the new and good. When a new year starts everything must be good, everything must be positive. This goes for the individual, the family and the village.

While he's chanting, those gathered walk slowly around the 'tree' and through the rope which is held up. They do this three times in all. If anyone is missing we carry their jacket in their place. Once we've walked around three times the old man will cut the cock's throat and throw it to the ground.

The bird is thrown to the ground with some force. This emphasises all the more the casting off of the bad influences of the previous year.

Then the grass crowns, the cock, the rope and 'tree' are taken out of the village by young men. They go towards the west, to the sunset side of the village. These things have to be thrown away into the 'sunset hole', the place where the sun goes down at the end of the day. So, when the sun sinks it will take them down with it.

The Hmong believe the earth is flat and is supported by four god-like figures, one at each corner. Sometimes the gods get tired of their burdens and change shoulders: this results in earthquakes (Chindarsi 1976:19).
The 'sunset hole' is the hole into which the sun sinks at the end of every day. The phrase 'come on, get a move on, it's almost into the hole', for instance, is commonly heard at dusk when Hmong villagers, tired and exhausted, are trudging back to the village after a hard day's work in the fields.
Knowing that other people do not discard the sacrificed birds after this ritual, we asked Laobor to explain further.

Oh, well, in the old days we used to throw away the cocks, but yes, you're right, now we keep the birds, and just throw away all the other stuff. It's because these days we have to buy the birds with money. And they're expensive. So instead of throwing them away we just burn some of their feathers and pretend to discard the body. Really we take them home to cook and eat.

The next morning everybody has a shower and washes their clothes so they will be clean for the new year. Thus we wash away all the dirt from the old year.

This special wash is a symbolic cleansing ready for the New Year and, however it may sound, is not the only wash and scrub-up of the year. There then follows at least three days of celebrations, sometimes as many as seven, crammed full with ancestor offerings, much feasting, during which quantities of rice liquor are consumed, the playing of a ritual ball-throwing courtship game (similar to the Lahu), top spinning, bull fighting – two bulls against each other – and the singing of courtship songs. One glorious week of respite in a long, hard year.

38 – Laodeng Sewa – Hmong

Laodeng is a man in his forties living in Kiew Khan. He is married, has three children, and has recently been enrolled as a recruit to the border police post in the village. He is recognised in the village as being one of the most successful hunters in the community; it was partly for his skill in procuring meat that he was originally asked to join the Hmong recruits at the police post. Unfortunately for the Thai NCO's, expectations of having their rations supplemented with delicious local jungle game – wild pig, deer, armadillo and one metre long lizard – proved to be groundless. For unknown to them, their renowned hunter is far more apt to slink off home for a sleep, rather than head up into the hills on their behalf. As Laodeng himself says, 'Why should I hunt for them? If I hunt, I hunt for myself, and my family. Hunting is hard work, you know.'

Paying One's Hunting Debts

Interested to hear something of the special rituals conducted by hunters, we asked Laodeng to tell us something of the ritual offering performed by a hunter after every kill.

Every time I get a pig or deer I hold a little ritual. You see, just as we feed the pigs in the village, which makes them ours, so is it the same with the wild pigs. Every wild pig is owned by a spirit in the jungle. So, whenever I get a wild pig, I have to do something for the spirit.

First I cut off the pig's head; then I butcher the body. I cook a small portion of the meat, and along with some rice and some spirit money, I offer it to the spirits. What I do is place everything on the floor by the door and light some incense sticks and burn the paper money. I then tell the spirit that the offering is for him.

Spirit money? Oh, it's white paper. But it's really money for the spirit. When we burn it we send it up to the spirits. As it burns I call out to the spirit who owns the pig and tell him to eat the meat and collect the money.

Oh, I forgot to tell you, I also leave the severed head on the floor by the door as well. You see, I catch the pig and then give the spirit some money and a share of the meat. Then the next time I go hunting the same spirit will aid me to find another pig. The spirit will make a pig come towards me for me to shoot. And later I'd give him some more money. If I didn't offer something, well, then of course the spirit would think I was mean. It would think I was too stingy. And the next time he wouldn't help me when I'm out hunting. I'd be just wasting my time out there in the jungle.

The people of Kiew Khan have been warned by the authorities to cease hunting in the surrounding forests, as these forests are under a protection order. To date, no action has been taken to enforce this ban. However, a new Forestry Department station has been planned for a site just fifteen kilometres from the village, and in all likelihood hunting and small-scale logging by villagers will soon be a thing of the past.

Christianity, or the Spirits?

Last year Laodeng's baby son went down with a very high fever. With the help of a missionary staying in the village at that time, Laodeng took the child to the hospital in Chiang Khong. The baby was given a cot in the ward and Laodeng was told to wait for the doctor, who at the time was not in the hospital. After waiting a number of hours, and with no sign yet of the doctor's arrival, Laodeng picked up his child and returned home, complaining that the Thai nurses had ignored him simply because he was dirty, and only a Hmong. On hearing this, the missionary once again persuaded him to take the child to seek medical care, but this time to the smaller hospital in Chiang Saen. Unfortunately the child died in the missionary's Land-Rover just two hundred metres out of the village.

I had always believed in the spirits, but then I went through a period when I was often unwell. It was the same with my daughter. We were both poorly for a long time, even though we appealed to the spirits for help. So I turned to the Christian way and looked to Jesus. I was a Christian for quite a few years, and eventually my health returned.

Then about a year ago my wife gave birth to a son. When he was five months old he fell ill and I took him to the hospital in

Chiang Khong. Oh, it was very crowded, there were people milling about everywhere. I had to wait in a long queue for ages just to see a nurse. Then I had to wait for a doctor to come and examine my baby. But he never came, so I brought my baby back home. He died later that day and I buried him. I was very upset.

And then Laodeng describes how, under pressure from his kinsmen in the village, he was persuaded to 'return to the way of the spirits'.

Our family has often been plagued by illness. Someone is always sick in our house. Sometimes it was me or my wife; at other times it was the children. At first when I became a Christian, things had been better. But then slowly things got bad again, even worse than before. My relatives in the village thought we were stupid not to try the ritual cures. They kept telling me to go back to the spirits, to ask the spirits for help. At first we didn't know what to do, but then finally my wife and I agreed that this would be for the best.

We invited the shaman to come to our house to determine why we were unwell. We also asked him to divine the future for us, to see if there was any luck coming our way. He said the household spirit that looks after our family was angry because I had become a Christian. This spirit was causing the sickness to come to our house. Oh, I was very worried about my family's health. It was upsetting for me to see one family member after another falling ill and not getting better.

The shaman informed me if I wanted to see an improvement in my family's health I should go back to our old beliefs. So I went over to see the missionary in the village—our teacher—to let him know I wanted to stop being a Christian, and to stop going to church every Sunday. He said it was alright, and that I should do whatever I thought was right.

The missionary is an American who was living in Kiew Khan with his wife and four children for a while. He has lived and worked in Hmong villages for a number of years and speaks fluent Hmong—even his children speak Hmong! They are Protestants, and in common with most Protestant missionaries in the region, refer to non-Christian Hmong (the vast majority in Kiew Khan) as demon-worshippers and heathens.

We return to Laodeng to ask him whether he was worried about leaving the Christian fold having already been baptised.

Oh, even though I was a Christian for a few years I was never baptised. Our teacher asked me to do it, but I was always a bit afraid to go through with it.

Where are they held? Oh, they do it in water, either in a stream or a pond. At first I wanted to be baptised, but then later I started having second thoughts. It's not that I expected to return to the spirits, or anything like that. It's just that people who are baptised have to be very good. They have to be nice people. I'm poor, I have to hunt for a living. If I had been baptised, and had therefore made those promises to Jesus that they make, there would've been many things I wouldn't have been allowed to do. If you make these promises you have to keep them. You can't do anything that goes against the Christian teachings. And once you've been baptised you can't ever go back to the old ways, back to the spirits. If you did, you'd probably die.

You know, if you make these promises to Jesus you can't play around with somebody else's wife. You can't tell lies or smoke opium; you can't even smoke cigarettes. You have to be good all the time.

The various Christian missions currently working among tribal people in northern Thailand can be divided into three principal denominations: Catholic, Protestant, and Seventh Day Adventist. Many Christians of our acquaintance seem to be uncertain as to the meaning of these divisions, and when asked to which faith they belong, simply reply 'Saturday Christian' (Seventh Day Adventist) or 'Sunday Christian' (Protestant or Catholic), according to which day church services are held.

Apart from the day of worship, another factor which helps them classify the various Christian sects is the differences in that what is forbidden them by the church. For instance, the Catholics permit smoking, drinking and the performing of almost all the ancestral rituals, whereas the Protestants come down harder on the traditional customs, and also forbid the drinking of whisky. The Seventh Day Adventists, however, are seen to impose the greatest demands, prohibiting drinking, smoking and the eating of pork.

The work of the missionaries constitutes a significant threat to the traditional cultures of the various tribal groups – particularly with regard to belief. To date, the Akha, with their high regard for the Akhazan, and the Yao, whose culture is so intricately linked with Taoism, have perhaps been least affected by missionary activity in the region. Whereas the Lahu, who have been subject to missionary pressure for many years (particularly in Burma in the past), arguably have been the most influenced.

I wasn't done [baptised], so I can go back to the old ways. My teacher had asked me to get baptised, but I wasn't sure, so I said I would later on, but not yet. He said it was up to me and there was no rush. Ha! Ha! Just think, if I'd given my promise to the river, I wouldn't be able to go back to the spirits now. If I had taken the oath, I'd be dead by now for sure. Ha!

Sadly, while in England preparing the manuscript for this book, we have received a letter telling us of Laodeng's death. The letter, which has been dictated by our close friend Laopia to one of the Thai police sergeants, makes no mention of how he died.

39 - Janoo – Lahu

Janoo is a forty-five year old Lahu Nyi man from the village of Huai Jai Yin I (the nearby Huai Jai Yin II is an Akha community). The village is located in the mountains south of Chiang Khong astride the winding 1155 highroad – an army-built strategic road which runs through a range of hills parallel to the Laotian border. The settlement is not large, and two-thirds of the population are non-Lahu: these being Kuomintang Chinese, and Dai from Sipsongpanna in Yunnan. Most of the Chinese are Christian, and the Dai are Buddhists.

Janoo, whose small, ramshackle ground-built house is more typical of a Yunnanese Chinese house than Lahu, has lived in Huai Jai Yin I for more than fifteen years. He is a former soldier, and was originally drafted into the area from Fang in Chiang Mai Province to protect road gangs working on the new road. The area was at one time a stronghold controlled by anti-government (communist) forces.

Losing the Old Ways

Ideally every Lahu, Akha, Lisu and Karen village in which the traditional belief systems are still adhered to – and this is the vast majority in northern Thailand – should have amongst their inhabitants a village priest. However, in practice not every village will have a priest. For instance, in many very small villages there may not be a suitable candidate among the population, and it will therefore be necessary to borrow a priest from a neighbouring village to conduct all the important ceremonies. Sometimes there will be no available priest within easy reach, however, and then the traditional culture may start to weaken, making it easier for other faiths, such as Christianity and Buddhism, to take root.

This is precisely the situation with the Lahu in Huai Jai Yin I. They originally came to the area from Doi Tung near Mae Sai to work on the new road and, being without a priest, they are now finding it increasingly difficult to continue in the old ways. Many have never even seen a Lahu temple! Increasingly the elders are heard to complain about the young: how the young are allowing themselves to be enticed into the Christian fold and, most frequently, how the young are leaving them, the old ones, to conduct the traditional – and often time-consuming, and expensive – ceremonies all on their own. As time goes by, the old ways of the Lahu are likely to disappear completely from this particular village.

Invited to enter Janoo's house and share a small bottle of Thai whisky in the company of two Thai border policemen already there, we noticed his house altar – a simple shelf-like construction – hanging from one wall. It was covered in cobwebs and cluttered with ordinary household items.

INTERVIEWER: Is that a Buddhist or Lahu altar? Or is it Chinese?

JANOO: I'm not Chinese, I'm Lahu. That's a Lahu altar.

INTERVIEWER: Do you still use it?

JANOO: Yes, of course. I'm Lahu, I believe in the spirits. Are you Christian missionaries?

INTERVIEWER: No, not at all. I'm Buddhist. The Westerner is Christian though, but he doesn't go to church. He's half Christian, half Buddhist.

JANOO: That's good. That's clever [laughing].

INTERVIEWER: How many families are there in this village?

JANOO: About fifty-eight. Some are Dai from Sipsongpanna, and some are Jin Haw [Yunnanese Chinese]. The others are Lahu. The families are all mixed in with each other.

INTERVIEWER: We noticed there is no Lahu temple in the village. Has there ever been one here?

JANOO: A long time ago, when I was living in my old village, we had a temple. I had to join the army in those days, and I was sent to this area to protect the men building the road. After the troubles, when it was all quiet again, I came to live here. I brought my wife with me. There were only four houses here then, it was a very small village. That was fourteen years ago. In this village there is no dominant clan, or group; everybody comes from different places. Chinese, Dai and Lahu, we all like each other and get on well.

INTERVIEWER: If the village has been here fourteen years, then why haven't you built a Lahu temple yet?

JANOO: Oh, there aren't enough people to warrant it. Some of the villagers are Christian, and the Dai are all Buddhists. There aren't enough non-Christian Lahu here to make building a temple worthwhile. I would like to have one for us Lahu, for our people, but there is just not enough of us. Now, whenever we hold a celebration, or whenever we want to make an offering to the spirits, we go over to the big tree up there. You see [pointing], up there at the top of the village, on the hill behind the village shop. Over there we've built a simple hut with an altar inside. The altar is for the local spirits.

The hut is indeed small. It is three metres square, built of bamboo posts, with walls of flattened bamboo and a thatched grass roof. Inside there is a single altar set against the far wall. It consists of a one metre long plank of wood raised on two posts. On the shelf are three small ceramic bowls containing incense sticks, and two stones on which a number of shop-bought candles have been stuck. A pile of unused candles lie to one side. Chicken feathers from past sacrifices have been stuck onto the posts. On the ground immediately in front of the altar there are more incense sticks, grouped together in three separate clusters.

INTERVIEWER: Is there a shaman in the village?

JANOO: We used to have one, but he died and nobody wanted to take over. Nowadays if people are ill they go to the hospital. It's a lot easier that way. There are more Christians than animists in this village. Do you believe me when I say that some Lahu people in the village have never seen a Lahu temple?

You know, not every Lahu subgroup has temples; it's only us Lahu Nyi who usually have them. There are many different Lahu subgroups, and we all speak different dialects. Did you know that? Here we have Lahu Shi as well as Lahu Nyi. I'm Lahu Nyi.

INTERVIEWER: Why haven't you become a Christian like many of the other people in the village?

JANOO: Oh, I'd like to, but I have to consider my brothers and sisters. I have eight altogether. None of them live here; I'm on my own. They live in Fang district in Chiang Mai Province. My brothers and sisters would be terribly upset if I were to become a Christian. Once I went to see them to ask permission for me to convert to Christianity. Oh, they were really against the idea. They told me if I were to do that, they'd no longer think of me as their brother.

There's nothing wrong with being Christian, though. They are very good people. In our village we get a lot of help from a Christian group from Singapore. They're Chinese. They built the school for the village, and they gave out clothing to all the Christian families. And the church pays for the Christians to study in the town; they pay for board and lodging. If it wasn't for my family I'd become one. They have a lot of fun at the church. I'd like to go along too.

INTERVIEWER: Do the non-Christian Lahu still retain their traditional beliefs? Do they keep the Lahu holy days?

JANOO: Yes, some do. We have a Lahu holy day once a month. It's a bit like a Buddhist holy day. We call it a *ghi-ee* day. On those days we don't work in the fields, it's a day of rest. But I think most of the young people in the village will eventually become Christians, and then the day will come when nobody will follow the old ways.

40 – Laoseu Seyang – Hmong

Laoseu Seyang is fifty-eight, widowed, and has five children. He lives in Kiew Khan, where he is known as Laoseu Khayao – Longlegs Laoseu – due to his above-average height. He is an energetic, talkative person, who spends much of his time out of the village on trips into Laos, looking for items with which to trade. In the past he has turned up at our house with a beautiful set of Yao Taoist paintings, a Yao priest's headgear, a jar full of uncut 'rubies' – they weren't, a gall stone from a bear, a rusty old iron cooking pot, which Laoseu swore was an ancient Chinese pot worth thousands of baht, teeth from a wild pig and an elegant old bottle, originally from Dijon, France, which another friend reliably informed us is just the sort of container in which chemicals used in the heroin-making process are usually stored.

A Non-believer

Sitting round the fire inside Laoseu's large house one dark, windy night, he told us the following story of a man who doubted the power of the spirits.

There was once a man who didn't believe in the spirits. He didn't even try to understand why people carry out the rituals and live their lives aware of the spirits. Every time people began talking about the spirits he'd get angry and say they were talking rubbish. But everything he said and did was known to the two great spirits: the 'Lord of the Land' and the 'Sky spirit'. They were watching all the time, and were rapidly losing patience with him.

The Lord and the Sky spirit knew this man owned a maize field, and one day they sent a spirit bear to his fields to eat the maize. Not only this, but the bear also trampled down a lot of the maize. The bear often went to his fields, and the destruction was great.

Sometimes he'd wait hidden nearby, and try and kill the bear, but he could never manage it. Then one day he saw tracks made by the bear. They led into a cave. He followed them for a long time, going deeper and deeper into the darkness. Ha! What he didn't know at the time was that the bear he was following was a spirit bear, and the cave led straight to the heavens.

Underground caves and holes in the earth are often depicted in Hmong mythology as ways to enter the Otherworld.

He kept following the tracks up into the sky, and when he emerged from the cave he was in the heavens. Here he met the two great spirits, the Lord of the Land and the Sky spirit. For a while he lived with them in the sky. He ate with them and they gave him some money to spend.

We asked Laoseu whether the two great spirits were the dreaded 'Lords' of the Otherworld, Ntxwj Nyug and Nyuj Vaj Tuam Teem?
  'Yes, yes, the sky spirit, he's one. The other was the Lord of the Land.'
  'But which is the sky spirit?'
  'Ntxwj Nyug', replied Laoseu, before continuing his story, the flow of which was apparently unaffected by our interruptions.

After a while he began thinking of his family, and he asked the two great spirits the way to go home. The Lord showed him by pointing, saying 'Follow that path and you'll get to your village'.
  So he left, walking along the path into the mountains. He walked all day, and then as night fell he lay down to sleep—still in the mountains. But on waking the next morning he found himself back in the heavens with the two spirits. He was back where he started! He tried to leave many times, but every time he woke up—having lain down to sleep somewhere in the mountains, he'd find himself back in the heavens with the two spirits. Eventually he gave up trying to leave and decided to remain in the heavens for a while.
  Then some time later he again asked the two spirits to send him back home. He told them he was missing his wife and desperately wanted to return to his family. The Lord and the Sky spirit said if he wanted to go back to his village he'd have to wait until the New Year festival. He asked why, and they answered 'You will wait until the New Year festival. When the time comes you'll see why, and then you'll believe in spirits.'

And then the time to return came at last.

Then two days before the festival the Lord told him if he wanted to go back home he should go and wait on the track at the place where three paths meet. The Lord pointed to the place to show him where. He was told to sit there and wait with his eyes closed. He had to promise to keep his eyes tightly shut. Then the Lord instructed him on what he must do. The Lord said, 'You must sit there at the junction, and the first time you hear harness bells jingle as a horse passes, you mustn't do anything. Just sit there and wait. But when you hear the bells for the second time, you must quickly make a grab for them just as they are passing you.'

He was then told not to forget to keep his eyes shut all the time. The Lord said, 'You can open them once you've succeeded in grabbing the bells. But don't make your move until the bells are really loud, otherwise you may not reach your village.'

So, he sat at the junction and waited. It was already late in the day—and getting dark—when he heard the bells pass him. They weren't particularly loud, so he continued waiting. Then he heard some really loud ones approach him. He knew these were the ones and so just as they were right in front of him he made his move. He grabbed hold of them tightly and opened his eyes. Ha! Guess what? He found himself lying under a shaman's bench, clasping hold of its legs.

The shaman's wooden bench is, of course, the 'winged horse' which carries the cosmic traveller into the Otherworld. The rattle shaken by him during shamanic rituals represents the harness bells worn by the horse.

The shaman was in a trance at the time, and an onlooker cried out 'Hey, what are you doing there? Where did you come from?' He told them everything that had happened, telling them how, when he had first made the grab, he had felt something warm and sweaty, but then on opening his eyes had found himself holding wood.

The man then stated that from then on he believed totally in the shaman and the spirits. After this he invited the shaman to perform a ritual for his family. He wanted to make an offering to the spirits to mark the New Year.

Cultural Integrity Under Threat

The richness and variety of our neighbours' beliefs and traditions has been found to be in evidence at every turn. In the course of a single year interviewing tribal people in their villages and homes, we have encountered beliefs and ritual practices which permeate every single aspect of their lives, from using chicken-bones to divine the outcome of a proposed business venture to the steps necessary to ward off the dreaded smallpox spirit; from building soul-calling bridges to facilitate the return of a wandering or lost soul to the placing of death spells on wrong-doers. In village after village we have listened to, and recorded, descriptions, explanations, reminiscences—even warnings—of all manner of spiritual activity and conviction including: possession, exorcism, shamanic curing, thanksgiving, reincarnation, attack by vampire and weretiger, the rituals of birth and death, the various methods of dealing with ghosts—and crop pests, and much, much more.

However, we have also encountered many instances in villages where the traditional culture seems to be under threat, or indeed, lost completely. As forests are felled, so game disappears and the hunter finds himself redundant—along with his special hunting rituals. Similarly, the proliferation of guns (and bowie knives) has replaced the need for black magic, after all, who would willingly spend long secretive hours embroiled in the intricacies of sending death magically, when a single shot fired out of the darkness would do the job just as surely?

In some communities we've visited, patients have availed themselves of ritual cures only after having first tried the local hospitals—in the past the opposite had been the case: shaman first, Western methods second. In many Yao settlements, the ancient writings of their forefathers, penned in Chinese characters, are increasingly illegible to the young, who can now only read Thai script. And in some Lahu villages, Christian churches are replacing temples, and in these, and others, the young are turning their backs on the old ways of their ancestors.

One only has to review the events of the 1992 Hmong New Year celebrations in Kiew Khan for an indication of the things to come. Excited rumours of a Hmong dance troupe coming to the village that year began circulating two weeks before the festival. They were to arrive, we were told, on the first day of the New Year, and the order went out for one member from every household to assist in the building of a stage in front of the school for their use. Illegally cut hardwood planks were taken from their hiding places and construction commenced almost immediately. The police, in the spirit of the occasion, refrained from asking any awkward questions.

Nobody, however, seemed to know exactly who these dancers were who were coming to entertain us. Rumours abounded. They were either from a village south of Chiang Khong, or from Chiang Mai. They would be fifteen, or fifty strong, and planned to stay a day, or a week. There was even some talk of their being from the United States.

Finally, New Year's day came. Under bright blue winter skies, and watched by crowds of excited onlookers, beautifully bedecked village women, many carrying brightly coloured sun-shading umbrellas and covered from top to bottom in intricate silver jewellery, ambled onto the little field in groups of four or five, eventually to form themselves into ragged lines to face similarly elaborately dressed young men.

Many of the men were strangers, having made their way to Kiew Khan in the hope of finding a bride. Aiming to impress, they sported dark sunglasses and, like some of the women, carried large cassette recorders, both being important status symbols for teenagers in Hmong villages.

And so the ritual courtship ball-throwing game got under way once again. All day long the homemade black cloth balls were tossed backwards and forwards between the opposing lines of smooth-talking men and regal-looking women, with the partners being changed regularly to increase the chances of a match.

And then, at last, towards four in the afternoon, the first of the visiting dance group arrived. Almost exactly one year after the building of the new church in the village, the Seventh Day Adventists were back. Not from the United States this time, but Hmong boys and girls from a SDA college in Chiang Mai—the first Hmong women I'd ever seen wearing jeans! Under the discreet guidance of an Australian woman named Mary, they had come to put on a show the likes of which Kiew Khan had never seen before.

Dressed in elaborately embroidered Hmong costumes and bedecked in silver jewellery, they performed that night for a village bathed in moonlight. In front of a large banner which proclaimed in Hmong in prominent white letters, 'Christ the Saviour', and accompanied by a rock band, they sang, danced, and acted out simple comic sketches—many with a Christian message. One sketch even had an anti-government flavour, depicting the rounding up and, far from comic, execution of Hmong by robot-like Thai soldiers (a reference to a Hmong insurgency in the 1960's).

The audience loved it! Beautiful young women in exquisite costumes and dashing young men with drums and electric guitars: for many, the very picture of wealth and success. And to top it all, they were Hmong, not rich Westerners, or city-living Thais, but Hmong, from villages just like their own. Some were even related to local families. Mad cheers and clapping resounded when each performer introduced himself or herself—members of the Selee clan (Kiew Khan's predominate clan) being awarded the biggest cheers of all. Many were proudly saying that night, that not even in the towns could you see such an extravaganza.

However, beneath the self-praise, the swellings of many a Hmong chest, the declarations of pride in their race, there were also mumblings of discontent. People quickly tired of the repeated references to God and Jesus. At first, during the long bible readings, feet were shuffled. But as the reader continued unabashed the audience soon began talking amongst itself. 'Why all the talk of Jesus, the King spirit of the Westerners?' some were asking. 'Why is Jesus always so eager to gather peoples under him?' others wondered. The children, however, continued to stare unabatedly throughout, all but lost to the glamorous dream-world above them on the stage.

That New Year there were more Thais in the village than in previous years. A number of women from nearby villages were selling food and drink from makeshift stalls—papaya salad, noodle soup and bottled soft drinks, and a steady stream of Thai youths turned up on motorbikes to investigate the party and give the Hmong young women the once-over.

At one point, Jonglao had needed to mount the stage carrying a carbine to warn off an unruly group of drunken Thais who were shouting out suggestive comments to the young women on the stage. With the gun in full view he reminded them that they were guests in the village and should behave accordingly. They apparently understood the meaning of the display and quickly faded into the background. However, from then on, armed villagers patrolled the crowd as a precaution—a sad state of affairs indeed.

The developers were absent over the New Year period, although in the months running up to the festival they had been particularly active in the village, holding endless village meetings to discuss their plans, and making sure that projects already decided on successfully got off the ground.

While many of the villagers appreciated the help they were being offered by the various organisations, they were naturally wary of the reasons behind this good-natured action. Many felt the projects most favoured by the developers, for example, were those of a high profile nature—toilets, clean streets, the removal of unsightly cow-sheds (this one raised a real storm), the terracing of fields near the entrance to the village and the placement of litter bins outside every house. Some wondered whether they were being used as part of a public relations exercise. Was their community to be a model village, a fund-raising showpiece, or, even worse, a social experiment?

There were surprisingly few tourists in the village during the week-long festival. Perhaps the two luxury hotels on the other side of Chiang Saen were unaware of the occasion. Certainly there had been a marked increase in tourists during November and the first half of December. On one November day alone, a group of forty Germans in five mini-buses from the Golden Triangle Resort Hotel had stopped in the village, as had a number of Westerners on motorbikes—Germans, Australians and Britons, followed by a group of sixteen Thai bank employees from Bangkok (who chose to stay the night in the village), and three Norwegian women accompanied by a Thai guide, who arrived in a dust-covered jeep late at night. They were lost, and were desperately looking for somewhere to sleep.

As on other occasions, it was the day-trippers who had made the most impact. Ever smiling, and clutching their video cameras, they had wandered around the lower part of the village dishing out handfuls of sweets to dazed children (wife hands out one sweet per native while her man records it for the folks back home). In the search for those photo opportunities of 'daily tribal life' promised them by their brochure, the more adventurous had ploughed through people's back yards, catching villagers totally by surprise, including one little group of startled young women sitting at their embroidery, and Laosong's wife showering topless at an outside tap.

And there were others, too, that winter, eagerly making their way up the mountain in the wake of the giant yellow earth-movers of the Highway Department. There was, for instance, the man from a luxurious resort hotel (the expatriate manager himself, no less) who came to outline how the community could profit from the establishment of an open-air tourist market in the village. He had been closely followed by an elderly Dutch man, a collector of artifacts for museums in Europe, who paid cash for wooden carrying frames, agricultural tools, bracelets, opium pipes, woven baskets and such like.

Then there were the men from the electricity company, offering extra-cheap installation charges, and also a number of well-dressed Thais, typically driving new pick-up trucks, who came to offer young village women, particularly the pretty ones, employment opportunities in the towns as maids, waitresses and shop women. The latter were, in reality, scouts for the brothels; the more unscrupulous of the unprincipled even offered marriage. The road was not yet finished, but already the difference was showing.

Of course, change is happening all the time, in all societies. After all, it is mainly through contact with other groups that cultures develop. However, in northern Thailand the magnitude and rapidness of changes currently being forced upon minority cultures is simply breathtaking; it is the very speed of the events which calls for concern.

Government officers, development workers, tourists, missionaries, drug traffickers, illegal loggers, land speculators and even Bangkokians in search of a second home far from the smog and confusion of the metropolis, are all, in one way or another, exerting influences of varying degrees on tribal people's long-held ways of life—and thus, consequently, also on those beliefs and rituals which constitute such a large part of that life.

However, if it were only cultural dilution—or collapse—that the highlanders had to contend with, perhaps there could still be room for hope, for, historically, highlanders are extremely resilient. They have kept their independent way of life over centuries, and are no strangers to war, mass migration, racial persecution and a life, for many, of the barest subsistence. Alarmingly though, within the last few years the spectre of an AIDS epidemic in the hills has raised its ugly head. One leading AIDS specialist in Chiang Rai has even predicted the decimation of tribal populations in Thailand within the next ten years! According to this expert, unless a cure is soon found, the tragedy will not end there, but will be repeated further afield, as girls returning home from the brothels, traders, migrating highlanders and others, carry the disease deep into neighbouring lands.

This more recent, and very deadly, threat to their way of life, coupled with the projected rapid economic development of the entire Golden Triangle region by Thailand, Burma, Laos and China, in which new roads and railways may be thrown across the formerly impenetrable mountains, air services between important towns upgraded, hydrofoil services on the Mekong introduced, industrial concerns developed, and holiday resorts and even a casino built, may serve to overwhelm minority cultures already under much strain.

Significant changes in the region are inevitable. Whether the hilltribe peoples can retain a sizeable portion of their unique cultures in the face of so many adversaries is still yet to be seen. What no-one can deny is that the erosion and possible extinction of such rich and highly individualistic cultures would be a tragic and irreplaceable loss to us all.

Bibliography

Beattie, John. (1964). *Other Cultures – Aims, Methods and Achievements in Social Anthropology*. London: Routledge & Kegan Paul.

Bhrukasari, Wanat, and John McKinnon. (Eds.). (1983). *The Highlanders of Thailand*. Kuala Lumpur: Oxford University Press.

Chindarsi, Nusit. (1976). *The Religion of the Hmong Njua*. Bangkok: The Siam Society.

Cooper, R., Tapp, N., Lee, Gary Yia, and Schwoer-Kohl, Gretel. (1991) *The Hmong*. Bangkok: Artasia Press.

Encyclopaedia Britannica. 15th edition. (1989).

Frazer, J. G. (1922). *The Golden Bough – A Study in Magic and Religion*. Abridged edition. London: The Macmillon Press.

Grunfeld, Frederic. (1982). *Wayfarers of the Thai Forest: The Akha*. Amsterdam: Time-Life Books.

Hurley, T. (1985). Placebo: The hidden asset in healing. *Investigations* 2 (1).

Kammerer, Cornelia. (1986). *Gateway to the Akha World – Kinship, Ritual and Community among Highlanders of Thailand*. Unpublished thesis: University of Chicago.

Lewis, I. M. (1971). *Ecstatic Religion – An Anthropological Study of Spirit Possession and Shamanism*. London: Penguin Books.

Opie, Iona, and Tatem, Moira. (1992). *A Dictionary of Superstitions*. Oxford University Press.

Park, George K. 'Divination and its Social Contexts' in Middleton, John. (Ed.). (1967). *Magic, Witchcraft and Curing*. New York: The National History Press.

Symonds, Patricia Veronica. (1991). *Cosmology and the Cycle of Life: Hmong Views of Birth, Death and Gender in a Mountain Village in Northern Thailand*. Unpublished PhD thesis: Brown University.

Trevelyan, Marie. (1909). *Folk-Lore and Folk-Stories of Wales.*

Walker, Anthony. (1970). 'The Lahu Nyi (Red Lahu) New Year Celebrations.' *The Journal of the Siam Society* 58/1: 1-44.

Walsh, Roger N. (1990). *The Spirit of Shamanism.* London: Mandala.

Wilde, Lady 'Speranza'. (1887). *Ancient Legends, Mystic Charms, and Superstitions of Ireland.* 2 vols.

Index

A Life Apart, 8
afterlife (*see also* Hmong afterlife), 18-20, 74, 144, 148-50
Ai Ma (Lahu creator, wife of G'ui-sha), 116
AIDS, 34, 254
Akha (people), 13-4; Akha Way, The (Akhazan), 56-7; Apoe Miyeh (creator), 17, 55-6, 215; blacksmiths, 68; books, mythological, 56; 'chasing out' ritual, 194; days and name-day omens, 217-8; houses, 212; *neh mui neh ceh* (unnamed baby spirits), 67-8; *pee-hah* spirits, 62; pig liver divination, 194, 196; *pong* spirits, 62, 66-7; rice rituals, 212-7; shamans, 68-70; soul-calling, 68-9; spirit gates (village gates), 62-4, 194, 214; spirit priests, 68-9; spirits and humans living in harmony, myth, 60-2; vampires, 65-6, 67; village priests, 55, 57-8, 64, 68, 213; village site, 58-60; writing, the loss of, 56-7
Akhazan (The Akha Way), 56-7
ancestral spirits, 18, 52, 77-8
animism, definition, 15
Apoe Miyeh (Akha creator) (*see also* Akhazan), 17, 55-6, 215

Apollo Diradiotes, temple of, 95
Argentina, 12
Australia, 12
authors(s), the: interviewing for *Tiger-Men And Tofu Dolls*, 20-5; living in Kiew Khan, 3, 4, 5-8, 20, 21, 24, 25, 199-200; past research, 8, 22

Baby Goddess (Hmong), 111
bad death, 16, 144-5, 147, 148-9, 174-5, 178; other references, 18, 182
Bangkok, 9, 64, 90, 158, 159, 180, 253
beeswax, used in rituals, 45, 142
belief, interviewee statements concerning, 57, 105-6, 159, 196, 227
beyond, the, *see* afterlife
birth, 108-11, 114-5, 116-7
black magic, 82, 84, 112, 206, 249; an attack on a man's father, 82-4; curse on a Hmong father, 118-20; death spells, 204, 206, 208, 210-11; a Yao practitioner, 88-9
Border Patrol Police (BPP), 118, 199, 237
Buddhism, 6, 242, 243; among the Karen, 14, 90; in Kiew Khan, 6, 133, 182; Lahu exposed to, 141
Burma (Myanmar), 5, 10, 90, 192, 193, 225, 254; highlanders living in, 12, 13, 14

Canada, 12
cat(s): man changed into a, 193; as omens, 124; as sacrifices, 34; as vampires, 65-6
Chiang Khong, 24, 161, 166, 176, 204, 208-9, 238, 250
Chiang Mai, 64, 73, 94, 159, 208, 223, 224, 228, 250, 251
Chiang Rai, 73, 159, 167, 182, 223, 254
Chiang Saen, 4-5, 130, 223, 238, 252
chicken and egg, which came first, 159
China, 10, 159, 254; Chinese, 56, 57, 121, 226, 242-4; highlanders living in, 10, 12, 13, 14, 100, 159; Hmong ancestors, flight from, 103; Jin Haw (people), 134, 243; Jin Haw Country, 134, 136-7; Kuomintang refugees from, 6; the Mongol invasion of (and the Akha account of the 'big burning'), 56-7; Yao fleeing coastal provinces of, 74-5
Chindarsi, Nusit, on the Hmong and earthquakes, 236
Christian converts, 47, 188, 189, 238-41, 242-5; other references, 6, 173, 197, 227, 229
Christianity (*see also* Christian converts; Seventh Day Adventists): and cultural dilution, 240-1, 242-3, 250, 254; missionary activity, 9, 238, 239, 240-1, 244-5, 251, 254; schools, Christian, 208, 245
cockerel, seen by Hmong as heavenly messenger, 235
creation myths: 'Creation, The', (Lisu), 80-1
'Crossing to the other side' (Yao myth), 73-5
cultural change, *see* culture, traditional, under threat
cultural diversity, decreasing, 9
culture, traditional, under threat, (*see also* Christianity; development projects; health care; Thai-isation; tourism), 249-54
curing rituals (*see also* soul-calling), 18; changing the name of a sick baby (Lisu), 117; procuring the return of a lost soul (Hmong), 154-5; ritual to imprison a semi-malevolent spirit (Hmong), 42; ritual involving the Three Ancestor spirit (Hmong), 102-7; 'spraying' of a sickness (Lisu), 113
curses, *see* black magic

Dai (people), 242, 243
days and weeks, 217
death drum (Hmong), 177
death spells (*see also* black magic), 204, 206, 208, 210-11
development projects: in Kiew Khan, 8-9, 158, 252; regional, 254
divination, 95-6; by chicken-bones, 88, 94, 96, 120-3, 138; with divination sticks (horns), 38-9, 50, 51, 104, 117, 170; by dropping coins and shells into water, 115; egg balancing, 49-50; egg-drop test, 59-60, 71; palmistry, 134, 137; with pig livers, 194, 196; rice-grain test, 60, 71-2
divination sticks (horns), 38-9, 50, 51, 104, 117, 170
dogs, able to see spirits, 124, 185
Doi Luang (mountain), 34, 151
Doi Tung (mountain), 242
dragons, 162, 168
dreams, 43, 159; other references, 78, 145
drug trafficking, 4-5, 58; Ban Hin Taek, battle at, 58; mining the Thai/Lao border to stop, 172; other references, 20, 246, 254

earthquakes, Hmong, explanation of, 236
effigies, 82, 98
egg-drop test (*see also* divination), 59-60
exorcism, 54; of *pong* spirits, 67; of the smallpox spirit, 31, 32; 'spraying' of a sickness, 113; of a vampire, 66

familiar spirits, *see under* Hmong shaman(s)

Index

Fang (town), 116, 242, 244
farts: as socially undesirable, 39; and spirits, 38-9
fireballs, the blowing of, 113
fire-walking, 85-7
flaming torch dog-on-a-string ritual (Hmong), 32
France, 12
Frazer, Sir James: on souls, 17; on divination, 95
funeral rites, 144-5, 176-8; other references, 74, 111, 147, 148, 175, 187-8

ghost(s), 16, 151, 202; at a Buddhist temple in a Hmong village, 179-82; of a mother and child, 183-84; sightings in a Lahu village, 145-6; waiting for passers-by, 153
Golden Triangle, The (*see also* drug trafficking), 20, 224, 254
gong-goy spirits (Hmong), 37-9
Gospelles of Dystaues, 158
G'ui-sha (Lahu creator), 17, 116, 128, 141
gunban spirit (Hmong), 31

Hani (people), 13
head-butting, see under Jin Haw Country
health-care, Western, 108, 116-7, 238-9, 250; in Laos, in the past, 33; as integral component of Thai-isation policy, 144; vaccinations against smallpox, 34; other references, 47, 107, 129, 164, 166, 167
Heavenly Archer, The (Hmong), 235
hen that crows, 93
herbal medicines (see also traditional remedies), 33, 114, 166, 167
Hin Taek (Shan/Akha village), 58
Hmong (people) (*see also* Ban Kiew Khan; Hmong afterlife; Hmong shamans; Hmong souls), 10-2; Baby Goddess, 111; chicken-bone divination, 121-3; childbirth practice, 108-11; courtship, 97-9, 250-51; courtship taboos, 97-9;

death drum, 177; death spells, 204; divination sticks (horns), 38-9; earthquakes, explanation of, 236; flaming torch dog-on-a-string ritual, 32; funeral practice, 175, 176-8, 187-8; *gong-goy* spirit, 37-9; *gunban* spirit, 31; Heavenly Archer, The, 235; household spirits, 72, 97-8, 111, 175, 239; houses, 72, 97, 98; hunting rituals, 237-8; New Year festival, 25, 40, 234-6, 247, 248, 250-2; Ntxwj Nyug, 17, 19, 211, 247; Poosu (evil spirit), 155-6, 157-8; rainbow spirit (Zai Laug), 161-2, 166-7, 168; smallpox and the smallpox spirit, 30-4; spirit gates, 31, 32; spirit heads, 29-31, 33, 34; 'sunset hole', 236; three ancestors, spirit of the, 102-7; tofu spirit, 35-6; tree spirit (Lord of the Tree), 129-30
Hmong afterlife (The Otherworld), 18-9, 44, 162, 177, 247-8; 'opening of the way' incantation, 177-8; supernatural forces accompanying a shaman to the, 44
Hmong shaman(s) (*see also* shaman(s); shamanic ritual activity; shamanism), 6; candidate chosen by *neeb* spirits, 41, 44; consulting a, 49-50; familiar spirits (*neeb* spirits), 41, 44; function of, 53-4; master shaman, 44; payment and material benefit of being a, 46, 49; ritual paraphernalia, 46, 48, 248; shamanic session, components of, 51-3; special altar of, 44, 48; in trance, 51-2; work load, 46
Hmong souls: identifying aids for wandering souls, 133-4; soul loss, 50, 125, 129, 130, 154-5; soul-calling bridges, 125-8; souls at birth, 111
Hmong Voices, 8
H'tin (people), 20
hungry ghosts, see ghost(s)

Ida ma (Lisu mountain spirit), 17, 79-81
India, 12, 180

In-jia-nee (Lisu water spirit), 76-7

Japanese, 56, 94, 226
Ja-pu'er (headman of Ja-pu'er village), 116, 140, 143
Jin Haw (a Chinese people), 134, 243
Jin Haw Country, 134, 136-7; and giant skulls, 137; and head-butting, 136-7
Jor-wor-lu (Lahu village guardian spirit), 232

Kammerer, Cornelia, on the Akha ceremonial harvest, 215
Kamphaeng Phet, 225
Karen (people) (*see also* Karen taboos), 10, 14; views of afterlife, 18, 148-50; divination, 94, 96; house spirits, 91-3; Lord of the Land and Water, 220; rice rituals, 219-20; souls, 148-9; vampires, 148, 149-50; village priests, 94, 96; village shrine, 220-1
Karen taboos: entry of strangers to village and, 221-2; hen that crows, 93; sex of piglets and, 92-3; siting a house and, 91-2; sleeping arrangements of guests and, 92; strange behaviour of pigs and, 93
Kayah (people), 14
KGB (Soviet secret police), 135
Khamu (people), 3, 20, 202-3
Khun Sa (opium warlord) (*see also* drug trafficking), 58
Kiew Khan (Hmong village), 4-9, 29, 34, 58, 88, 126, 133, 158, 164, 187, 197, 204, 228, 234, 237, 238, 239, 246; authors living in, 3, 4, 5-8, 20, 21, 24, 25, 199-200; border police post in, 118, 197, 199, 237; curse on a thief living in, 208-11; death of a woman in (and resurrection as a weretiger's wife), 187-9; death of a Lahu woman with baby in, 147; ghost sightings, 179-82, 183-4; growing outside influence on, 250-3; other references, 47, 97, 102, 108, 157, 161, 169, 174, 175, 176, 208
Kiew Khan Kickers, 7

Kublai Khan, 57
Kuomintang (Chinese), 6, 242

Lahu (people), 6, 13; Ai Ma (creator, wife of G'ui-sha), 116; bad death, 144-5, 147; bathing the elders, 140-1, 232-3; black magic, 82; childbirth practice, 116-7; G'ui-sha (creator), 17, 116, 128, 141; holy days, 140-3; Jor-wor-lu (village guardian spirit), 232; *leh-o* (taboo device), 143; locality spirit, shrine for, 244; name divination, 117; new year festival, 229-33; new water, 232-3; rice cakes (*hk'aw-buk*), 230-2; shaman, 143; soul-calling, 128, 138-9, 146; spirit gate, 147; temple, 141, 243, 244; temple offerings, 141-3; year tree (*hk'aw-dur*), 230-2
Lampang, 94
Lan Na (ancient Tai kingdom), 4
land of the ancestors, *see* afterlife
Laoleuer Sewa (Lazy Leuer), 1-3, 5, 9, 24, 29, 199
Laos: bone-seller from, 135; highlanders living in, 10, 11, 12, 13, 202; Hmong fleeing from, 11-2, 133; Laoseu's trade goods from, 246; mining of the Thai/Lao border, 172; smallpox epidemic in, 33-4; United States MIA's in, 135; other references, 1, 182, 185, 197, 200, 203, 254
laughter, spirits manifesting themselves through, 45
leh-o (Lahu taboo device), 143
Lewis, Paul: on the Lahu drawing of 'new water', 233; on the Lahu 'Tree of Life', 230
Lhwyd, E, on 'snake stones', 168
Lisu (people), 12-3; black magic, 82-4, 112; childbirth practice, 114-5; creation myth, 80-1; house spirits, 77-8; houses, 77-8; Ida ma (mountain spirit), 17, 79-81; *In-jia-nee* (water spirit), 76-7; *lu khwa* leaves, the use of, 78; name divination, 115; naming ceremony, 115; 'Old

Index

Grandfather' (village guardian spirit), 78-9; spraying fireballs, 113; village guardian spirit shrine, 78-9, 80; village location, 76-7; village priest, 79; Wu sa (creator), 17, 80-1
living world, the (World of Light), 16, 18
locality spirit (Lord of the Land), *see under* owner spirits
logging, illegal, 234, 238, 254
Lord of the Land (and Water), *see under* owner spirits
Lua (people), 20

Mae Chan, 21, 24-5, 138, 183, 208, 223
Mae Sai, 73, 225, 242
Mae Salong, 24, 25, 55, 58, 192, 193, 223
malicious spirits (*see also* bad death; ghosts; vampires; weretigers), 16; *pee-hah* spirits (Akha), 62; Poosu spirit (Hmong), 155-6, 157-8; smallpox spirit (Hmong), 30-4; unnamed babies, spirits of (Akha), 67-8; *meh* spirits (Lahu bad death spirit), 147
Mekong river, 4, 254
Meo, *see* Hmong
missionary activity (Christian), *see under* Christianity
Mongolia, 136-7

name changing, 34-5, 115, 117
naming, 111, 115, 117
nature spirits, 15, 69
neeb spirits, *see under* Hmong shaman(s)
'new rice', 141
'new water', 232-3
new year festivities, 25, 40, 79, 229-33, 234-6, 247, 248, 250-2
northern Thailand: a cultural mishmash in, 20; economic development of, 254; migration of highlanders into, 10, 11, 12, 13, 14; missionary activity in (*see also under* Christianity), 240-1; rapid cultural change in (*see also* culture, traditional, under threat), 9, 144, 253-4; tourism in (*see also* tourism), 224-5; tribal peoples of, 10
Ntxwj Nyug (Hmong), 17, 19, 211, 247

Old Grandfather (Lisu village guardian spirit), 78-9
omens (*see also* divination), 124; associated with animal-name days, 217-8; a death blamed on an omen disregarded, 161-3; ominous black birds (Western tradition), 158
opium (*see also* drug trafficking), 6, 9, 144, 180, 228, 240
Otherworld, *see* afterlife
owner spirits, 15; locality spirit (Lord of the Land), 59, 127, 182, 218, 220-1, 244, 247-8; rice owner, 213; wild pig owner, 237-8

palmistry (*see also* divination), 134, 137
Park, George, on diviners, 96
peanut spots, 31, 33
phlyng (Karen afterlife), 18, 148-50
Pien Hung, Emperor, 100
placebo effect, 54
Pliny the Elder, on 'snake stones', 168
pong spirits (Akha), 62, 66-7
Poosu (Hmong evil spirit), 155-6, 157-8
Population and Community Development Association (PDA), 47
possession, *see* spirit possession
protective spirits, 15-6; Akha spirit gates, 62-4; Hmong *gunban* spirit, 31; Hmong household spirits, 72, 97-8, 111, 175, 239; Hmong spirit heads, 29, 31, 33, 34; Karen house spirits, 91-3; Lisu house spirits, 77-8; Lisu village guardian spirit (Old Grandfather), 78-9

rainbow spirit (Zai Laug) (Hmong), 161-2, 166-7, 168
refugee camps (and detention centres), 12, 133, 134
reincarnation (*see also* afterlife; souls), 18-20, 203
rice rituals, 212-7, 219-20

rice-grain test (*see also* divination), 60, 71-2
Russians, 135

sacrifices, 32-3, 52-3, 54, 86, 213-4; consequences if not made, 104, 106, 162, 170; other references, 34, 40, 64, 70, 72, 74, 77, 79, 92, 102, 104, 105, 107, 127, 128, 153, 154-5, 158, 176, 177, 234-6, 237-8, 244
schools, special, sending tribal children to, 144; other references, 71, 138
Seventh Day Adventists (*see also* Christianity), 9, 197, 198, 208, 240, 251
shaman(s) (*see also* Hmong shaman(s); shamanic ritual activity; shamanism), 17, 18, 24, 68-70, 85-8, 244
shamanic ritual activity (*see also* Hmong shaman(s); shaman(s); shamanism): changing the name of a sick baby (Lisu), 117; combating the smallpox spirit (Hmong), 31-2; conducting a ritual to imprison a spirit (Hmong), 42; conducting a curing ritual with the Three Ancestor spirit (Hmong), 102-7; entreating the Lord of the Land for permission to build a soul-calling bridge (Hmong), 126-7; fire-walking (Yao), 85-7; negotiating with an angered spirit (Hmong), 170; pacifying the house spirit after improper lovemaking (Hmong), 98; procuring the return of a lost soul (Hmong), 154-5; 'spraying' of a sickness (Lisu), 113
shamanism (*see also* Hmong shaman(s); shaman(s); shamanic ritual activity), 24; benefits to a community, 54
Siberia, 9, 24, 136
Singapore, 244
Sipsongpanna, Yunnan, 13, 242, 243
Siv Yis (Hmong), 48
'sky stones' (flint implements), 66
smallpox and the smallpox spirit (Hmong), 31-4

'snake splash', medical condition referred to as, 164-7
'snake stones', mythical occurrence and curative use of, 167-8
snakes: attitude towards eating of, 88; as omens, 124, 162-3
soul-calling (*see also* Hmong souls; souls), 18, 68-70, 128, 138-9, 146
soul-calling bridges, 125-8
souls (*see also* afterlife; Hmong souls; soul-calling), 17, 148-50; soul force, 37, 184; soul-loss, 18; vulnerability to attack, 18
spirit gates, 31, 32, 62-4, 147, 194, 214
spirit heads (Hmong), 29-31, 33, 34
spirit money (votive offerings), 51, 237
spirit possession (*see also neeb* spirits): by a Khamu 'hungry ghost', 201-3; by Akha *pong* spirits, 67; by Akha vampires, 65; by Karen vampires, 150; of Nayua, by an evil spirit, 32
spirits (*see also* ancestral spirits; ghosts; malicious spirits; nature spirits; owner spirits; protective spirits; supernatural spirits), 15-7; forests as domain of, 164-5; living a life that mirrors human existence, 16, 194
'spraying' of a sickness (fireballs) (Lisu), 113
'sunset hole' (Hmong), 236
supernatural spirits (*see also* Apoe Miyeh; G'ui sha; Ntxwj Nyug; Wu Sa), 17
Symmonds, Patricia, on Hmong 'birth shirts', 109, 110

taboo devices, 143, 147
taboos, *see* Karen taboos
Tai (people), 4, 141
Taoism, 12, 39, 246
temples, *see under* Lahu
Thai-isation (*see also* culture, traditional, under threat), 144
thread-tying (binding), 35, 117, 125-6, 129-30, 143, 146
Tibet, 10, 14, 136, 192, 193

tiger spirit, 36
tiger-men (see also weretigers), 189-91, 192-3
'tiger's paw' (vegetable), 36-7
tourism, 224-5; and cultural dilution, 254; effect on village economies, four stages, 227-8; in Kiew Khan, 8, 252-3; in Padua Yao village, 223-4, 225-7, 228; other references, 73
traditional remedies: gunpowder (smeared over wounds), 188; heated coin-on-the-forehead, 165; heated stones, 117; herbal, 33, 114, 166; pressure-point medicine, 165; rainbow-tooth cure, 166-7
trance, 48, 51-2, 53, 68, 85-7, 126-7, 248
tree spirit (Lord of the Tree) (Hmong), 129-30
Trevelyan, Marie, on 'snake stones', 168
Tungas (people), 24

United States of America, 11-2, 133, 161, 250, 251; American pilot living in Laos, story of, 134-5; MIA's (Missing In Action), the search for, 135
unnamed babies, spirits of (Akha), 67-8

vampires, 16, 18, 65-6, 67, 145, 148, 150
Vietnam, 10, 12, 13
village leaders, 55
village priests (see also under Akha; Karen; Lisu), 242
villages: A-bey (Akha), 22, 55, 58; Ar Lae (Akha), 22; Bon Pa Kaem (Yao), 22, 87; Doi (Karen), 58, 90, 148, 219, 221-2; Doi Pui (Hmong), 228; Hin Taek (Shan/Akha), 58; Hmong Gahn (Hmong), 37, 177, 202; Hoor Mae Kham (Hmong/Akha), 193, 205; Huai Haan (Hmong), 137, 169, 171, 172, 174-5, 177, 188-9; Huai Jai Yin I (Lahu/Dai/Chinese), 242; Huai Lu (Hmong), 71; Huai Pu (Lahu), 22; Huai Sa (Lahu), 197-8, 228, 229; Huai Sak (Karen), 148, 219, 221; Huai Tu (Lao/Hmong/ Lahu), 197-8; Ja-pu'er (Lahu/Lisu), 22, 116, 138, 141, 145; Kiew Khan (Hmong), see under Kiew Khan; Lao Shi Guai (Yao), 22, 23, 58, 85, 86, 100, 120, 228; Lao Sip (Yao), 87; Mae Tur (Akha), 192, 212; Pa Car (Yao), 73; Paca Sup Jai (Akha), 192; Padua (Yao), 223, 228; Pang Sa (Lisu), 22, 76, 77, 78, 112, 120; Terd Thai (Shan/Akha) 58; Tung Sai (Hmong), 41, 58, 130, 131, 185

Walker, Anthony, on themes to the Lahu New Year festival, 230
weretigers (see also tiger-men), 16, 18, 112, 187, 189; A Lahu weretiger, 197-8; A weretiger's bride, 187-9
Wilde, Lady 'Speranza', on hens that crow being considered as unlucky, 93
World of Dark (see also afterlife), 17
World of Light (The Living World), 16, 18
Wu sa (Lisu High God), 17, 80-1

Yao (people), 12; afterlife, 18, 74; black magic, 88-9; Book of Days, 100; 'Crossing to the other side' (myth), 73-5; divination, 88; houses, 85; paper and banana-leaf funeral boat, 74; priests, 85, 87; shaman, 85-8; soul-calling bridge ceremony, 128; walking on fire ritual, 85-7; writing, tradition of, 12, 100-1, 250
Yao charter (Mien Passport), 100
year tree (Lahu), 230-2
Yunnan: highlanders living in, 12, 13; other references, 56, 75, 76, 134, 136, 242, 243